easy guide
to the
Bb5 Sicilian

by Steffen Pedersen

EVERYMAN CHESS

Everyman Chess, formerly Cadogan Chess, is published by Everyman Publishers, London

First published in 1999 by Everyman Publishers plc, formerly Cadogan Books plc, Gloucester Mansions, 140A Shaftesbury Avenue, London WC2H 8HD in association with Gambit Publications Ltd, 69 Masbro Road, London W14 0LS.

British Library Cataloguing in Publication Data
A CIP catalogue record for this book is available from the British Library.

ISBN 1 85744 230 X

Distributed in North America by The Globe Pequot Press, 6 Business Park Road, P.O. Box 833, Old Saybrook, Connecticut 06475-0833.
Telephone 1-800 243 0495 (toll free)

All other sales enquiries should be directed to Everyman Chess, Gloucester Mansions, 140A Shaftesbury Avenue, London WC2H 8HD tel: 0171 539 7600 fax: 0171 379 4060

EVERYMAN CHESS SERIES (formerly Cadogan Chess)
Chief Advisor: Garry Kasparov
Series Editor: Murray Chandler

Edited by Graham Burgess and typeset by Petra Nunn for Gambit Publications Ltd.

Printed in Great Britain by Redwood Books, Trowbridge, Wilts.

Contents

Symbols

+	check	Wch	world championship
++	double check	Ct	candidates event
#	checkmate	IZ	interzonal event
x	capture	Z	zonal event
!!	brilliant move	OL	olympiad
!	good move	ECC	European Clubs Cup
!?	interesting move	jr	junior event
?!	dubious move	wom	women's event
?	bad move	mem	memorial event
??	blunder	rpd	rapidplay game
+–	White is winning	corr	correspondence game
±	White has a large advantage	qual	qualifying event
⩲	White is slightly better	1-0	the game ends in a win for White
=	the game is equal		
⩱	Black is slightly better	½-½	the game ends in a draw
∓	Black has a large advantage	0-1	the game ends in a win for Black
–+	Black is winning		
Ch	championship	(n)	nth match game
Cht	team championship	(D)	see next diagram

Bibliography

Books
ECO B (3rd edition), Šahovski
  Informator 1997
ECO B (2nd edition), Šahovski
  Informator 1984
Nunn, Burgess, Emms, Gallagher:
  Nunn's Chess Openings,
  Gambit/Everyman 1999
Gallagher: *Beating the Anti-Sicilians*,
  Batsford 1994
Kraut: *Sicilianisch mit 3.Lb5(+)*,
  Schachverlag Kania 1996

Razuvaev, Matsukevich:
  The Anti-Sicilian: 3 ♗b5 (+),
  Batsford 1984

Periodicals
Informator 1-73
New In Chess Yearbook 1-49
Various magazines

Electronic
ChessBase, Chess Assistant,
The Week In Chess

Introduction

The main-line Sicilian is one of the most complex of all opening systems, and with its immense number of branches, it can be a full-time job to keep up to date with the latest developments. Therefore we have seen a strong tendency for White to avoid the main lines in recent practice. There has been a move towards systems where a general understanding of the ideas is more important than being able to memorize lots of variations. The 2 c3 Sicilian is one such line, while the ♗b5 Sicilian, the subject of this book, is a more aggressive and increasingly popular way to avoid the main lines.

This book covers both main forms of ♗b5 Sicilian:

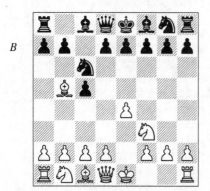

The **Rossolimo Variation** (1 e4 c5 2 ♘f3 ♘c6 3 ♗b5).

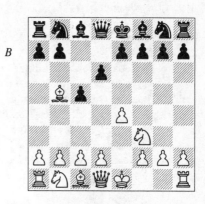

The **Moscow Variation** (1 e4 c5 2 ♘f3 d6 3 ♗b5+).

Is the ♗b5 Sicilian better than the Open Sicilian (i.e. 3 d4 in either case)? Objectively, it is simply impossible to answer that question as the two approaches lead to wholly different types of game. The Open Sicilian gives rise to wide-open positions with lots of possibilities for both sides. Those who are fortunate enough to possess fine developed calculating skills, and are tactically alert, will find themselves at ease in such positions – Kasparov being one such person.

The ♗b5 Sicilian leads to completely different positions, where it is more important to *understand* and *know* why and where to put your pieces. There are of course exceptions, but generally the positions become more closed, and knowing the common ideas and strategies will be of great benefit.

In this book, I have tried to emphasize this aspect without neglecting the theoretical coverage.

The Scope of this Book and the ♗b5 Sicilian

3 ♗b5(+) is not a universal antidote to the Sicilian – it can only be used against Black's two most popular moves after 1 e4 c5 2 ♘f3, viz. 2...d6 and 2...♘c6. Therefore to build a complete anti-Sicilian repertoire, you will need to learn some lines against the rarer lines like 2...g6, 2...♘f6 and 2...a6.

"Are you not forgetting one move?" I hear some of you think. Yes, it is also necessary to decide what to do against 2...e6. One can still try to lure Black into a ♗b5 Sicilian with 3 ♘c3, intending 3...♘c6 4 ♗b5 (Line B of Chapter 2), but here White needs an answer to 3...a6.

Repertoires for White *and* Black

The theoretical coverage of the Rossolimo Variation (2...♘c6 3 ♗b5) and the Moscow Variation (2...d6 3 ♗b5+) is enough to form a repertoire for White in both these variations. Where the choice between White's options is largely a matter of taste, I have frequently provided some alternatives for White by covering more than one line.

This book also provides coverage for those who play the black side of the Rossolimo or Moscow, though here I have been rather more ruthless in my selection of lines. Against 1 e4 c5 2 ♘f3 d6 3 ♗b5+ I advocate 3...♗d7 4 ♗xd7+ ♘xd7, while after 1 e4 c5 2 ♘f3 ♘c6 3 ♗b5, it is the main line, 3...g6, that I have chosen, and hence have provided enough coverage of this line for Black to form a repertoire with it.

Therefore, the Theory Sections of Chapters 2, 3, 5 and 6, and Line B of Chapter 4, are designed primarily to equip White to play these lines. In Chapter 1 and Line A of Chapter 4 I have given material for both sides – including recommendations for Black against inferior white moves, and recommendations for White against inferior black moves, in addition to a particularly detailed discussion of the critical variations.

The introduction to each chapter discusses the key themes in that variation, and is relevant to players of either colour.

Pawn Structures

Before we enter the main body of this book, I think it is worth getting acquainted with some of the most common structures arising in the ♗b5 Sicilian (i.e. both after 2...♘c6 3 ♗b5 and 2...d6 3 ♗b5+). In my opinion it is most important that you have a good understanding of how to play the positions arising. Often White's advantage is not very great out of the opening but all the same players such as the young Russian stars Morozevich and Rublevsky keep winning with White – simply because they know so well what to do after the opening. Here, we shall first take a brief look at some of the most common pawn structures that arise. They will be referred to extensively throughout this book, so it is worth familiarizing yourself with them. The main structures are:

- The Maroczy Bind
- The Hedgehog
- The French Structure

One could easily mention a few more, but these are the most important.

The Maroczy Bind

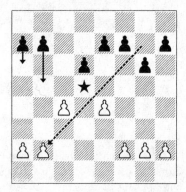

The diagram shows the typical structure of the Maroczy Bind. White's e- and c-pawns exert a firm grip on the centre, while Black's structure is solid. The d5-square almost screams for a white knight to occupy it, while Black usually seeks his counterplay by means of a ...b5 break on the queenside, which is in general ably assisted by pressure from the strong fianchettoed bishop on g7. This advance might not always be so easy for Black to carry out, but Black's position tends in any event to be quite solid.

The Hedgehog

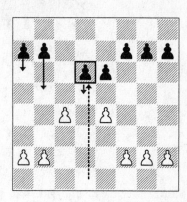

The Hedgehog structure looks quite similar to the Maroczy Bind. The only difference is that in the Hedgehog Black does not fianchetto his dark-squared bishop. Here Black's control of the centre is stronger, but at the cost of a backward pawn on d6, which can easily end up terribly weak. On the other hand, the modern interpretation is that the Hedgehog contains a lot of hidden dynamism. White must be very careful not to over-extend, and must be constantly watching out for ...b5 and ...d5 breaks.

The French Structure

The French structure (*see diagram overleaf*) can arise when White adopts a plan involving c3 and d4, and Black counters with ...d5. The fixed centre that results is highly reminiscent of the French Defence, except that Black has often managed to exchange off his 'bad' light-squared bishop. Black's structure is the more solid, and he would be doing well in most endings.

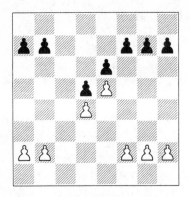

However, in the middlegame White's space advantage is an important factor, and he often tries to turn it to account by launching a kingside attack.

Inspirational Games

The following four games serve as nice appetizers before the main dish. While there is undoubtedly much to be learned from these games, they have not been selected with any particular intention of them being of prime historical or theoretical importance.

Game 1
Kasparov – Salov
Dortmund 1992

1 e4 c5 2 ♘f3 ♘c6 3 ♗b5 g6 4 ♗xc6

This was not exactly a revolution around this time but it was notable that the World Champion preferred to surrender his bishop-pair at this early stage, and it was only after Kasparov's use of it that interest in this particular system exploded.

4...bxc6 5 0-0 ♗g7 6 ♖e1 ♘f6

This system is now considered quite difficult to handle for Black as White develops a strong initiative based on his large space advantage. One year later Salov played 6...f6!? and achieved a good position against the very same opponent.

7 e5 ♘d5 8 c4 ♘c7 9 d4 cxd4 10 ♕xd4 *(D)*

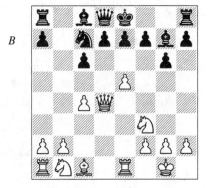

This is a critical position. I do not think that Black is able to equalize here, but for more details, please see Chapter 1.

10...0-0?! 11 ♕h4 d6

In order to free his position Black needs to get rid of White's e-pawn. Black would like to challenge it with 11...f6 but this would be wrong in this position in view of 12 exf6 exf6 (12...♗xf6 13 ♘g5!) 13 c5! ±.

12 ♗h6 ♘e6 13 ♘c3 f6

This is forced, as White was ready to strengthen his position even further with 14 ♖ad1.

14 ♗xg7?!

This turns out well in the game but only with a little cooperation from

Salov. White should instead play 14 exf6!, when Black is in a very difficult situation after 14...♖xf6 (14...♗xf6 also runs into trouble after 15 ♘g5 ♖b8 16 ♘ce4) 15 ♘g5! ♘xg5 16 ♗xg5.

14...♔xg7?

Black could hope for counterplay with 14...♘xg7! 15 exf6 ♖xf6 16 ♘g5 ♘h5 since the direct attempt 17 g4 is probably bending the bow a little too much in view of 17...♖f4 18 ♖e4 ♕f8.

15 exf6+ ♖xf6 16 ♘g5 ♘xg5 17 ♕xg5 ♕f8 18 ♖e2 ♗a6 19 b3 *(D)*

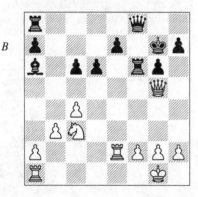

White has a clear advantage. While he has some prospects of a successful kingside attack, the vital factor is his pressure against Black's centre. Moreover, the white knight is far superior to the black bishop, which is struggling to find something useful to do.

19...e5

Not 19...d5? 20 ♖ae1 ♖e8 21 ♕e3! and White is clearly better.

20 ♖d1?

A serious inaccuracy. 20 ♕e3! is far more accurate, returning the queen to its ideal square, while targeting the

a7-pawn and preparing to double on the d-file.

20...♖f4! 21 ♖ed2 ♖d8 22 ♕g3

Black's position stands up well after 22 c5? h6 23 ♕g3 d5.

22...c5 23 ♘e2 ♖f5 24 ♕e3 ♗b7 25 f3 h5 26 ♖d3 *(D)*

Making sure not to run into a tactic involving ...♗xf3, which would be the case after the casual 26 ♘c3?.

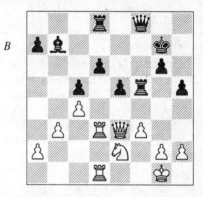

26...♖d7?

Black spoils his chance to harvest the fruits of his earlier efforts. Much stronger is 26...e4! 27 fxe4 ♗xe4!, when Black is doing well, for example 28 ♕xe4 ♖e8 29 ♕c6 ♖xe2 with an attack.

27 ♘c3 ♗c6 28 ♕d2 ♖f6 29 ♘d5

White is back in the driver's seat and the rest of the game sees no more wobbling by the World Champion.

29...♖e6 30 h3 ♕f5 31 ♖e1 ♕f7 32 a3 ♖d8 33 b4 cxb4 34 axb4 ♕b7 35 b5 ♗xd5 36 ♖xd5 ♕b6+ 37 ♔h2 ♖c8

Or 37...♖f8 38 ♖a1!.

38 f4! ♖ce8 39 fxe5 dxe5 40 ♖d7+ ♖8e7 *(D)*

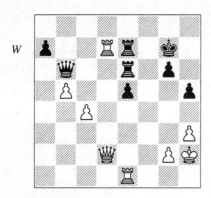

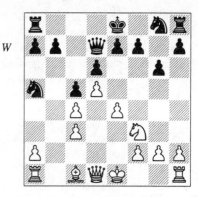

41 ♕d5

Kasparov later admitted that 41 ♖a1! would have won far more quickly, e.g. 41...♕c5 42 ♖axa7 ♕xa7 43 ♖xa7 ♖xa7 44 c5 +–.

41...♔h6 42 ♕d2+ ♔h7 43 ♖f1

With the king on h7 rather than g7, Black could, after 43 ♖a1, try to mix things up with 43...e4!.

43...e4 44 ♖f7+ ♖xf7 45 ♖xf7+ ♔g8 46 ♕d7! ♕b8+ 47 ♔g1 ♕e5 48 ♖g7+ ♕xg7 49 ♕xe6+ ♔h7 50 ♕xe4

The queen ending is a very easy win as White has no weaknesses around his king.

50...♕c3 51 ♕e7+ ♔h6 52 ♕xa7 ♕c1+ 53 ♔h2 ♕xc4

Or 53...♕f4+ 54 ♔h1 ♕c1+ 55 ♕g1 ♕xc4 56 ♕b1 and White wins.

54 ♕b8 1-0

Game 2
Shirov – Kasparov
Erevan OL 1996

1 e4 c5 2 ♘f3 d6 3 ♗b5+ ♗d7 4 ♗xd7+ ♕xd7 5 c4 ♘c6 6 ♘c3 g6 7 d4 ♗g7!? 8 d5 ♗xc3+ 9 bxc3 ♘a5 *(D)*

Black's strategic motifs closely resemble those in the Nimzo-Indian. Having doubled White's c-pawns, Black would now like to keep the position closed and then slowly attempt to exploit White's inferior pawn-structure.

10 0-0 f6!

10...♘xc4 is too dangerous because White develops a strong initiative after 11 ♕e2 ♘e5 12 ♘xe5 dxe5 13 f4.

11 ♘d2 b6 12 ♕e2?

This poor move allows Black to step up his pressure against the c4-pawn. It is noteworthy, however, that it is not the pawn in itself that makes it troublesome for White but rather that his pieces are rendered passive by the need to defend it, and thus White is not able to make much use of his army. 12 f4 or 12 a4 would be much better.

12...♕a4! *(D)*

13 f4 ♘h6 14 e5

White's only chance is to throw everything forward and hope for the best. Surprisingly, it works in this game.

14...0-0-0 15 ♖b1 ♘f5?!

It is understandable that Kasparov was dissatisfied with this move, which

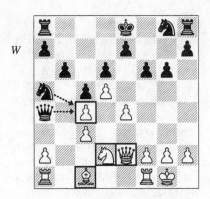

almost returns the favour. Instead he suggests 15...罝hf8!, with the idea of meeting 16 e6 with 16...f5!, followed by ...公g8-f6-e4.

16 g4! *(D)*

16...公h4?!

This makes things very complicated. Black should play 16...公g7, when after 17 exf6 exf6, 18 豐e7 罝d7 19 豐xf6 公xc4 is still better for Black. Shirov had planned 18 f5!? but did not really trust it.

17 exf6 exf6 18 豐f2! g5 19 公e4 豐e8

With this subtle move, Black intends to bring his queen to the kingside.

20 罝e1

Not, of course, falling for 20 公xf6 豐g6, hitting the knight and rook.

20...豐g6 21 fxg5

21 f5 is another very interesting idea. After 21...豐g7 (21...豐f7, with the idea that 公h5 will not gain a tempo, loses to 22 公xg5 fxg5 23 奧xg5) 22 公g3 公xc4 23 公h5 豐f7 24 罝e6 公e5, White's best, according to Shirov, is 25 豐e2! 罝he8 26 豐e4! with good compensation. Indeed, it does not look easy for Black to cover his f-pawn; 26...罝xe6 27 dxe6 d5 (27...豐b7 28 豐xb7+ 含xb7 29 公xf6 +−) 28 豐xe5 豐xh5 29 豐e2 豐e8 should be very good for White in view of the trapped black knight and White's good attacking prospects on the queenside, not to mention his powerful passed e-pawn.

21...罝he8! 22 公xd6+! 罝xd6 23 罝xe8+ 豐xe8 24 奧f4!

24 豐xh4 is mistaken on account of 24...豐e4 25 罝a1 公xc4, when Black's knight gallops into the game.

24...公xc4!

The tactics just about work for Black. Black cannot count on full equality after 24...豐g6 25 罝e1 罝d8! (best) 26 豐xh4 fxg5 27 豐xg5 豐xg5 28 奧xg5 罝g8 29 h4!, when, for example, after 29...h6 30 奧xh6 罝xg4+ 31 含f2 罝xh4 32 奧g5 罝h2+ 33 含g3 White is somewhere between clearly better and winning in view of his menacing d-pawn.

25 奧xd6 公d2! 26 罝d1 豐e4! 27 奧g3

White's planned 27 罝xd2? fails since after 27...豐b1+ 28 豐f1 公f3+

29 ♔f2 ♕xf1+ 30 ♔xf1 Black takes the rook with check and then safely returns his knight, creating new problems for White: 30...♘xd2+ 31 ♔e2 ♘e4 ∓ (Shirov).

½-½

Shirov analysed 27...♘hf3+ 28 ♔h1 ♘e1+ 29 ♔g1 ♘df3+ (29...♘ef3+ is just a perpetual check) 30 ♔f1 ♘c2 31 d6! (31 ♗f4 ♕xf4 32 ♕xc2 ♘xh2++ 33 ♔g1 ♘xg4 ∓) 31...♔d7 32 ♗f4 ♕xf4 33 ♕xc2 ♘xg5+ 34 ♕f2 ♕xg4 35 ♕e2! with an unclear position.

Game 3
Morozevich – Yakovich
Samara 1998

1 e4 c5 2 ♘f3 ♘c6 3 ♗b5 g6 4 0-0 ♗g7 5 ♘c3 d6 6 e5!?

This pawn sacrifice is currently regarded as the most dangerous, for Black has a very reasonable game if he is left in peace and gets time for ...♗d7 and ...♘f6. However, I am not quite sure that I trust it.

6...dxe5 7 ♗xc6+ bxc6 8 ♖e1 f6 9 b3 (D)

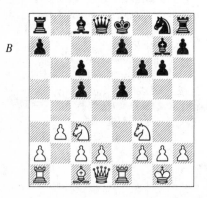

This is the point of Morozevich's play. By opening a path for the bishop to a3, he is now ready to target the c5-pawn.

9...♘h6 10 ♗a3 ♕a5 11 ♘a4 c4

It is interesting that both Morozevich and Yakovich let this move pass without comment in their annotations. In my opinion 11...♘f7!? deserves attention too, e.g. 12 ♗xc5 f5. Perhaps the reason for their silence is that White can ignore the pawn and, for example, continue 12 c4 f5 13 d3, when 13...e4 14 dxe4 ♗xa1 15 ♕xa1 looks too risky for Black.

12 d4 cxd3 13 cxd3 ♗g4 14 d4! (D)

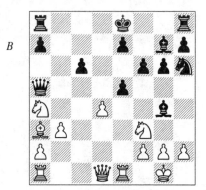

This is the critical position for evaluating this whole line. Up to now the game has proceeded along methodical lines, but now it is time for some fireworks.

14...♕d5

This move is very logical since White will have little joy in taking on e5. There are at least two other possibilities, both pressurizing the d4-pawn, which should be examined. These are (analysis based on the players' notes):

a) 14...♖d8 15 h3 and now:

a1) 15...♗xf3 16 ♕xf3 ♕d5 should simply be met by 17 ♕e2! ♕xd4 18 ♖ad1 ± (Yakovich).

a2) 15...♗h5!? is left without further comment by Morozevich but I am not quite sure where Black's compensation is after 16 g4 ♘xg4 17 hxg4 ♗xg4 18 ♗c5.

a3) 15...♖xd4 16 ♕xd4! exd4 17 ♖xe7+ ♔d8 18 hxg4 (this is the correct move; Morozevich gives 18 ♘xd4 '±', but that can be met by the very strong 18...♕d5) 18...♗f8 19 ♘xd4 ± Yakovich.

b) 14...♘f5! is much more testing; White must now play very energetically to maintain his initiative. 15 dxe5 ♖d8 (15...fxe5 16 h3 ♖d8 17 hxg4!? ♖xd1 18 ♖axd1 gives White compensation – Morozevich) 16 ♕e2 and then:

b1) 16...fxe5 17 ♕e4 ♗xf3 18 ♕xf3 e4 (Black can more or less force a queen exchange with 18...♕d5 19 ♕g4 ♕d4 20 ♕e2 ♕d3 but White is not doing so badly after 21 ♕xd3 ♖xd3 22 ♘c5) 19 ♕xe4 ♗xa1 20 ♕xc6+ (after 20 ♗xe7 Black's defensive queen manoeuvre would rescue him, viz. 20...♕d5 21 ♕e2 ♕d3) 20...♔f7!? is unclear according to Morozevich. I will not disagree.

b2) 16...♘d4 17 ♕e3! ♘c2 18 exf6!! (Morozevich; Yakovich gave only 18 ♕e4 ♘xe1 19 ♖xe1 ♗xf3 20 gxf3 ♕d5 −+) 18...♘xe3 19 fxg7 ♖g8 20 ♖xe3 ♖xg7 21 ♘e5! ♖d1+ 22 ♖xd1 ♗xd1 23 ♘xc6 ♕d2 24 ♘c3

♖f7 25 ♘e4 ♕xa2 26 ♗c5 gives White only two pieces for the queen but they cooperate splendidly.

15 ♘c3! *(D)*

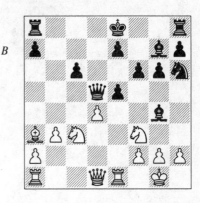

15...♗xf3

Black can try 15...♕a5!, seeking a repetition after 16 ♘a4. If White wants more he has to try the suspicious-looking 16 h3!?. Then 16...♗xf3 17 ♕xf3 ♕xa3? 18 ♕xc6+ ♔f7 19 ♘b5 reveals the point of White's idea, but 16...♕xa3 17 hxg4 ♘xg4 18 ♘xe5 ♘xe5 19 dxe5 0-0 is much better, when White still has a lot to prove but can claim some sort of compensation with 20 ♕d7.

16 ♕d3!

This is the point, and now it does in fact look like White has enough initiative to compensate for the sacrificed pawn.

16...♕e6

16...♕a5 17 ♕xf3 ♕xa3? is similar to 15...♕a5 16 h3 ♗xf3 above, while 16...♕xd4 17 ♕xd4 exd4 18 ♖xe7+ ♔d8 19 ♖xg7 also looks dangerous for Black.

17 ♕xf3 0-0 18 ♖ad1 ♘f5 19 dxe5 fxe5 20 ♕e4 ♖ad8 21 ♗c5 ♖d7 22 h3! *(D)*

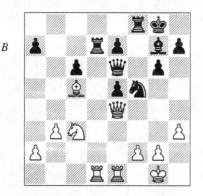

Now White is getting something tangible. Black is a pawn up, but his extra pawn is one of the doubled e-pawns, which only seem to be obstructing his own bishop.

22...♖fd8 23 ♖xd7 ♕xd7 24 ♕c4+ ♔h8 25 ♕a6 ♕c7?

This move is a little too cooperative. 25...♖a8 is more resilient.

26 ♕xa7 ♕xa7 27 ♗xa7 e4!? 28 ♘xe4 ♖a8 29 ♖d1! *(D)*

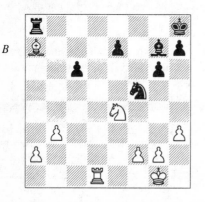

With this clever move, White prepares to defend his bishop with 30 ♖d7. If he instead moved the bishop, Black would get reasonable counterplay with 29...♖xa2.

29...♖xa7 30 ♖d8+ ♗f8 31 ♖xf8+ ♔g7 32 ♖c8 ♘d4 33 ♘c3

White's work is nearly finished; he must now only show that his technique is all right.

33...♖a5 34 ♖d8 ♘b5 35 ♘a4 ♔f6 36 ♖d2 e5 37 ♘b6 ♘d4 38 f4! ♔e6 39 fxe5 ♖b5 40 ♘c4 ♘f5 41 g4 ♘h6 42 ♖d6+ ♔e7 43 ♖xc6 1-0

Game 4
Timman – Kramnik
Riga Tal mem 1995

1 e4 c5 2 ♘f3 ♘c6 3 ♗b5 g6 4 0-0 ♗g7 5 ♖e1 ♘f6

5...e5 is another option, which is now even more popular.

6 e5 ♘d5 7 ♘c3 ♘c7

Despite it being played in some games, I do not think that Black should really consider 7...♘xc3, because 8 dxc3 opens the d-file and activates White's dark-squared bishop, while the e5-pawn does a good job restraining any possible space-gaining actions by Black.

8 ♗xc6 dxc6 9 ♘e4 *(D)*

9...b6

The later game, Kramnik-Kasparov, Moscow PCA rpd 1996, continued 9...♘e6 10 d3 0-0 11 ♗e3 b6 12 ♕d2 f5!? 13 exf6 exf6 14 ♗h6 a5 15 ♗xg7 ♔xg7 16 ♖e2 ♖a7 with a roughly equal position.

10 ♘f6+ ♔f8

10...exf6? 11 exf6+ ♔f8 12 fxg7+ ♔xg7 13 b3 is very good for White, while 10...♗xf6?! 11 exf6 e6 12 d4! also looks suspicious for Black.

11 ♘e4 ♗g4 12 d3!? *(D)*

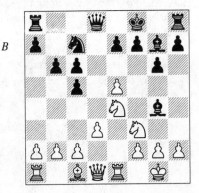

12...♗xe5?

It is quite astonishing that Kramnik erred with this greedy move, since 12...♘e6 gave Black a reasonable position in the earlier game Lutz-Piket, Wijk aan Zee 1995, of which Kramnik was undoubtedly aware. The explanation for Kramnik not following Piket's path could only be that either he was

not convinced that Black solves all his problems with 12...♘e6, or he just could not refute the text-move.

13 ♘xe5!!

A fantastic move, and since Timman does not find the right follow-up I suspect it was over-the-board inspiration.

13...♗xd1 14 ♗h6+ ♔g8

The only move, as 14...♔e8 15 ♘xc6 (threatening 16 ♘f6#) 15...f5 16 ♘xd8 ♖xd8 17 ♖axd1 fxe4 18 ♖xe4 would give White a winning endgame.

15 ♘xc6 ♗xc2 *(D)*

Black has no chance of surviving 15...♕d7 16 ♘f6+! exf6 17 ♘e7+ ♕xe7 18 ♖xe7 ♘d5 19 ♖d7, as the h8-rook is buried alive.

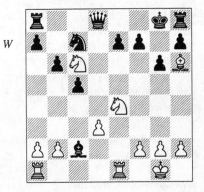

16 ♘c3?

This looks very sensible but unfortunately Timman misses the pretty 16 ♘xd8 ♖xd8 17 ♘xc5!, as suggested by Kramnik in *Informator*. Whether this is really enough to win is, however, not so clear. The idea is that after 17...bxc5 18 ♖xe7 the h8-rook is boxed in and will have problems ever getting out. This means that Black is never able to activate his other rook due to back-rank mates. Some sample lines (based on Kramnik's analysis):

a) 18...♘d5 19 ♖xa7 ♗xd3 (after 19...♘f6 White replies 20 h3) 20 a4 and White's a-pawn races forward, while Black is still struggling desperately to free his h8-rook.

b) 18...♘e6 19 b3! is, according to Kramnik, very good for White, who threatens 20 ♖c1 ♗xd3 21 ♖d1, but Black seems to have some hopes after 19...♘g7, e.g. 20 ♖xa7 ♘f5 21 ♗g5 ♖d6. The key element in Black's defence is the move ...♘f5, so White should prevent this with 20 g4!, renewing the threat. It is difficult to see how Black is ever going to untangle. A sample line is 20...♗xd3? 21 ♖d1 ♖d4 22 f3 ♗b5 23 ♖xd4 cxd4 24 a4 ♗e8 25 ♖xa7 and White wins. Black should, of course, prefer 20...a6 or 20...a5, but even if Black keeps his a-pawn, White will be winning due to the boxed-in rook on h8.

16...e6! *(D)*

This superb defensive move seems to hold the balance. Timman had

probably prayed for 16...♘e6?, after which 17 ♘d5! decides the game.

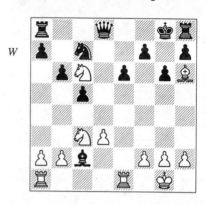

17 ♘xd8 ♖xd8 18 ♗g5 ♔g7! 19 ♗xd8 ♖xd8 20 ♖ac1 ♗xd3

Two pawns constitute enough compensation to encourage White to sue for peace.

21 ♖ed1 e5 22 ♖e1 ♖e8 23 b3!

This strong restraining move comes in handy before Black succeeds in advancing his pawns too far.

23...♘b5 ½-½

The game would be approximately equal after 24 ♘xb5 ♗xb5 25 ♖cd1.

Acknowledgements

I would like to thank a few people for helping out with this book:

GM Peter Heine Nielsen for analytical help;

GM Ian Rogers for sending one of his games;

FM Graham Burgess of Gambit for editing and various suggestions (not to mention his patience when the deadline had been exceeded several times); and

last but not least my fiancée, Mona Andersen, for her never-ending support in the course of writing this book.

Steffen Pedersen
Odense, April 1999

1 Rossolimo Variation with 3...g6

1 e4 c5 2 ♘f3 ♘c6 3 ♗b5 g6 *(D)*

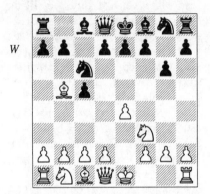

3...g6 remains the most popular defence against the Rossolimo, and it is also the defence I am advocating for Black. The further evolution of the game is rich in possibilities for both sides. As early as move 4, White needs to decide on a strategy: he can either double Black's c-pawns by eliminating the knight on c6, or he can try for an immediate advance in the centre with c3 and d4. The most common, however, is the flexible continuation 4 0-0, by which White keeps both options open.

Sacrificing for the initiative

Although White's strategy is in essence rather slow and positional, there are many positions where it is worth considering a pawn sacrifice in order to obtain a lead in development and thus usually a strong initiative. These pawn sacrifices usually involve White venturing an early b4 or an early c3 and d4, despite Black trying to prevent this by playing ...e5.

The following position arises after the moves **1 e4 c5 2 ♘f3 ♘c6 3 ♗b5 g6 4 0-0 ♗g7 5 ♖e1 e5 6 b4!?** *(D)*.

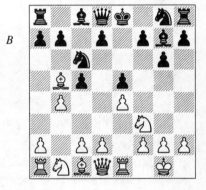

As a consequence of moving first, White enjoys a small lead in development, and tries to turn this to account by this violent move, aiming to open the centre, or files on the queenside. Those familiar with the Benko Gambit will know how effective such pressure on semi-open a- and b-files can be.

Black faces a major decision, and must decide which way to accept the sacrifice: **6...cxb4** and **6...♘xb4** are the possibilities (note that declining the sacrifice with, for example, 6...d6 would lead to a horrible position after 7 bxc5 dxc5 8 ♗xc6+ bxc6). 6...♘xb4 has the better reputation but White obtains very good practical chances with 7 ♗b2, or even 7 c3 ♘c6 8 d4.

The b4 sacrifice comes in many slightly different shapes and sizes, and one even more common than the previous example is when White exchanges on c6 first. An example:

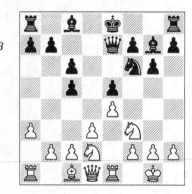

Motwani – Lanka
Vienna 1991

White has just played 9 a3 and is obviously planning to continue 10 b4. It is questionable whether it is worth Black preventing this with, for example, 9...a5. White would then change strategy, and proceed 10 ♘c4 ♘d7 11 a4, when he can claim a small advantage in view of so many black pawns

being fixed on dark squares. Lanka's reaction was much better:

9...0-0 10 b4 ♗e6 11 bxc5 ♛xc5 12 a4 b5! 13 ♗b2 ♘h5 14 c3 ♛b6 15 d4 ♖fd8

The position is messy, but I would rather be Black.

It is very common for Black to defend with ...e5. Not only does Black try to stop White expanding in the centre with c3 and d4, but he also provides a good square for his king's knight on e7. Here it supports future activities such as ...d5 or ...f5, and removes White's threat to double Black's c-pawns by ♗xc6. For this reason, White usually exchanges on c6 before the knight reaches e7, but an interesting alternative is to sacrifice a pawn with an early d4. For example, the following position arises after the moves **1 e4 c5 2 ♘f3 ♘c6 3 ♗b5 g6 4 0-0 ♗g7 5 c3 e5 6 d4!? cxd4 7 cxd4 exd4 8 ♗f4** *(D)*:

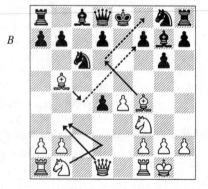

White obtains a strong initiative at the cost of a pawn. White has simple positional ideas of just regaining the pawn with ♘d2-b3, but Black must also be alert not to fall victim to an early attack. Things would be quite easy for Black if he had time for ...♘ge7, ...0-0 and ...d5, but the problem is that White plants a bishop on d6, thereby making further development troublesome.

Black attacks on the kingside

It is rare for Black to resort to an early attack on the kingside, but the prospect of a positionally inferior game sometimes provokes such actions. The following excerpt shows that this plan should not be underestimated.

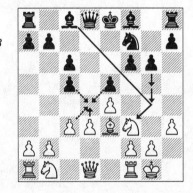

B

Shirov – Kramnik
Novgorod 1994

White is about to play d4, which would give him the better game owing to his space advantage and Black's slightly weakened kingside. In addition, Black's light-squared bishop, despite having plenty of scope, would be pretty useless as a white knight on d4 would do a good job of restricting its activity.

Kramnik decided to burn most of his bridges with...

9...g5!?

Later, it was discovered that 9...♗d6 is perhaps a more solid alternative, but it is worth familiarizing ourselves with Kramnik's idea. Although I have described this as a kingside attack, it is also a fight for the centre.

10 ♕e2

10 d4 represents a more serious test of Black's idea, but is also more risky, e.g. 10...cxd4 11 cxd4 g4, when White can choose between 12 hxg4 ♗xg4 13 ♘bd2 ♖g8, which Kramnik assesses as being quite promising for Black, and 12 ♘h4 gxh3 13 g3 with a mess. See Line B21 for a more detailed analysis of this.

10...h5 11 ♘e1 ♗e6 12 a3 a5 13 ♘d2 b6 14 ♘c2 ♖a7! 15 d4?!

15 ♖fd1 ♖d7 16 ♘f1 leads to equality.

15...cxd4 16 cxd4 ♖d7 17 dxe5 ♘xe5 *(D)*

Black is better.

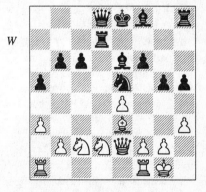

W

Black remains solid and flexible

While White usually obtains a space advantage in the Rossolimo, Black often gains the pair of bishops and this has to be reckoned as a strong long-term asset. Hence a popular variation amongst many grandmasters is **1 e4 c5 2 ♘f3 ♘c6 3 ♗b5 g6 4 ♗xc6 bxc6 5 0-0 ♗g7 6 ♖e1 ♘h6 7 c3 0-0 8 d4 cxd4 9 cxd4 f6 10 ♘c3 d6 11 h3 ♘f7 12 ♕c2 ♗d7** *(D)*. This is rich on ideas for both sides – one has to weigh up a space advantage against Black's longer-term assets.

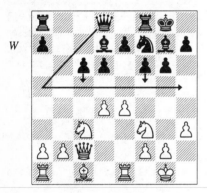

W

Brodsky – Beshukov
St Petersburg 1997

Black will not be able to tolerate a cramped position indefinitely, hence space-gaining actions are called for. White needs to watch out for the ...c5 and ...f5 thrusts, while Black's queen can join the game from a5, and even in some cases swing over to h5. Often the best White can do is to be ready to answer ...c5 with d5, and ...f5 with e5.

13 ♗d2 ♖c8 14 ♖ad1 ♕b6

14...c5!? 15 ♗e3 cxd4 16 ♗xd4 ♕a5 deserves serious consideration.

15 ♗c1 ♕b7 16 ♘e2 ♖fe8

16...c5 looks right.

17 ♕d3 ♖cd8 18 ♘c3 g5? 19 ♘d2 e5 20 d5 c5 21 ♘f1 *(D)*

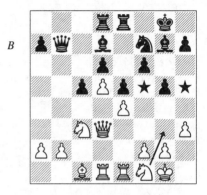

B

White has a strategically won position.

The Theory of the Rossolimo with 3...g6

1 e4 c5 2 ♘f3 ♘c6 3 ♗b5 g6

We shall now look at White's three main choices, of which the last two are the most popular:

A: 4 c3		20
B: 4 ♗xc6		21
C: 4 0-0		34

A)

4 c3 *(D)*

4...♗g7

4...♘f6 5 e5 ♘d5 6 0-0 ♗g7 is also possible, with a transposition to Line C2.

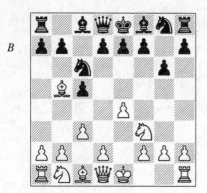

5 d4 ♕a5!

I am surprised I have been able to find so few games with this move. More popular (but inferior) options are:

a) 5...cxd4 6 cxd4 ♘f6 7 ♘c3 0-0 8 d5 ♘b8 9 0-0 d6 10 h3 ♘bd7 11 ♖e1 ♘c5 12 ♗f1 ± Kr.Georgiev-Ignatiadis, Athens 1993.

b) 5...♕b6 6 a4 and now:

b1) 6...a6?! 7 dxc5 ♕xc5 8 ♗e3 ♕h5 9 ♗e2 ♕a5 10 ♘bd2 ♘f6 11 ♘c4 ♕c7 12 ♘b6 ♖b8 13 ♘d5 ♘xd5 14 exd5 ♘a5 15 0-0 ± Magem-Granero Roca, Spanish Ch (Linares) 1998.

b2) 6...cxd4 7 0-0 ♘f6 (7...dxc3 8 ♘xc3 e6 9 ♗e3 gives White compensation *à la* Morra Gambit, but Black can also decline the sacrifice with 7...d3, though White probably has a slight edge following 8 ♘a3 ♘f6 9 ♗xd3) 8 e5 ♘d5 9 cxd4 0-0 (9...a6 10 ♗c4!) 10 ♘c3 ♘xc3 11 bxc3 d6 12 exd6 exd6 13 ♗a3 ♘a5 14 ♘g5 h6 15 ♘e4 ♖d8 16 ♖e1 ♗f5 17 ♕f3 with an edge for White, Smirin-Schmittdiel, Wijk aan Zee 1993.

6 ♗xc6

Razuvaev and Matsukevich also analyse 6 ♕e2!?, which might be a better try for White, e.g. 6...cxd4 7 0-0 d3 (7...a6!?) 8 ♗xd3 and now 8...♘f6 9 b4 ♕c7 10 b5 ♘d8 (10...♘e5) 11 e5 ♘g4 12 ♖e1 ♘e6 13 h3 ♘h6 14 c4 0-0 15 ♘c3 leaves White with a good game. However, Black's play in this line was poor; he would do much better to play 8...d6 before developing his king's knight.

6...dxc6 7 dxc5

7 0-0 ♗g4 is fine for Black.

7...♕xc5 8 ♗e3 ♕a5 9 0-0 ♘f6 10 ♘bd2 0-0 11 h3 ♖d8 12 ♕c2 ♕c7

Black already has the better game in view of his bishop-pair, Ellenbroek-Van der Weide, Dutch Ch 1996.

B)

4 ♗xc6 *(D)*

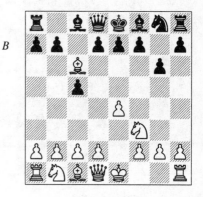

Prior to the 1990s there were very few examples of White giving up his bishop-pair at this early stage, but nowadays most top players prefer the immediate exchange over the more stereotyped 4 0-0, and, it seems, with good reason. Since most set-ups with c3 and d4 cause Black few problems, White has been increasingly investigating the exchange on c6. By doing so as early as possible, White retains maximum flexibility – and might in some cases even castle queenside. I have always been rather suspicious about this strategy since I am usually quite fond of having the bishop-pair, but Black's centre, albeit especially solid, is not very dynamic as most pawn moves will leave weaknesses.

We now examine the two possible recaptures:

B1: 4...bxc6   22
B2: 4...dxc6   28

B1)

4...bxc6 5 0-0

There is definitely no need for White to consider castling queenside when Black has a semi-open b-file, so this is without doubt the most logical move.

5...♗g7 *(D)*

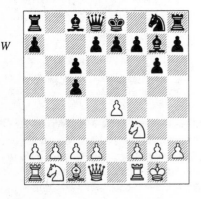

6 ♖e1

Flexibility is White's watchword in this opening and so he does not commit himself to a specific plan as yet. However, 6 c3!? also deserves a brief look:

a) 6...d6 7 h3 ♘h6!? (7...e5 8 d4 cxd4 9 cxd4 exd4 10 ♘xd4 ♘e7 11 ♘c3 ± Smyslov) 8 d4 cxd4 9 cxd4 0-0 10 ♘c3 f6 11 b3!? (usually White arrives at this type of position with the rook on e1, but here White can try to economize on this move) 11...♕a5 12 ♗b2 ♕h5?! (12...♘f7 with the idea of ...e5 is better) 13 ♘d2! ♕xd1 14 ♘xd1 f5 15 e5 f4 16 ♖c1 ♗d7 17 ♘f3 (White has a space advantage and the better pawn-structure; furthermore Black's bishops are not very useful) 17...♘f5 18 ♘c3 h6 19 ♖fe1 ♖fd8 (Matulović-Velimirović, Yugoslavia 1997) and now White should play 20 ♘e4! with the rather annoying threat of 21 g4!.

b) In my opinion 6...♘f6 is more logical; the lines with e5 and c4 followed by d4 are hardly more challenging without the rook on e1 (compare with note 'c' to the next move), so White should play 7 ♖e1, transposing to note 'c1' to Black's 6th move.

6...♘h6

Black intends to play solidly with ...f6 and ...♘f7 and makes sure the knight is brought out in time. Other options:

a) 6...e5 is considered under Line C321.

b) After the immediate 6...f6, White can transpose to our main lines with 7 c3 ♘h6!? 8 d4 cxd4 9 cxd4. The other option is 7 d4 cxd4 8 ♘xd4:

b1) 8...e5 9 ♘b3 ♘h6 10 c4 ♘f7 11 c5! 0-0 (11...a5 12 a4 0-0 13 ♘a3 d5 14 cxd6 ♘xd6 15 ♗d2 ± Hector-Ikonnikov, Geneva 1994) and now 12 ♘a3? a5! 13 ♘c4? a4 14 ♘b6 ♖a7 15 ♘xc8 ♕xc8 16 ♘d2 ♕a6! left Black in command in Kasparov-Salov, French Cht 1993. However, 12 ♕c2, as suggested by Salov, is much stronger; White is probably slightly better.

b2) The reason Salov rejected 8...♘h6 was 9 ♗xh6 ♗xh6 10 ♘f5, when 10...♗f8 11 e5 gives White some attacking possibilities. Even though this is not quite clear, Black has the much stronger 10...♗f4!. I do not see anything better for White than to retreat the knight to d4, which is obviously embarrassing. 9 ♘f5 ♘xf5 10 exf5 d5 11 fxg6 hxg6 also seems perfectly OK for Black, so White probably has nothing better than 9 ♘c3.

c) 6...♘f6 and here:

c1) 7 c3 0-0 8 e5 ♘d5 9 d4 cxd4 10 cxd4 is nothing to worry about; Nevednichy-Hübner, Elista OL 1998 went 10...d6 11 ♘bd2 ♗f5 12 ♘c4 ♕d7 13 ♗d2 ♖ab8, favouring Black.

c2) 7 e5 ♘d5 8 c4 ♘c7 9 d4 cxd4 10 ♕xd4 gives White a big space advantage and good attacking chances on the kingside. Black has a difficult defensive task:

c21) 10...♗b7?! 11 ♘c3 ♘e6 12 ♕h4 h6 13 ♘d4 c5 (neither does 13...♘xd4 14 ♕xd4 d6 15 ♗f4 solve Black's problems) 14 ♘xe6 dxe6 15 ♕g3 0-0 16 h4! ± Kasparov.

c22) 10...0-0?! 11 ♕h4 d6 12 ♗h6 ♘e6 13 ♘c3 f6 (Kasparov-Salov, Dortmund 1992) and now Kasparov

suggests 14 exf6! ♖xf6 15 ♘g5! ♘xg5 16 ♗xg5 ♖b8 17 ♘e4 ♖xb2 18 ♘xf6+ exf6 19 ♗h6 ±.

c23) 10...d5!? 11 ♘c3 ♘e6 12 ♕h4 h6 transposes to line 'c24', note to Black's 12th, but denies White the possibility of capturing the d-pawn *en passant*.

c24) 10...♘e6 11 ♕h4 h6!? 12 ♘c3 d6 (after 12...d5!?, 13 ♘d4 ♘xd4 14 ♕xd4 ♗e6 15 cxd5 cxd5 16 b3 gives White a slight advantage according to Kasparov, but White might try for even more with 13 exd6 exd6 14 ♕g3!?) 13 ♖d1 ♗b7 14 ♗e3 (14 exd6 exd6 15 ♕g3 is also interesting) 14...c5 15 exd6! (15 ♘d5? gives Black excellent play after the queen sacrifice 15...dxe5! 16 ♘f6+ ♗xf6 17 ♖xd8+ ♖xd8, Kharlov-Andersson, Haninge 1992) 15...exd6 16 ♕g3 ♗xf3 (after 16...0-0 17 ♖xd6 ♕b8 18 ♖d2 White is just a pawn up for insufficient compensation) 17 ♖xd6! ♕b8 and now White wins with 18 ♖xe6+! fxe6 19 ♕xg6+ ♔f8 20 ♗xc5+ ♔g8 21 ♕xe6+ ♔h7 22 ♕f5+ ♔g8 23 ♕xf3.

Returning to the position after 6...♘h6 *(D)*:

7 c3

Alternatively there is 7 ♘c3 f6 8 ♕e2, which is a very flexible approach. Black should of course avoid 8...0-0, which drops a pawn to 9 ♕c4+. Kaidanov suggests 8...e5 since in Orlov-Kaidanov, USA Ch 1994 he came out much worse after the opening following 8...♘f7?! 9 a3! ♖b8 (9...a5 10 ♕c4 d6 11 d4 cxd4 12 ♘xd4 c5 13 ♘e6 gives White a clear advantage according to Kaidanov and demonstrates

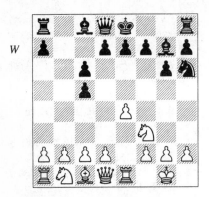

why Black should play 8...e5 rather than 8...♘f7?!) 10 b4! cxb4 11 axb4 a6 12 ♖a4! 0-0 13 d4 e5 14 ♗e3 ♔h8 15 d5! f5 16 dxc6 dxc6 17 ♗c5 ♖e8 18 ♖d1 with a tremendous position.

7...0-0 8 d4 *(D)*

8 h3!? can hardly be considered better than the text-move, although it is a move White tends to make later on anyway. It might be worth trying, since it contains a little trick:

a) 8...d5? 9 d3! (Black is rather uncomfortable after this; he can now easily end up in a position with weak c-pawns) 9...f6 10 ♗e3 c4 11 exd5 cxd3 12 ♕xd3 cxd5 13 ♗c5 ♗f5 14 ♕d1 ♗e4 15 ♘bd2 ♖c8 16 ♘xe4!? (16 ♗a3 also looks good) 16...dxe4 17 ♕xd8 ♖fxd8 18 ♗xe7 exf3 19 ♗xd8 ♖xd8 20 ♖ad1 ♖b8 21 ♖d7 a5 22 gxf3 ♘f5 23 b4! and White has a clearly better ending as his rooks are very active and Black has very poor chances of blockading the queenside pawns, Rublevsky-Hraček, Polanica Zdroj 1996.

b) Black should play 8...f6, whereafter White does not have anything

better than 9 d4, transposing back into the main lines.

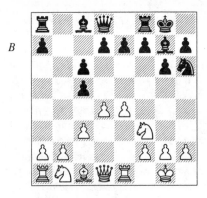

8...cxd4 9 cxd4 f6

This is the super-solid continuation which is currently preferred by Svidler (amongst others). Black hopes that if he just remains patient and does not allow anything terrible to happen, his bishop-pair will come into their own later in the game.

The alternative is 9...d5 10 e5 and now:

a) 10...♗g4 has ideas of swapping the bishop for the white knight, but is unpopular, maybe for the aforementioned reasons. Nevertheless, White was unable to gain any clear advantage in Psakhis-Dautov, Nîmes 1991: 11 ♘bd2 ♕b6 12 b3 c5 (otherwise White would prevent this thrust with ♗a3) 13 ♗a3!? cxd4 14 ♗xe7 ♖fe8 15 ♗g5 ♗d7! 16 ♘f1 ♘f5 with an unclear position.

b) 10...f6 leaves White with a difficult decision as to how to handle the situation in the centre. He can exchange on f6, but this relieves the tension and gives Black an easier life. However, if White does not exchange, Black might eventually be able to capture on e5, forcing White to take back with the d-pawn, whereupon Black will obtain a potentially dangerous passed d-pawn. We have:

b1) 11 ♘bd2 g5?! (too ambitious; 11...♘f7 is more circumspect) 12 e6! (an excellent move as long as the pawn is not simply being lost) 12...♕d6 13 ♕e2 ♘f5 14 ♘b3 and then:

b11) 14...g4 15 ♘fd2 a5 16 ♘f1 a4 17 ♕xg4 ♗xe6 18 ♗f4 h5! 19 ♕f3 ♕d8 20 ♘c5 ♘xd4 21 ♕e3 ♗f7 22 ♕xd4 e5 23 ♕d2 exf4 24 ♕xf4 ± Timman-Yakovich, Køge 1997.

b12) 14...a5!? 15 g4 ♘h6 16 h3 f5 17 ♗xg5 fxg4 and now 18 ♘e5 ♗xe6 19 ♗xh6 ♗xh6 20 ♘xg4 gives White clearly the better of it according to Timman, but this does not look entirely conclusive, e.g. 20...♗xg4 21 ♕xg4+ (21 hxg4 ♗g7!?) 21...♔h8 22 ♖e6 ♖g8 23 ♖xd6 ♖xg4+ 24 hxg4 exd6 25 ♖e1 a4 and Black might even be better. A riskier (but maybe superior) approach is 18 ♘h4 gxh3 19 ♘c5!?, but White can only indulge in this as long as he can keep the bishop on c8 buried, e.g. 19...h2+ 20 ♔h1 ♖b8 21 ♖ad1 with a mess.

b2) 11 h3 ♘f7 12 ♘c3!? ♗f5? (12...fxe5 must be critical) 13 e6! ♘d6 14 ♘h4 ♗e4 15 f3 g5 16 fxe4 gxh4 17 exd5 cxd5 18 ♘xd5 ± Sutovsky-de la Riva, Pamplona 1998/9.

b3) 11 exf6 exf6 12 h3 ♘f7 and now:

b31) 13 b3 ♗f5 (13...♘g5!? 14 ♘bd2 ♖e8 15 ♖xe8+ ♕xe8 16 ♘xg5

fxg5 17 ♘f1 was roughly equal in Nevednichy-Poluliakhov, Yugoslavia 1994) 14 ♘c3 ♖e8 15 ♖xe8+ ♕xe8 16 ♗a3 ♕d7 17 ♘a4 ♖e8 18 ♕f1 ♘g5 19 ♘xg5 fxg5 20 ♗c5 g4 21 hxg4 ♗xg4 22 ♖e1 ♖xe1 23 ♕xe1 h5! and Black has just about sufficient activity to compensate for the hole on c5, Kuczynski-Khalifman, Bundesliga 1998/9.

b32) 13 ♗f4 ♘g5!? 14 ♘bd2 ♘e6 (14...♗f5 15 ♘xg5 fxg5 16 ♗e5 gives White an edge) 15 ♗g3 c5 16 ♘b3 (Brodsky also suggests 16 ♖c1 c4 17 b3 as a fair chance of obtaining an advantage) 16...c4 17 ♘c5 ♕b6 18 ♘a4 ♕c6 19 b3 ♗d7 20 ♕d2 cxb3?! (20...♖fc8 is better) 21 axb3 ♖fc8 22 ♕a5! ± Brodsky-Hendriks, Wijk aan Zee 1998.

10 ♘c3 d6 *(D)*

11 h3

This flexible move serves the useful purpose of preparing ♗e3. Alternatives:

a) 11 ♗e3 ♘g4 12 ♗d2 ♗d7 13 ♕c2 ♕b6 14 ♖ad1 ♖ac8 15 ♗c1 (15

h3 ♘h6 16 ♗e3 f5 should be fine for Black) and now:

a1) 15...c5!? 16 ♘d5 ♕d8 17 h3 cxd4 18 ♕b3 ♖b8 (or 18...e6 19 hxg4 exd5 20 ♕xd5+ ♔h8 21 ♘xd4 with an edge) 19 ♕c4 ♗b5 20 ♘xe7+ ♔h8 21 ♕xd4 ♘xf2 22 ♘xg6+ ± Sulskis.

a2) 15...♕b7 16 e5!? fxe5 17 h3 ♘h6 (17...exd4 18 hxg4 dxc3 19 ♖xe7 ♗f6 20 ♖xd6 ♗xe7 21 ♖xg6+ and now 21...hxg6 22 ♕xg6+ is a draw, while 21...♔f7 22 ♖h6 is very risky for Black) 18 dxe5 ♗xh3 19 ♗xh6 ♗xh6 20 gxh3 ♖xf3 21 exd6 exd6 22 ♖xd6 with good attacking chances for White, Sulskis-Svidler, Pula Echt 1997.

b) 11 b3 and then:

b1) 11...♗d7 12 ♗b2 ♘f7 13 ♖c1 (13 ♕c2 ♖c8 14 h3 ♕c7 15 ♖ad1 ♖fe8 16 ♕d2 ♕a5!? 17 d5 cxd5 18 exd5 ♗h6 19 ♕d4 ♘e5 20 ♘h2!? ♕b6 21 ♕h4 ♗g7 22 ♘e4 ♖c2 23 ♗d4 ♕a5 24 a4 ♗f5 with counterplay, Rublev-sky-Svidler, Russia 1996) 13...♕b6 14 ♖c2 ♕b7 15 ♘d2!? f5 16 e5 c5 (16...dxe5 17 ♘a4! e4 18 ♘c5 ♕c7 19 f3 gives White good compensation) 17 e6 cxd4 18 exd7 dxc3 19 ♖xe7 ♕b4 20 a3 ♕h4 21 ♖e8 ♖axe8 22 dxe8♕ ♖xe8 23 ♘f3 ♕e4 24 ♗xc3 ♖c8 25 ♖e2 and, with the dust about to settle, White has obtained a slight advantage, Yakovich-Izkuznykh, Russian Club Cup (Maikop) 1998.

b2) 11...♘f7 12 ♗b2 ♕a5 13 ♕c2 ♗d7 14 ♘d2 ♖ac8 15 ♘c4 ♕a6 16 ♖ad1 ♗e6 17 ♘e3 ♗h6 18 ♕b1 ♖fe8 19 d5 cxd5 20 ♘cxd5 ± Illescas-Kramnik, Alcobendas (5) 1993.

c) 11 ♕a4 ♕b6 (11...♗d7!? suggests itself as a reasonable alternative)

12 ♘d2 ♘f7 13 ♘c4 ♕a6 and now, rather than 14 ♗e3?! ♕xa4 15 ♘xa4 f5, when Black has good counterplay, Fischer-Spassky, Belgrade (13) 1992, White should play 14 ♕xa6 ♗xa6 15 ♘a5 ♖fc8 16 ♗e3 ♖ab8 17 b3 f5 18 exf5 gxf5 19 ♖ac1 ± Matulović.

Returning to the position after 11 h3 *(D)*:

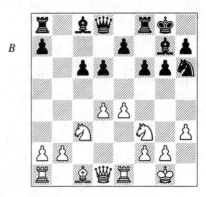

B

11...♘f7 12 ♗e3

This position is very interesting from a strategic point of view. Black has quite good long-term prospects in view of his bishop-pair, but right now the bishops are rather dormant. White has a space advantage and will seek to improve his position further, possibly by ♖c1 and sometimes ♘d2-c4. He must also watch out for possible space-gaining actions from Black such as ...c5 and/or ...f5, as discussed in the introduction to this chapter.

White has a few alternatives at this juncture:

a) 12 ♕c2!? ♗d7 and then:

a1) 13 ♗e3 ♕a5! (the most flexible; Black still intends ...f5 but now introduces the additional idea ...♕h5; 13...f5 is not so bad either though) 14 ♘d2! f5 15 ♖ad1 (planning e5; the immediate 15 e5 is not quite good enough, since Black can defend with 15...dxe5 16 ♘c4 ♕c7 17 ♘xe5 ♘xe5 18 dxe5 ♗xe5 19 ♗c5 ♖ae8) 15...fxe4 16 ♕xe4 ♖ae8 17 ♕d3 ♘h6! with an unclear game, Yudasin-Morović, Leon 1993.

a2) 13 ♗d2 ♖c8 14 ♖ad1 and now:

a21) 14...♕b6 15 ♗c1 ♕b7 16 ♘e2 ♖fe8 (Black seems to be unsure what to play for; 16...c5 looks like the right move, although he might have feared 17 d5 f5 18 ♘g3 fxe4 19 ♕xe4) 17 ♕d3 ♖cd8 18 ♘c3 (White's play does not look very consistent either) 18...g5? 19 ♘d2 e5 20 d5 c5 21 ♘f1 and Black's position is in ruins, Brodsky-Beshukov, St Petersburg 1997.

a22) Breaking out with 14...c5 is a logical reaction when White has played ♗d2 rather than ♗e3. White's best is probably 15 ♗e3 cxd4 16 ♗xd4, but I doubt that Black has any problems after 16...♕a5.

b) 12 b3 and here:

b1) 12...f5!? 13 ♗b2 fxe4 14 ♘xe4 ♗d7 (14...♕a5!?) and now:

b11) 15 ♖c1 ♕a5! 16 ♗c3 ♕d5! 17 ♖c2 ♘h6 18 ♘eg5 ♘f5 19 ♖ce2, Arkhipov-Yakovich, Russia 1994, and now 19...♖ae8!?, with the idea 20 ♘e6 ♗xe6 21 ♖xe6 c5, gives Black sufficient counterplay.

b12) Arkhipov claims an advantage for White after 15 ♕d2! a5 16 ♖e2 a4 17 b4 a3 18 ♗c3 ♕b6 19 ♖ae1.

b2) 12...♗d7 13 ♗b2 ♕b6 14 ♖c1 ♖ad8 15 ♕c2 e5 16 ♖ed1 ♖fe8 17

♘a4 ♕a6 18 ♘d2 ♗h6 19 ♖b1 ♕e2 20 ♘c3 ♕h5 21 ♘f1 ♕h4 22 ♘g3 ± Rublevsky-Izkuznykh, Russian Club Cup (Maikop) 1998.

12...♗d7 *(D)*

If Black plays 12...f5, White can reply 13 ♕a4, and after 13...♗d7, 14 exf5 forces Black to recapture with the pawn.

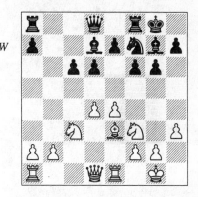

13 ♖c1

V.Spasov-Svidler, Erevan OL 1996 instead went 13 ♕d2 ♕c7 (13...♕a5!?) 14 ♖ac1 ♕b7 15 b3 ♖ad8 (Black needs to prepare the ...f5 advance, because 15...f5 16 e5 dxe5 17 dxe5 ♘xe5 18 ♘xe5 ♗xe5 19 ♗h6 is very good for White) 16 ♕c2 (16 ♘a4!?) 16...f5! 17 e5 c5! (it is time to open the position for those bishops) 18 exd6 exd6 19 ♖cd1! (19 dxc5 ♗c6! gives Black a strong initiative) 19...♗c6 20 d5 ♗d7 with a roughly level position.

13...♕a5 14 ♘d2! ♕b4

14...♕a6!?.

15 b3 f5 16 ♘c4 fxe4 17 ♘xe4 ♖ae8 18 ♖e2!? ♗f5 19 ♘g3 ♗d7 20 ♗d2 ♕b5 21 ♗c3

White has a clear plus, T.Wall-Din-eley, British League (4NCL) 1997/8. He has done a good job of neutralizing any activity from Black and is now ready pressurize the e7-pawn.

B2)
4...dxc6 *(D)*

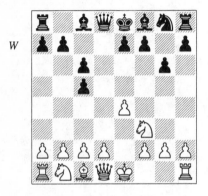

Now White usually plays d3 and h3 in one order or the other. There is, however, a small but significant differ-ence between the two orders. We shall discuss them as follows:

B21: 5 h3   28
B22: 5 d3   30

B21)
5 h3

It is now more or less established that this is inferior to 5 d3. There seems no reason to prevent Black from playing ...&g4 as long as White has the possibility of replying &bd2 and recapturing on f3 with the knight.

5...e5! *(D)*

The king's bishop is going to be much better on d6 than on g7, so Black

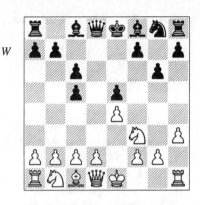

takes advantage of the possibility to play ...e5 without playing ...&g7 first.

6 d3

6 &xe5 &d4 reveals why Black can play 5...e5! against 5 h3 but not against 5 d3.

6...f6!

6...&g7 transposes to Line B222.

7 0-0

7 c3 &h6 8 &e3 &f7 9 0-0 leads to the same thing, but another possibility is 7 &c3. However, in my opinion White needs to execute the d4 advance in order to claim an advantage, and in this respect 7 &c3 is of course useless. Yudasin has played it with success, but it seems like Black has plenty of possi-bilities to improve: 7...&h6 8 &e3 &f7 9 &d2! (according to Yudasin, 9 &d2 is well met by 9...&e6 with the idea of playing ...&d7, ...0-0-0 and ...f5) and now:

a) 9...b6 10 0-0 &g7 11 a3!? f5?! (generally Black should be rather pa-tient in these positions, and this seems premature; 11...&e7 is an obvious im-provement, e.g. 12 &b1 0-0 13 b4 cxb4 14 axb4 f5 with strong counterplay)

12 exf5 gxf5 13 f4! 0-0 14 ♕f3 ♕f6 15 ♘c4 exf4 16 ♗xf4 ♗d7 17 ♔h1 ♖ae8 18 a4 and White is better due to his much superior pawn structure, Yudasin-Soffer, Israeli Cht 1996.

b) Black would stand quite well if he could bring his knight to d4, so I am very much in favour of 9...♘g5! (another route is d6-b5-c4, but that is more troublesome to achieve), when 10 f4 exf4 11 ♗xf4 ♘e6 is fine for Black and 10 ♗xg5 fxg5 11 ♘c4 ♕e7 also looks quite good as all possible knight entrances are well covered by the black pawns.

7...♘h6 8 ♗e3 ♘f7 9 c3 (D)

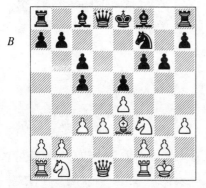

9...♗d6

This looks a lot sounder than the alternative 9...g5!?. In fact, if it had not been used by some very strong players, I would have severe doubts about such a move – Black's only developed piece is his knight on f7. However, it is not so clear how White should reply:

a) After 10 ♕e2 h5 11 ♘e1 ♗e6 12 a3 a5 13 ♘d2, Shirov-Kramnik, Novgorod 1994 went 13...b6 14 ♘c2 ♖a7!

15 d4?! (15 ♖fd1! ♖d7 16 ♘f1 should be about equal) 15...cxd4 16 cxd4 ♖d7 17 dxe5 ♘xe5 with an edge for Black. Kramnik even suggests the acrobatic 13...♖h7 14 ♘c2 ♘h8! 15 d4 cxd4 16 cxd4 ♘g6 with good counterplay; for example, 17 ♖fd1 g4!? 18 dxe5 fxe5 19 ♘c4 ♕f6.

b) 10 d4 looks like a more serious test of Black's experiment, but again Black seems to be surprisingly well placed to meet this: 10...cxd4 11 cxd4 g4, with two possibilities for White:

b1) 12 hxg4 ♗xg4 13 ♘bd2 ♖g8! gives Black a strong attack according to Kramnik, who continues his analysis with 14 ♕a4 ♗h3 15 ♘e1 ♕d7 16 f3 b5 17 ♕c2 exd4 and 14 ♕b3 ♗h3 15 ♘h4 f5 (15...exd4 is simple and good) 16 ♕xb7 ♖xh4 17 ♕xc6+ ♔e7 18 ♕b7+ ♔f6; in both cases Black gains a clear advantage. Presumably White should not allow ...♗h3, but 14 ♔h1 ♕d7 is also very pleasant for Black.

b2) 12 ♘h4 gxh3 13 g3 was Krasenkow's suggestion in *Informator 65*, but this had already been tried. Oral-Krakops, Guarapuava U-18 Wch 1995 continued 13...exd4 14 ♗xd4 (maybe White should play 14 ♕xd4 but I find it hard to believe that White is anywhere near being better) 14...♖g8 15 ♘c3 (15 ♘f5?? ♗xf5 16 exf5 was played in Ovechkin-Gagarin, Russian Cht (Briansk) 1995, but both players must have had a little too much vodka to miss 16...♕d5! with the dual threats of 17...♕g2# and 17...0-0-0) 15...♗g4 16 ♕a4 ♕d6 with a strong attack for Black.

10 d4

10 a3 0-0 11 b4 ♕e7 12 ♘bd2 ♗e6 13 ♘c4 ♗xc4 14 dxc4 a5!? 15 b5 a4 was equal in Ulybin-Krasenkov, Russian Ch 1995.

10...cxd4 11 cxd4 0-0 12 ♘c3 ♕e7 13 ♖e1 ♔g7 14 ♕c2 ♗e6 15 ♖ad1 ♖fd8 16 a3 ♗c4

16...exd4 17 ♘xd4 ♘e5 18 ♘xe6+ ♕xe6 is worth considering but White probably has a slight edge.

17 d5! ♖dc8 18 dxc6 ♖xc6

Black could also choose to cover d5 with 18...bxc6 but then White clamps down on the c5-square by 19 ♘a4 ♗b5 20 ♘c5.

19 ♘d2 ♗e6 20 ♕d3 b6 21 ♘d5 ♕b7 22 ♘b1 ♖ac8 23 ♘bc3

White's firm control of d5 gives him a small advantage, Svidler-Vyzhmanavin, Russian Ch 1995.

B22)

5 d3 ♗g7 *(D)*

Or:

a) As long as the position remains closed, Black's bishops are not particularly useful, so another logical move is 5...♗g4, intending to exchange this bishop for White's knight on f3. This would increase Black's control of the central dark squares at the cost of parting with one of his long-term assets, the bishop-pair. This exchange will give Black good play if White has to recapture on f3 with his queen, as we see:

a1) 6 0-0 ♗g7 7 h3 ♗xf3 8 ♕xf3 ♘f6 9 ♘c3 ♘d7 10 ♕e3 b6 11 ♘e2 e5 12 ♕g3 ♕e7! and Black, with the manoeuvre ...♘f8-e6, is ready to seize maximum control of the d4-square,

Kobaliya-And.Tzermiadianos, Ano Liosia 1997.

a2) 6 ♘bd2! ♗g7 7 h3 ♗xf3 8 ♘xf3 ♘f6 9 0-0 ♘d7 10 ♗e3 b6 11 c3 0-0 12 ♕c2 and White has a slight but enduring edge, Khalifman-Schekachev, Russian Ch (Elista) 1996.

b) Another idea for Black is 5...f6, intending to transpose to Line B21 after 6 h3 e5. However, in Anand-Krasenkow, Moscow PCA rpd 1996 White saw no need to engage in this, and instead continued 6 e5!? ♗g4 7 exf6 exf6 8 h3 ♗e6 9 0-0 ♕d7 10 ♗e3 ♘h6 11 ♘c3 with a solid advantage.

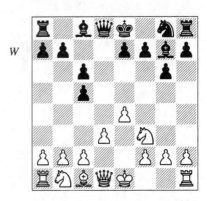

White should now choose between:

B221: 6 0-0   30
B222: 6 h3   32

A third possibility is 6 ♘c3, but this can now be well met by 6...♗g4 since White will then be forced to recapture with the queen on f3.

B221)

6 0-0 ♘f6

This looks most sensible to me.

6...♗g4 7 ♘bd2 transposes to note 'a' to Black's 5th move in Line B22.

6...e5 is another option, but I do not like the latter for the simple reason that compared to Line C322 White does not have to play ♖e1, and is thus basically a tempo up on similar variations. For example: 7 ♗e3 (7 a3!?) 7...♕e7 (7...b6 is feasible, but since the queen belongs on e7 anyway, I see no reason why Black should not play it immediately; after 8 ♘bd2 f6 9 a3! ♘h6 10 h3 ♕e7 11 b4 cxb4 12 axb4 ♕xb4 13 c3 ♕xc3 14 ♕b1! and White is probably already winning, Stefansson-McShane, Copenhagen 1998) 8 h3 (Yudasin-Vyzhmanavin, Leon 1993 continued in rather unorthodox fashion: 8 a4 ♘f6 9 ♘a3 0-0 10 ♖b1!? ♖d8! 11 ♕e1!? ♗g4! 12 ♘d2 ♗e6 13 ♘dc4 ♘d7 14 ♘a5!? ♘b8! 15 ♔h1 ♘a6 with an unclear position) 8...♘f6 9 ♕d2 ♘d7 10 ♗h6 0-0 (I prefer 10...f6, hoping to be in time with the manoeuvre ...♘f8-e6) 11 ♗xg7 ♔xg7 12 ♕c3 ♖e8 13 ♘bd2 ♘f8 14 ♘h2! f6 15 f4 exf4 16 ♖xf4 with an advantage for White, Chandler-Cummings, British League (4NCL) 1997/8.

7 h3

I consider this to be more accurate than 7 ♘c3. Black usually meets 7 ♘c3 with something like 7...♘d7, but Black should play 7...♗g4!, e.g. 8 h3 ♗xf3 9 ♕xf3 ♘d7, transposing to note 'a1' to Black's 5th move in Line B22.

7...0-0

Playing 7...♘d7 before castling does not make any difference if White simply continues 8 ♘c3 but in the game Lobron-Khalifman, Bad Wiessee 1998 White tried to take advantage of the fact that Black has already committed his knight: 8 c3!? (this would make much less sense if the knight had stayed on f6) 8...0-0 9 d4 b6 10 ♖e1 cxd4 11 cxd4 e5 12 ♗g5 ♕c7 13 ♗e7! (this, together with White's next move, suggests that Black's 11th or 12th move might be wrong) 13...♖e8 14 d5! cxd5 15 exd5 ±.

8 ♘c3 (D)

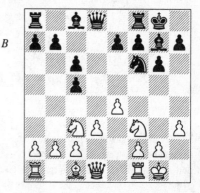

8...♘d7

This is slightly more flexible than 8...♘e8, which only contains one idea, namely the manoeuvre ...♘c7-e6-d4 (with or without ...e5). After 9 ♗e3 b6 10 a4 a5 (White is better if he gets in a5) 11 ♕d2 e5 (this is virtually essential as 11...♘c7 12 ♗h6 ♘e6 13 ♗xg7 ♔xg7 14 ♘e2 gives White an edge) 12 ♗h6 f6 13 ♘h2 g5!? (13...♕d6 looks like a safer alternative) 14 ♗xg7 ♘xg7 with an unclear game, Becerra Rivero-Fraschini, Havana 1994.

9 ♗e3 e5 10 a3 a5

10...♕e7!?.

11 ♘d2 ♕e7 12 ♘c4 b5 13 ♘d2
Anand-Kramnik, Villarrobledo rpd 1998. Now 13...a4 is roughly equal.

B222)
6 h3 *(D)*

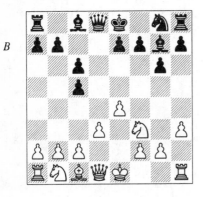

6...e5
It is difficult for Black to do without this move. It stakes out space in the centre, while restricting White's piece play.

The main alternative, 6...♘f6, is entirely feasible as long as Black follows it up with a quick ...♘d7 and ...e5. 7 ♘c3 and then:

a) 7...b6 8 ♗e3 ♘d7 9 ♕d2 h6 10 ♘h2 e5 11 0-0-0 ♘f8 12 f4 exf4 13 ♗xf4 ♘e6 14 ♗e3 ♕e7 15 ♖df1 ♘d4 16 ♘g4 ♗e6! 17 ♗xh6 ♗xh6 18 ♘xh6 ♕h4 19 ♘g4 ♗xg4 20 hxg4 ♕xh1 21 ♖xh1 ♖xh1+ 22 ♘d1 c4! with just sufficient counterplay for Black, Oratovsky-Ulybin, Cappelle la Grande 1996.

b) 7...♕c7 8 ♗e3 b6 9 ♕d2 e5 10 ♗h6 0-0 11 ♗xg7 ♔xg7 12 g4!? ♘e8 13 0-0-0 f6 14 ♖dg1 ♔g8 15 h4 with a

promising attack for White, Sutovsky-Kotronias, Buenos Aires 1997.

c) 7...0-0 8 ♗e3 b6 9 ♕d2 and then any attempt to withhold ...e5 seems to fail:

c1) 9...♖e8 10 a3 (White plays very flexibly but a more direct approach is also possible, e.g. 10 0-0-0 e5 11 ♗h6 ♕c7 12 ♘h2! ♗e6 13 ♘g4 ♘h5 14 ♗xg7 ♔xg7 15 ♕h6+ ♔h8 16 f4! exf4 17 e5 with a strong attack, Ziatdinov-C.Horvath, Nikšić 1991) 10...a5 11 0-0 ♘d7 12 ♘h2! ♘f8 13 f4 f5 (after 13...♘e6 14 f5 ♘d4 15 ♘g4 White is also much better) 14 ♖ae1 ♘e6 15 exf5 gxf5 16 ♘f3 ♘d4 17 ♘e5 with a distinct advantage for White, Rublevsky-Andersson, Polanica Zdroj 1997.

c2) 9...♘e8 10 0-0-0 ♘c7 11 ♗h6 ♘e6 12 h4 ♗xh6 13 ♕xh6 f6 14 ♘e2 ♖f7 15 g4 ♘d4 16 ♘fxd4 cxd4 17 ♖dg1 ± Bologan-Kharlov, USSR 1991.

c3) 9...e5! 10 ♗h6 (after 10 ♘xe5?! ♘xe4 11 ♘xf7 ♘xd2 12 ♘xd8 ♘f3+! 13 gxf3 ♖xd8 Black has enough compensation in view of White's weak pawns) 10...♕e7 11 0-0-0 (there is no need to exchange too soon on g7; an example is 11 ♗xg7 ♔xg7 12 ♕g5 ♖e8 13 0-0-0 a5 14 ♘d2 a4 15 ♖df1 h6 16 ♕e3 b5, when Black is doing well, Kaidanov-D.Gurevich, Chicago 1996) 11...♘h5 12 ♘e2 (Black would be happy to get a chance to play ...♘f4, even at the cost of a pawn, but only if it meant White having to part with his dark-squared bishop) 12...f6 13 ♖df1 ♗e6 14 g4 ♗xh6 15 ♕xh6 ♘g7 16 ♘d2! is slightly better for White, Rublevsky-Lanka, Budapest ECC 1996. White is ready to play f4, while it would take something drastic to speed up Black's attack.

d) 7...♘d7 8 ♗e3 e5 9 ♕d2 ♕e7 10 ♗h6 ♗xh6 11 ♕xh6 f6 12 ♘d2 ♘f8 13 f4 and now:

d1) 13...♘e6? 14 fxe5 fxe5 15 ♘e2! (White has a clear advantage, and in the following stage of the game he aims at reducing any possible counterplay while keeping his own assets, i.e. control of the f-file and an attack against the e5-pawn) 15...♗d7 (presumably Black should at least try to put up a fight for the f-file with 15...♖f8) 15...♗d7 16 0-0 0-0-0 17 ♘c4 ♗e8 18 ♖f2 ♘c7 19 a4 ♘a6 20 ♖af1 ♘b4 21 ♘c1 ± Wells-Chandler, British League (4NCL) 1997/8.

d2) Black should definitely continue 13...exf4 14 ♕xf4. Nevertheless, White maintains an edge, since his knights are significantly stronger than Black's bishop and knight, and the pawn structure will always be in White's favour.

7 ♗e3

7 ♘c3 ♕e7 8 ♗e3 ♘f6 9 ♕d2 ♘d7 transposes to note 'd' to Black's 6th move.

7...♕e7 8 ♕d2 (D)

This seems to be the most accurate move-order for White. First of all it prevents ideas like ...f6 and ...♘h6-f7, but it also introduces the idea of moving the queen to c3. For example after 8...f5, 9 ♕c3! b6 10 a4 would be very strong.

8...♘f6 9 ♗h6

The most direct, and it stops Black transposing to Wells-Chandler (note 'd' to Black's 6th move; whether this

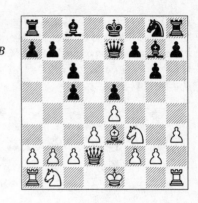

is anything for Black to strive for is another question), but other moves are also available:

a) 9 ♕c3 ♘d7 10 a3 a5 11 a4 b6 12 ♘a3 f5 13 ♘c4 f4 14 ♗c1 ♗a6 15 b3 0-0 16 ♗b2 ♖ae8 was roughly equal in Nevednichy-Kiseliov, USSR Cht (Azov) 1991.

b) After 9 ♘c3, 9...0-0 is likely to transpose to the main line below as White will have to play ♗h6 sooner or later, while 9...♘d7 transposes directly into Wells-Chandler.

9...0-0 10 ♘c3 ♖e8

Alternatives:

a) 10...♘h5!? 11 ♘e2 ♗xh6 12 ♕xh6 c4! 13 0-0 cxd3 14 cxd3 f6 = Svidler-Sutovsky, Tilburg 1996.

b) 10...♘e8!? intends to recapture with the knight when White exchanges on g7. Black will then play ...f6, whereafter the knight can join the game via e6. 11 0-0-0 b5 12 ♘h2 a5 13 ♘g4 (I prefer the immediate 13 ♗xg7 ♘xg7 14 f4) 13...a4 14 ♖de1? (I do not quite see the idea of this move; an exchange on g7 followed by f4 would still be preferable) 14...a3 15 b3 c4! 16

f4 cxb3 17 cxb3 exf4 18 ♗xg7 ♘xg7
19 ♘h6+ ♚h8 20 ♕xf4 ♗e6 and Black
has a promising position, Shaked-Van
der Weide, Groningen 1996.

11 ♗xg7 ♚xg7 *(D)*

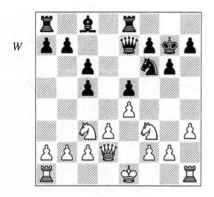

12 0-0-0

12 ♘h2!? h5 13 0-0-0 ♘h7 14 ♘e2
gave White an edge in Wells-Silman,
Budapest 1994, and there may indeed
be a case for making some kingside
threats before committing the king.

**12...b5 13 ♚b1 a5 14 ♘h2 a4 15
♘e2**

15 ♘g4 or 15 f4!? looks much stronger.

**15...a3 16 b3 c4 17 ♘c3 cxb3 18
cxb3 ♗e6**

Black is doing well, Khasangatin-
Gagarin, Russian Club Cup (Maikop)
1998.

C)

4 0-0 ♗g7 *(D)*
Now we branch into:

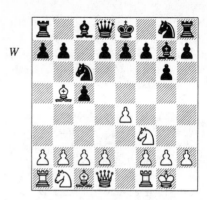

5 ♕e2 is the only reasonable alternative to the above-mentioned options;
5...e5 (5...♘f6 would also be met by a
♕c4 idea, namely 6 e5 ♘d5 7 ♕c4!?
♘c7 8 ♗xc6 dxc6 9 ♕xc5 ♗g4 10
♘d4! 0-0 11 h3 ♗d7 12 ♘f3 ♘e6,
Kosikov-Tukmakov, USSR 1976, and
now White should play 13 ♕e3!, when
it is difficult for Black to prove that he
has enough for the pawn) 6 ♕c4!?.
Now Morozevich considers the following possibilities for Black:

a) 6...d6 7 b4 ♘ge7!? (7...cxb4 8
♗xc6+ bxc6 9 ♕xc6+ ♗d7 10 ♕xd6
gives White a clear advantage, while
7...♗e6 8 ♕c3 cxb4 9 ♗xc6+ ♚f8 10
♕xb4 bxc6 11 ♗a3 c5 12 ♕a4 also
looks better for White) 8 bxc5 ♗e6
(8...0-0 9 cxd6 ♕xd6 10 ♗a3 ±) 9
♕c3 d5! with compensation.

b) 6...♘d4!? 7 ♕xc5 (7 ♘xd4 cxd4
is fine for Black) 7...♘xf3+ 8 gxf3
♘e7! (intending ...0-0 followed by
...d5) 9 d4 a6 (9...exd4 10 ♗f4 is awkward for Black due to White's powerful
bishops) 10 ♗a4 b5 11 dxe5 (11 ♗b3
d6 should be quite OK) 11...bxa4 12
♗g5 gives White compensation, but I

will leave it up to the reader to judge whether it is enough to compensate. Black will have to do a lot of preparatory work before he is ready to castle.

c) 6...b6 is definitely the safest option. Then Morozevich-Ivanchuk, Moscow OL 1994 continued 7 &xc6 dxc6 8 ♕c3 ♕c7 9 a3 a5 10 d3 ♘e7 11 &e3 0-0 12 ♘bd2 &e6 13 b4 cxb4 14 axb4 axb4 15 ♕xb4 c5 16 ♕b5, whereafter 16...&d7! 17 ♕b3 ♘c6 18 ♖xa8 ♖xa8 19 ♘g5 ♖f8 20 f4 h6 21 ♘h3 &xh3 22 gxh3 exf4 23 &xf4 &e5!? 24 &xe5 ♘xe5 25 ♘c4 ♘xc4 26 ♕xc4 would have led to an equal ending.

C1)

5 ♘c3 *(D)*

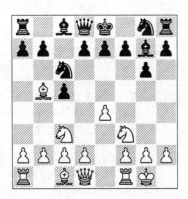

B

This has not exactly been Black's main worry until very recently. But with Kasparov having actually used it in a rapidplay game against Kramnik and young Russian star Alexander Morozevich's addiction to it, one has to treat it with respect. Surprisingly, it is not very easy for Black to find a suitable reply.

5...d6

With this move Black plans ...&d7 followed by ...♘f6, with quite a decent position. The problem with 5...♘f6 straight away is, naturally, that White can continue 6 e5, and here Black does not have 6...♘d5 as in Line C3. Hence he must play 6...♘g4, whereafter White secures an advantage with 7 &xc6 dxc6 8 ♖e1 0-0 9 d3. Two other options for Black are:

a) 5...e5 and now:

a1) 6 d3 ♘ge7 and here:

a11) 7 ♘d2 0-0 (7...♘d4 8 ♘c4 ♘xb5 9 ♘xb5 0-0 10 ♘bd6 ±) 8 ♘c4 d6 9 ♘e3 f5 10 &c4+ ♔h8 11 ♘ed5 f4 12 f3 (Ashley-Cao, Budapest 1997) 12...h5 with an unclear position.

a12) 7 &g5 0-0 8 &c4 h6 9 &h4 ♔h7!? 10 ♘d5 f6 11 ♘d2 d6 = Planinc-Parma, Belgrade 1978.

a13) 7 ♘e1 0-0 8 f4 exf4 9 &xf4 d6 10 ♘f3 &g4 11 ♕d2 ♘d4 12 ♘xd4 cxd4 13 ♘e2 ♖c8 14 &a4 ♘c6 15 &b3 ♕d7 16 ♖f2 &e6 = Morozevich-Christiansen, New York rpd 1995.

a2) 6 &xc6 bxc6 7 d3 ♘e7 8 a3 a5 9 &e3 d6 10 ♘d2 0-0 11 f4 exf4 12 &xf4, Kaidanov-Alterman, Erevan OL 1996, and now Kaidanov believes Black has a reasonable game after 12...h6.

b) 5...♘d4 and now:

b1) 6 ♘xd4 cxd4 7 ♘e2 ♕b6 (7...a6 8 &a4 e6 9 c3 b5 10 &c2 dxc3 11 dxc3 was very pleasant for White in Morozevich-Salov, Amsterdam 1995) 8 a4 ♘f6 9 &d3 0-0 10 a5 ♕c5 11 c3 dxc3 12 dxc3 d5 13 e5 ♘g4 14 b4 ♕c7 15 f4 f6 with good counterplay, Morozevich-Khalifman, Yalta 1995.

b2) 6 &a4!? ♕a5?! (again it is surprisingly difficult for Black to find a good reply; 6...a6 7 ♘xd4 cxd4 8 ♘e2 transposes to the game Morozevich-Salov in 'b1', while 6...e6 7 ♘xd4 cxd4 8 ♘b5 ♕b6 9 c3 likewise results in a good game for White) 7 ♖b1! e6 (one point of White's last move is revealed after 7...♘xf3+? 8 ♕xf3 ♗xc3 9 ♕xc3 ♕xc3 10 bxc3, when the b1-rook wakes up) 8 a3 b5 9 b4! ♕a6 10 bxc5! (this is a very strong sacrifice, exploiting Black's poor development) 10...♘xf3+ 11 ♕xf3 bxa4 12 ♘b5 ♔e7 13 d4! (White has more than enough compensation for the piece) 13...f6 (13...♕c6 is also insufficient: 14 d5! ♕xc5 15 ♗e3 ♕c4 16 ♖b4 ♕a2 17 ♗c5+ and White wins) 14 ♘c7 ♕c6 15 d5! ♕xc5 16 ♘xa8 ♗a6 17 ♖e1 and, in Morozevich-Yakovich, Russian Club Cup (Maikop) 1998, White won in a few more moves.

6 e5!? *(D)*

This disruptive pawn sacrifice is White's only chance for an advantage. Others:

a) 6 d3 ♗d7 7 a4 ♘f6 8 h3 0-0 9 ♗e3 e5 10 ♘d2 ♗e6 11 ♗c4 h6! 12 ♘e2 b6 13 ♗xe6 fxe6 14 f4 exf4 15 ♘xf4 ♕e8 and Black, with moves like ...d5 and ...g5 on the agenda, is doing fine, Adams-Anand, Groningen FIDE KO Wch 1997.

b) 6 h3 ♗d7 (this is necessary as a preparation for ...♘f6, because after 6...♘f6? 7 e5 dxe5 8 ♘xe5 Black cannot avoid doubled c-pawns) 7 ♖e1 ♘f6 8 ♗xc6 ♗xc6 9 e5 dxe5 10 ♘xe5 ♖c8 11 d3 0-0 12 ♗g5 ♖e8 13 ♕d2 ♘d7 14 ♘xc6 ♖xc6 = Kasparov-Kramnik, Paris rpd 1995.

6...dxe5 7 ♗xc6+ bxc6 8 ♖e1 f6

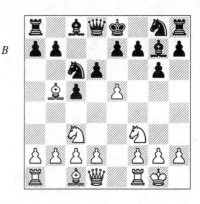

The problem for Black in this position is that he has very little hope of holding on to his extra pawn, and as soon as either the e5-pawn or the c5-pawn falls, White can concentrate on exploiting his positional advantage. Svidler-Van Wely, Tilburg 1998 instead saw Black giving up his e-pawn: 8...♕c7 9 d3 ♘f6 10 ♘xe5 ♘d5 11 ♕e2 ♘xc3 12 bxc3 ♕xe5 13 ♕xe5 ♗xe5 14 ♖xe5 c4 15 dxc4 f6 16 ♖c5 ♗d7 17 ♖a5 and White was better.

9 b3 ♘h6 10 ♗a3 ♕a5 11 ♘a4 c4

Since Black comes under some pressure after this move, it might be worth seeking a more dynamic solution, e.g. 11...♘f7 12 ♗xc5 f5 13 d3 ♕c7.

12 d4 cxd3 13 cxd3 ♗g4 14 d4!

This is Morozevich-Yakovich, Samara 1998. Black must play carefully to hold the balance, but with correct play he should have very good counterchances too. For a more detailed discussion of this position, see page 12 in the introduction.

C2)

5 c3 *(D)*

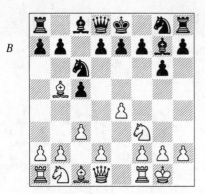

5...♘f6

This is the most common, and also the most logical against the c3 and d4 plan. Black's idea is to try to provoke e5. If White advances his e-pawn and follows with d4, Black will exchange pawns on d4 and hope to set up a blockade on the light squares, in the end trying to prove that White's pawn formation is weak.

Alternatives:

a) 5...♕b6 (this early queen sortie, which attempts to stop White playing d4, has a rather poor reputation) 6 ♘a3! a6 7 ♗a4 ♕c7 8 d4 b5 9 ♗b3 d6 10 ♗e3 c4 11 ♗c2 e5 12 b3 cxb3 13 axb3 ♖b8 14 d5 ♘ce7 15 c4 and White is better, Zaitsev-Apicella, Bucharest 1993.

b) 5...a6 6 ♗xc6 dxc6 7 d3 and then:

b1) 7...♘f6 8 h3 0-0 9 ♕e2 ♕c7? 10 e5 ♘e8 11 ♗f4 ♗e6 12 c4 b6 13 ♕e3 ♖d8 14 ♘c3 ♕d7 15 ♖fd1 ♘c7 16 b3 ± Minasian-Yermolinsky, New York 1993.

b2) 7...♗g4 8 a4 ♘f6 9 h3 ♗xf3 10 ♕xf3 ♘d7 11 ♕e2 e5 (11...a5 is better but White still has an edge after

12 ♘a3 e5 13 f4) 12 a5 ♘f8 13 f4 exf4 14 ♗xf4 ♘e6 15 ♗h2 0-0 16 ♘d2 ♕e7 17 ♘c4 ± Minasian-Goldin, New York 1993.

c) 5...e5 *(D)* with the options:

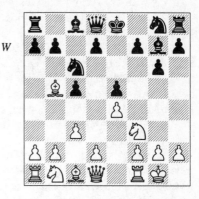

c1) 6 d3 ♘ge7 7 ♗e3 d6 8 d4 exd4 9 cxd4 0-0 10 ♘c3 b6 11 h3 a6 12 ♗c4! ♘a5 (Krasenkov mentions 12...b5 13 ♗d5 ♘xd5 14 exd5 ♘xd4 15 ♘xd4 cxd4 16 ♗xd4 and White is better) 13 ♗e2 ♗b7?! (Krasenkov suggests the more active 13...f5!? but I think Black still has some problems to solve after, for example, 14 dxc5 dxc5 15 ♕c1 ♗b7 16 ♖d1 ♕e8 17 ♘g5) 14 d5 b5 15 ♖c1 ♕d7, Kveinys-Krasenkov, Poland 1992, 16 b3! f5 17 e5 f4 18 ♗d2 dxe5 19 ♘e4 and White has a large advantage.

c2) 6 b4!? (this pawn sacrifice is quite interesting but we need a few more high-level games before a more precise evaluation can be established) 6...cxb4 7 d4 exd4 (7...bxc3 8 ♘xc3 exd4 9 ♘d5 also gives White a lot of initiative – Zaitsev) 8 cxd4 ♕b6 9 ♗c4 ♘xd4 10 e5 ♘e6 (Zaitsev also analyses other moves, but this appears best)

11 ♘bd2 ♘e7 12 ♘e4 0-0 13 ♘f6+ (13 ♘d6!?) 13...♗xf6?! (13...♔h8 14 ♗b2 d5 is better, with the idea 15 exd6 ♘g8, but White might try 15 ♗b3 with some compensation) 14 exf6 ♘f5 15 ♗b2 d5 16 ♗d3 with good attacking chances, Zaitsev-Krasenkov, USSR 1991.

c3) 6 d4 exd4 7 cxd4 cxd4 (7...♘xd4 8 ♘xd4 cxd4 9 f4 ♘e7 10 f5 ♘c6 11 f6! ♗f8 12 ♗c4 ♕b6 13 ♘d2 d6 14 b4!? ♘e5 15 ♗d5 ♗g4 16 ♕a4+ ♗d7 17 ♕b3 gave White fantastic compensation in W.Watson-Prasad, Thessaloniki OL 1988) 8 ♗f4 and now:

c31) 8...a6 (starting a plan of attacking White's b5-bishop) 9 ♗c4 d6 10 ♕b3 ♘a5 (10...♕e7? is bad in view of 11 ♗xd6! ♕xd6 12 ♗xf7+ ♔d7 13 ♗xg8 ♔c7 14 ♗d5 +– V.I.Ivanov-Goloshchapov, Sevastopol 1995) 11 ♗xf7+ ♔e7 12 ♕d5 ♘f6 13 ♗g5 (13 ♗xd6+ ♕xd6 14 ♕xd6+ ♔xd6 15 e5+ ♔e7 16 exf6+ ♔xf6 17 ♗d5 ♖d8 18 ♗e4 ♗g4 should be fine for Black) 13...♖f8 14 ♖e1 ♘c6 (14...♖xf7?! 15 e5 dxe5 16 ♖xe5+ ♗e6 17 ♖xe6+ ♔f8 18 ♕xd8+ ♖xd8 19 ♘e5 ♖c7 20 ♘a3 and White is better – Kraut) 15 e5 dxe5 16 ♕xd8+ ♖xd8 17 ♗b3 ♔f8 18 ♘xe5 ♖e8, and now Kraut suggests 19 f4!? rather than Razuvaev and Matsukevich's 19 ♘f3, when Black is quite OK after 19...♖xe1+ 20 ♘xe1 ♗f5.

c32) 8...♘ge7 9 ♗d6 (highlighting the main drawback of Black's 8th move) 9...0-0 10 ♘bd2 a6 11 ♗c4 b5 12 ♗d5 ♗b7 13 ♘b3 ♘xd5 (if 13...♖e8?, then 14 ♘c5 ♘xd5 15 exd5 ♘a5 16 b4, etc.) 14 ♗xf8 ♕xf8 15 exd5 ♘b4 16 a3 ♘xd5 17 ♘a5 and

Black does not have quite enough compensation, Dreev-Lputian, Simferopol 1988.

We return to the position after 5...♘f6 *(D)*.

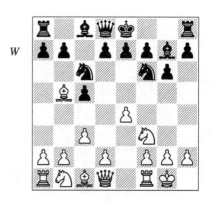

White has the following main possibilities:

C21: 6 ♕e2　　39
C22: 6 ♖e1　　41

Besides White's two main options, it is worth paying attention to two more:

a) 6 e5 ♘d5 7 d4 cxd4 8 cxd4 0-0 9 ♘c3 and now the simplest equalizing method for Black is probably to exchange on c3:

a1) 9...♘xc3 10 bxc3 d6 11 exd6 (the pawn sacrifice 11 e6 fxe6 12 ♗d3 has been tried but I do not quite trust it). Now both captures are fine for Black:

a11) 11...♕xd6 12 a4 a6 13 ♗a3 ♕c7 14 ♗xc6 (or 14 ♗d3 ♘a5, intending ...♗e6, controlling the c4-square) 14...♕xc6 15 ♗xe7 ♖e8 16 d5! ♕xc3 17 ♖c1 ♕a5 18 ♖c5 ♕b4 19 ♖xc8

Wxe7 20 d6 Wf6 21 Ixa8 Ixa8 =
Ardeleanu-Čabrilo, Star Dojran 1994.

a12) 11...exd6 12 &g5 Wc7 13 Ie1
a6 14 &a4 &d7 15 ②d2 h6 16 &f4
②a5 = G.Kuzmin-Zubarev, Donetsk Z
1998.

a2) 9...②c7 *(D)* and now White
should decide whether he wants to
play for quick development or to retain his light-squared bishop:

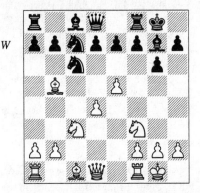

a21) 10 &g5?! h6 11 &h4 g5!
(11...②xb5 12 ②xb5 a6 13 ②d6!? g5
14 &xg5! hxg5 15 ②xg5 f6 16 exf6
Ixf6, Smirin-Vyzhmanavin, Groningen PCA qual 1993, 17 ②de4 If4 18
d5 ②e5 19 d6 e6 20 Ic1 with compensation – Smirin) 12 &g3 ②xb5 13
②xb5 a6 14 ②c3 d6 15 Ie1?! (15 exd6
exd6 16 d5 ②e7 ∓ Lanka) 15...&g4 16
h3 &h5 and Black is better, Leventić-
Lanka, Portorož 1994.

a22) 10 &a4 d6 11 &xc6 bxc6 12
Ie1 &g4 13 h3 &xf3 14 Wxf3 ②e6
15 &e3 dxe5 (Kraut's 15...c5 is interesting; he suggests that Black might
even be able to seize an initiative) 16
dxe5 Wc7 17 Iac1 &xe5 18 ②d5 Wb7

19 Ixc6 Wxb2 20 &c1, and now,
rather than 20...Wa1?!, as in Moreno-
Lopez, Havana 1993, Black should
play 20...Wd4 21 ②xe7+ &h8 with an
unclear position.

a23) 10 a4 a6 11 &c4 d6 12 exd6
Wxd6 13 d5 ②e5 14 ②e4!? ②xf3+ 15
Wxf3 Wb4, Zaitsev-Kiseliov, Orel
1994, 16 Wb3!? with an unclear position – Kiseliov and Gagarin.

a24) 10 &f4 (this was Bronstein's
preference in a few games, but it really
ought not to give Black problems)
10...②xb5 11 ②xb5 a6 12 ②c3 d6 13
exd6 exd6 14 h3 Ie8 15 &g5 Wa5 =
Bronstein-Dvoretsky, Moscow 1975.

b) 6 d4!? cxd4 7 cxd4 ②xe4 8 d5
②d6 9 &d3!? (9 ②a3 ②e5 10 ②xe5
&xe5 11 Ie1 &f6 12 h4!? gives White
some play for the pawn, according to
Mikhalchishin) 9...②b4 10 ②c3 0-0
11 &f4 b6 12 Ie1?! (12 &e5!? gives
White some compensation) 12...&b7
∓ Kotsur-Tzermiadianos, Sofia 1994.

C21)
6 We2 0-0 *(D)*

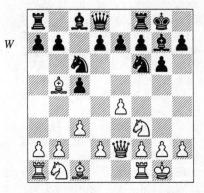

7 d4

This move clearly makes most sense. A few other options:

a) 7 ♖d1 ♘e8 8 d4 cxd4 9 cxd4 ♘c7 10 ♗xc6 dxc6 11 h3 and then:

a1) 11...f5?! is a little too optimistic; Black hopes that the opening of the position will do him some good in view of his possession of the two bishops, but objectively it is too weakening. 12 ♘c3 fxe4 13 ♕xe4 ♗f5 14 ♕h4 ♘e6 (14...♘d5 is safer) 15 d5! ♗xc3 16 bxc3 cxd5 17 c4 d4 18 ♗h6 ♖f6 19 ♘xd4 ± A.Fernandez-V.Spasov, Manila OL 1992.

a2) 11...b6 12 ♘c3 ♗a6 13 ♕c2 ♕c8 14 ♗g5 ♖e8 = A.Fernandes-Ra.Garcia, Lisbon Z 1993.

b) 7 e5 ♘e8 (7...♘d5 8 ♕c4 is one of White's points when playing ♕e2 rather than ♖e1, but whether this is as strong as intended is not so clear: 8...♘c7! 9 ♗xc6 dxc6 10 ♕xc5 ♗g4 11 ♘d4 ♕d7 with compensation according to Kraut) 8 d4 cxd4 9 cxd4 ♘c7 10 ♗a4 d6 (Spassky once tried 10...d5, which should be good enough too, but beginning an attack on White's centre looks more logical) 11 ♖d1 ♗g4 12 h3 ♗xf3 13 ♕xf3 dxe5 14 dxe5 ♕c8 15 ♗xc6 bxc6 16 ♕xc6 ♗xe5 17 ♘c3 ♘e6 18 ♘d5 ♖e8 19 ♕xc8 ♖axc8 and Black is at least equal, Rogers-Agdestein, Biel IZ 1993.

7...cxd4

7...d5 should also be possible (this move is seen in the related line 6 ♖e1 0-0 7 d4 d5!?, but against 6 ♕e2 the immediate 7...d5 is for some reason rarely seen). Utemov-Smirin, USSR Cht (Podolsk) 1990 went 8 e5 ♘e4 9 ♘bd2 (9 ♗e3) 9...cxd4 10 cxd4 ♕b6 11 ♘xe4?! dxe4 12 ♗xc6 ♕xc6 13 ♘g5 ♗f5 14 ♖e1 ♖ad8 15 ♘xe4 ♖xd4 with an edge for Black.

8 cxd4 d5 9 e5 ♘e4 10 ♗e3

Another possibility for White is 10 ♘c3 ♘xc3 11 bxc3 ♕a5 (Korchnoi suggests 11...♘a5 12 h3 a6 13 ♗d3 ♗d7 with equality) 12 ♗d2 (or 12 a4 ♗g4 13 ♕e3 f6 14 ♗a3 ♖fe8 15 ♖fe1 ♕d8 16 exf6 exf6 17 ♕f4 ♕d7 = Sepp-Gausel, Debrecen Echt 1992) 12...♗g4 13 ♖fb1 ♕c7 = A.Fernandes-Wells, Linares Z 1995.

10...f6

10...♕b6 11 ♘c3 ♘xc3 12 bxc3 ♗g4 13 ♖fb1 ♕c7 14 h3 ♗xf3 15 ♕xf3 e6 16 h4 ♘a5 was about equal in Bilek-Szilagyi, Budapest 1964.

11 exf6 exf6 12 ♘c3 ♘xc3 13 bxc3 ♘a5 14 ♘d2 ♗f5?!

A very natural developing move, but in my opinion a mistake. White is positionally worse unless he can get in c4. Black cannot prevent that (since ...a6 and ...b5 is too weakening) but he can attempt to make sure the light-squared bishops are exchanged when this happens. Beginning with 14...♔h8 would be an idea. Now 15 c4 fails in view of 15...a6 16 ♗a4 dxc4 17 ♘xc4 ♘xc4 18 ♕xc4 b5 (see the point of ...♔h8!), so a normal move would be 15 ♗d3, to which Black can reply 15...♗e6, intending to place the bishop on f7. White cannot really get in c4 now without exchanging the light-squared bishops, and this would ease Black's defence a lot.

15 c4! a6 16 ♗a4 ♘xc4 17 ♘xc4 dxc4 18 ♕xc4+ ♔h8 19 ♗b3

White is better due to his strong passed d-pawn, Minasian-Nikolaidis, Panormo Z 1998.

C22)
6 ♖e1 *(D)*

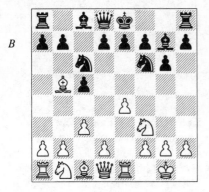

6...0-0

Instead, 6...a6 forces an immediate decision from White's light-squared bishop. White can retreat it to f1, but the best is 7 ♗xc6 dxc6 8 h3, when it is difficult to see a better move than 8...0-0, transposing to note 'd' to Black's 7th move.

7 h3!?

Even though this looks like one of those moves you just play and hope they turn out not to be completely wasted, this is actually a very good waiting move as it forces Black to 'show his cards'. White will most likely follow up with d4 but only after seeing what Black has in mind. Alternatives:

a) 7 e5 ♘d5 8 d4 cxd4 9 cxd4 d6 (9...♘c7 is also feasible) 10 ♘c3 ♘xc3 (10...dxe5 11 ♗xc6 bxc6 12 ♘xe5 is comfortable for White and 10...♘c7 11 ♗xc6 bxc6 12 h3 h6 13 ♕a4 ♗b7 14 ♗f4 c5 15 ♘e4 ♘e6 16 ♗g3 ♗xe4 17 ♖xe4 cxd4 18 ♕a3 d5 19 ♖e2 ♖e8 20 ♖d1 ♕b6 was good for Black in Stavrinov-Lanka, Latvian Ch 1993) 11 bxc3 ♗g4 12 exd6 ♕xd6 (12...exd6 13 h3 ♗xf3 14 ♕xf3 gives White an edge) and now:

a1) 13 h3 ♗xf3 14 ♕xf3 e5 15 ♗xc6 bxc6 16 dxe5 ♗xe5 17 ♗h6 ♖fe8 18 ♖ad1 ♕c7 19 ♖e4 ♖e6 = Yandemirov-Polovnikova, Perm 1997.

a2) 13 a4 ♕d5 14 ♗a3 ♖fc8 15 h3 ♗xf3 16 ♕xf3 ♕xf3 17 gxf3 e6 18 ♖ab1 ♘a5 and Black is better, Ribeiro-Turner, Athens 1997.

b) 7 d4 and then:

b1) 7...cxd4 8 cxd4 (8 e5 ♘d5 9 cxd4 d6 10 ♘c3 transposes to 'a') 8...a6 9 ♗xc6 dxc6 10 h3 c5 11 d5 e6?! (11...b5 is stronger but I would still prefer White after 12 ♘c3 ♗b7 13 ♗g5) 12 d6! (this pawn turns out to be very annoying) 12...e5 13 ♘c3 ♖e8 14 ♗e3 b6 15 ♕d3 and White is better, Rozentalis-Timman, Moscow OL 1994.

b2) 7...d5!? (this move has almost entirely superseded the older 7...cxd4; now White's knight will not have access to c3). Then:

b21) 8 exd5 ♕xd5! 9 dxc5 (9 c4 ♕d6 10 dxc5 ♕xd1 11 ♖xd1 ♘e4 12 ♗xc6 bxc6 13 ♘a3 ♗g4 14 ♘c2 ♘xc5 15 ♘cd4 ♖fc8 = Torre-Kotronias, Manila OL 1992) 9...♕xc5 10 ♗xc6?! (this is rather dubious, but Black would have absolutely no problems if the bishop retreated) 10...♕xc6! 11 ♖xe7 ♗e6 12 ♘d4 ♕d6! 13 ♖xb7 ♘g4 14 g3 ♖fd8! 15 ♗g5 ♗xd4! 16 ♕xd4

♕f8! with a winning attack for Black, Vedder-Yakovich, Leeuwarden 1992.

b22) 8 e5!? ♘e4 leading to a further branch:

b221) 9 h3 ♕b6 10 ♗a4 ♗f5 11 ♘a3 cxd4 12 cxd4 f6! 13 ♗b3 ♖ad8 14 exf6 exf6 15 ♘c2 ♖fe8 16 ♗f4 ♗e6 17 ♖e2 g5! 18 ♗h2 f5 19 ♕e1 ♗f7! ∓ Rozentalis-Kramnik, Bundesliga 1993/4.

b222) 9 ♗xc6 bxc6 10 ♘bd2 ♘xd2 11 ♘xd2 cxd4 12 cxd4 c5! 13 dxc5 ♕c7 14 ♘f3 ♕xc5 15 ♘d4 ♗d7 16 b3 ♖fc8 17 ♗b2 ♕a5 = Rozentalis-Degraeve, Belfort 1997.

b223) 9 ♘bd2 cxd4 10 cxd4 ♗d7!? (after 10...♕b6 11 ♗xc6 ♕xc6, 12 ♘xe4 dxe4 13 ♘g5 ♖d8! was comfortable for Black in J.Polgar-Kramnik, Monaco Amber blindfold 1994, but White should prefer 12 ♘b3!? followed by ♗e3 and ♖c1) 11 ♗d3 (11 ♘xe4 dxe4 12 ♖xe4 ♘xe5 {or 12...♕b6!?} 13 ♖xe5 ♗xe5 14 ♗xd7 ♗xh2+ 15 ♔xh2 ♕xd7 ± Nesis and Novik) 11...♘xd2 12 ♗xd2 ♕b6 13 ♗c3 ♗g4 14 ♗e2 e6 15 ♕d2 ♖fc8 ½-½ Shabanov-Novik, St Petersburg 1994.

Returning to the position after 7 h3 *(D)*:

7...e5

Black will now be left with the worse structure after White plays d4. Black's idea is to take twice, when he will end up with an isolated d-pawn, but he hopes that his slight lead in development and well-placed pieces will compensate for this. Other moves:

a) 7...d6!? 8 d4 (8 d3 ♗d7 9 a3 ♕c7 10 ♘bd2 a6 11 ♗c4 ♘e5 12

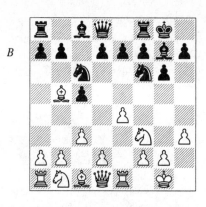

♘xe5 dxe5 13 ♘f3 ♖ad8 14 ♕e2 ♗c6 = Certić-Skembris, Kavala 1997) 8...cxd4 9 cxd4 a6 10 ♗f1 e5 11 ♘c3 ♖e8 12 d5 ♘d4 13 ♗e3 ♘xf3+ 14 ♕xf3 ± Hübner-Soltis, Ybbs 1968.

b) 7...♕b6 8 ♘a3 d5 9 e5 ♘e8 10 d3 ♘c7 11 ♗a4 ♘e6 12 ♘c2 d4 13 cxd4 ♘cxd4 14 ♘cxd4 cxd4 15 ♗b3 h6 16 a4! a5 17 ♗c4 ♘d8 18 b3 ♗e6 19 ♗a3 ± Smyslov-Zsu.Polgar, Prague 1995.

c) 7...♘e8 8 d4 cxd4 9 cxd4 ♘c7 10 ♗f1 d5 11 e5 ♘e6 12 ♘c3 f6 13 exf6 exf6 14 b3 with an edge for White, Ciocaltea-Ghitescu, Bucharest 1966.

d) 7...a6 8 ♗xc6 (8 ♗f1 e5 9 d4 cxd4 10 cxd4 exd4 seems to give Black a better version of the main lines) 8...dxc6 9 d4 cxd4 10 cxd4 c5 11 d5 transposes to note 'b1' to White's 7th move.

8 d4

Or:

a) 8 ♗xc6 dxc6 9 ♘xe5 (testing the tactical justification of Black's 7th move) 9...♖e8 10 f4 ♘h5! 11 d4 ♕h4 12 ♖f1 ♗xh3! 13 gxh3 ♕g3+ (Black has at least a perpetual check) 14 ♔h1

♕xh3+ 15 ♔g1 ♘g3 16 ♘d2 ♕h1+ 17 ♔f2 (Galdunts-Dreev, St Petersburg 1993) 17...♘xf1! 18 ♕xf1 (18 ♘xf1 ♕xe4 19 ♘g3 ♕d5 ∓) 18...♕xf1+ 19 ♘xf1 cxd4 20 cxd4 f6. The e4-pawn drops, with clearly the better ending for Black – Dreev.

b) 8 d3 (a quieter approach) 8...d6 9 ♘bd2 ♗d7 (9...h6 10 ♘f1 ♕c7 11 ♗a4 ♖b8 12 ♗e3 ♘h7 13 ♗c2 b6 14 d4 ♗d7 15 d5 ♘e7 16 g4 ♘fg8 17 ♘g3 ♔h8 18 ♘h2 b5 with counter-play, Stripunsky-Antunes, Wijk aan Zee 1996) 10 ♘f1 and then:

b1) 10...h6 11 ♘e3!? a6 12 ♗a4 b5 13 ♗c2 ♖e8 14 a3 ♗e6 15 ♗d2 ♔h7 16 ♕c1 ♕d7 17 b4 cxb4 (17...a5!?) 18 axb4 d5 19 exd5 ♘xd5 20 ♘g4! ♗xg4 21 hxg4 with some attacking prospects for White, Certić-Kotronias, Kavala 1997.

b2) 10...♘e8 11 ♗g5!? f6 12 ♗d2 ♔h8 13 b4! cxb4 (Kholmov's suggestion 13...♘c7 is better) 14 cxb4 f5 15 ♗c4 and White has a slight advantage, Kholmov-Vasiukov, Russia 1995.

8...cxd4 9 cxd4 *(D)*

9...exd4

White has a much easier game after 9...♘xd4 10 ♘xd4 exd4 11 ♕xd4!, when Black has serious problems justifying the weak d-pawn, e.g.:

a) 11...♖e8 12 e5 a6 13 ♗g5! h6 14 ♗xf6 ♗xf6 15 ♘c3 ♗g7 16 ♗c4 d6 (16...♕g5 17 ♘e4!) 17 ♕xd6 ♕g5 18 ♘e4 ♕f4 19 e6! ♕xd6 20 exf7+ 1-0 Stelting-Danschczyk, 2nd Bundesliga 1991.

b) 11...a6 12 ♗a4 ♖e8 13 e5 b5 14 ♗b3 (the same idea as above, 14 ♗g5, still looks interesting) 14...d6 15 ♖d1 ♘h5 16 ♕xd6 ± Kazhgaleev-Kožul, Pula Echt 1997.

10 e5

The best try. White can play 10 ♘xd4, hoping for 10...♘xd4 11 ♕xd4 with a transposition to the previous note. However, Black plays the much better 10...♕b6, forcing an exchange on c6: 11 ♘xc6 dxc6 12 ♗c4 ♖e8 13 ♘c3 ♗e6 14 ♗f1 ♖ad8 and Black has a comfortable game, Fusthy-Klundt, Berlin 1988.

10...♘d5

Gallagher's suggestion 10...♘e8!? is also very interesting, although White may be in a position to claim some compensation – but probably not more – after 11 ♗g5 f6 12 exf6 ♗xf6 13 ♗xf6 ♕xf6 14 ♘bd2 ♘d6 15 ♗d3.

11 ♗g5 ♕c7

Here 11...f6 is met by 12 ♕b3!, but Anand-Salov, Paris Immopar rpd 1992 instead saw 11...♕a5 12 ♘a3 a6 13 ♗c4 ♘b6?! (this embarrasses the queen; 13...♘de7 is better) 14 ♗b3 ♘xe5? (a further mistake, and this time a losing one) 15 ♘xe5 ♗xe5 16 ♗h6

d6? (16...♖e8 17 ♕f3 d5? 18 ♖xe5!)
17 ♗d2 ♕c5 18 ♖c1 ♕xc1 19 ♗xc1
♗d7 20 ♗h6 ♖fe8 21 ♕f3 1-0.

12 ♕b3! ♘b6 13 ♘bd2

13 ♗f4 a6 14 ♗f1 ♘a5 15 ♕d1 ♘d5
16 ♗g3 ♕b6 17 ♕xd4 ♕xd4 18 ♘xd4
♘c6 19 ♘xc6 dxc6 = Tkachev-Mortensen, Moscow OL 1994.

13...d5

13...♘xe5 14 ♘xe5 ♗xe5 15 ♖ac1
♕b8 16 ♗h6 is highly unpleasant.

**14 exd6 ♕xd6 15 ♘e4 ♕d5 16
♗xc6 ♕xc6 17 ♗e7 ♗e6 18 ♕d1
♖fe8 19 ♘xd4 ♕a4**

Black must still watch his step carefully. For example, 19...♗xd4? is a
mistake owing to 20 ♕xd4 ♖xe7 21
♘f6+ ♔f8 22 ♘xh7+ ♔g8 23 ♘f6+
♔f8 24 ♘d5! +–.

**20 ♘xe6 ♕xd1 21 ♖axd1 ♖xe7 22
♘xg7 ♔xg7 23 ♘d6 ♖xe1+ 24 ♖xe1
♖d8 25 ♘xb7 ♖d2**

The players agreed to a draw here in
Meier-Mednis, Hamburg 1997. Black
seems to have just about enough counterplay.

C3)

5 ♖e1 *(D)*
Now:
C31: 5...♘f6   44
C32: 5...e5   47

C31)

5...♘f6 6 e5

We have already looked at 6 c3,
which was covered in Line C22, but
another important alternative here is 6
♘c3 0-0 (6...♘d4? has been known as
a mistake since it was played in Rossolimo-Romanenko, Salzburg 1948: 7

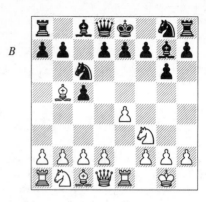

e5 ♘g8 8 d3 ♘xb5?! {in view of what
is coming, this is probably wrong} 9
♘xb5 a6 10 ♘d6+! exd6 {10...♔f8 is
more prudent, but White is better anyway} 11 ♗g5 ♕a5 12 exd6+ ♔f8 13
♖e8+! ♔xe8 14 ♕e2+ ♔f8 15 ♗e7+
♔e8 16 ♗d8+! ♔xd8 17 ♘g5 1-0) 7
e5 ♘e8, and now:

a) 8 d3 ♘d4!? (there is nothing
wrong with 8...♘c7 but Black tries to
take advantage of the fact that White
did not exchange on c6) 9 ♗g5 ♘c7
10 ♗c4 b5!? (very aggressive; a more
peace-minded player might choose
10...♘ce6 with the idea 11 ♗h4 ♘f5)
11 ♘xd4 bxc4 12 ♘db5 ♘e6 13 ♗h4
cxd3 14 ♕xd3 ♗b7 and Black is taking over the initiative, Ricardi-Smirin,
Moscow OL 1994.

b) 8 ♗xc6 dxc6 (8...bxc6 9 d4
cxd4 10 ♕xd4 d6 11 ♕h4 was better
for White in Sigurjonsson-Beliavsky,
Hastings 1974/5) 9 h3 ♘c7 with the
possibilities:

b1) 10 b3 (this has for a long time
been the choice of Rossolimo expert
Rainer Kraut) 10...♘e6 (an interesting
idea is to activate the bishop on d5

before playing ...♘e6; Kraut-Fahnen-schmidt, Tübingen 1994 saw an early peace agreement after 10...♗e6!? 11 d3 ♗d5 12 ♘e4 ♗e6 13 ♗b2 ♕d7 14 ♕c1 f5 15 exf6 exf6 =) 11 ♘e4 b6 12 ♗b2 ♘d4 13 d3 f5! (Black needs to gain some space) 14 exf6 exf6 15 ♘xd4 cxd4 16 ♕f3 f5 17 ♘d2 ♗b7 18 ♘c4 ♕c7 19 ♕e2 with perhaps a tiny advantage for White, Spangenberg-Fraschini, Buenos Aires 1991.

b2) 10 d3 ♘e6 (or 10...♗e6!? 11 ♗e3 b6 12 ♕d2 ♖e8 13 ♗h6 ♖h8 14 ♘e4 with an edge for White) 11 a4 (11 ♘e4 ♕c7 12 ♘eg5 h6 13 ♘xe6 ♗xe6 14 ♗f4 ♗h7 15 ♕e2 ♖ad8 16 b3 a5 17 a4 b6 18 ♕e3 ♕c8 19 ♖ab1 ♖d5 20 ♘d2 ♖fd8 21 ♗g3 ♗f5 22 ♘c4 ± Tseshkovsky-Mihalko, Budapest 1989) 11...a5 12 b3 b6 13 ♘e4 f5 14 exf6 exf6 15 ♗b2 ♖e8 16 ♘g3 ♖a7 17 ♕d2 ♖ae7 with a roughly equal position, Gdanski-Izbinski, Polish Cht (Krynica) 1997.

Returning to the position after 6 e5 *(D)*:

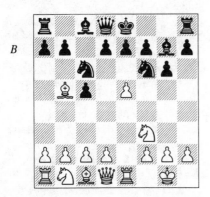

6...♘d5 7 ♘c3 ♘c7

7...♘xc3 8 dxc3 0-0 9 ♗c4 gives White lasting pressure, e.g. 9...b6 10 ♗f4 ♗b7 11 ♕d2 ♘a5 12 ♗d5 ♗xd5 13 ♕xd5 ♕c7 14 ♖ad1 ♖ad8 15 c4 ♕c6 16 b3 ± Golubović-Ptacnikova, Mitropa Cup 1997.

8 ♗xc6 dxc6 9 ♘e4 ♘e6

This is probably the most solid. The alternative is 9...b6 10 ♘f6+ (10 d4 cxd4 11 ♘xd4 ♘e6! is good for Black, who has the trick 12 ♘xc6? ♕xd1 13 ♖xd1 ♗b7 in mind) 10...♔f8 11 ♘e4 ♗g4 12 d3 (12 h3 ♗xf3 13 ♕xf3 ♘e6 14 d3 ♕d5 gave Black few worries in Glek-Wells, Wijk aan Zee 1995). The question is now whether it has been worth investing two tempi to interfere with Black's right to castle. This is without doubt somewhat awkward for Black, but White cannot relax either, since it is not so easy for him to defend his e-pawn:

a) 12...♗xe5? (this has already been examined in the Introduction {page 15}, and hence I will not go into much detail) 13 ♘xe5!! ♗xd1 14 ♗h6+ ♔g8 (14...♔e8 15 ♘xc6 f5 16 ♘xd8 ♖xd8 17 ♖axd1 fxe4 18 ♖xe4 +-) 15 ♘xc6 ♗xc2 (or 15...♕d7 16 ♘f6+! exf6 17 ♘e7+ ♕xe7 18 ♖xe7 ♘d5 19 ♖d7 and again White wins) and now:

a1) 16 ♘c3? e6 17 ♘xd8 ♖xd8 18 ♗g5 ♔g7 19 ♗xd8 ♖xd8 and Black has little to worry about, with a solid position and soon to be two pawns for the exchange, Timman-Kramnik, Riga Tal mem 1995.

a2) 16 ♘xd8! ♖xd8 17 ♘xc5! bxc5 18 ♖xe7 was Kramnik's suggestion afterwards, which he found very dangerous. For further analysis, see pages 15-16.

b) 12...♕d5?! 13 c4 ♕d7 (13...♕xe5 14 ♘xe5 ♗xd1 15 ♘xf7! ±) 14 h3 ♗xf3 15 ♕xf3 h6, Timman-Van der Wiel, Dutch Ch 1996, and now Timman claims a clear advantage for White after 16 b3 followed by ♗b2. In the game Timman played 16 ♗d2?! followed by ♗c3 but later had to play b3 and ♗b2, so I assume Timman decided these tempi could be better spent.

c) 12...♘e6! 13 ♘ed2 ♕d5 14 h3 ♗xf3 15 ♘xf3 ♖d8 16 ♕e2 h6! is the right solution. Black is ready to play ...♔g8-h7, with a comfortable position. Lutz-Piket, Wijk aan Zee 1995 now continued 17 ♗e3 ♔g8 18 c4! (it is already difficult to find a plan for White, so Lutz decided to gambit a pawn) 18...♕xd3 19 ♕xd3 ♖xd3 20 ♖ad1 ♖xd1 21 ♖xd1 f5! 22 exf6 ♗xf6 23 ♖d7 ♔f7 24 ♖xa7 ♗xb2 25 ♖b7 ♖a8 26 ♖xb6 ♖xa2 27 ♖xc6 and a draw was soon agreed.

10 d3 0-0 11 ♗e3 b6

11...♘d4 12 ♘xc5 leads to quite interesting play, e.g.:

a) 12...♗g4!? 13 ♗xd4 (13 ♘xb7 ♗xf3 14 gxf3 ♕d5 15 ♗xd4 ♕xd4 16 ♘a5 ♗xe5 17 ♘c4 ♗f4 and Black has plenty of play for the pawn) 13...♗xf3 14 ♕xf3 ♕xd4 15 ♕e3 ♕xb2 16 ♖ab1 ♕xa2 17 ♖xb7 with an unclear position – Lutz.

b) 12...♘xf3+ 13 ♕xf3 ♗xe5 14 d4 ♗g7 15 c4 and White's space advantage ensures an advantage, Lutz-Weemaes, Moscow OL 1994.

12 ♕d2 ♘d4!? *(D)*

12...f5!? 13 exf6 exf6 14 ♗h6 a5 15 ♗xg7 ♔xg7 16 ♖e2 ♖a7 was roughly equal in Kramnik-Kasparov, Moscow PCA rpd 1996.

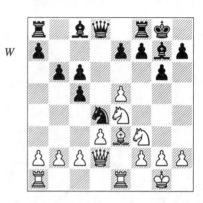

13 ♘xd4 cxd4 14 ♗h6

It is now rather easy to see the contours of White's plan. If Black does nothing, White will play ♕g5-h4 followed by ♘g5 and Black will soon be mated.

14...c5

Black has also tried a number of other moves:

a) 14...f6 15 exf6 exf6 16 ♗xg7 ♔xg7 17 ♕f4 ♕d5 18 ♖e2 ♗e6 19 ♖ae1 ♖ae8 20 ♘d6 ♖e7 21 ♘c4 ♖d8 22 a4 ♖ee8 23 h4 ♕d7 24 ♘d2 c5 25 a5 and White is better, Van den Doel-De Wachter, Zagan jr Wch 1997. Note a funny thing about the position: it is actually the king's rook on d8 and the queen's rook on e8!

b) 14...♕d5 15 ♗xg7 ♔xg7 16 ♕g5 ♕e6 17 ♕h4 h6 18 ♘g3 c5 19 f4 ♗b7 20 ♖e2 is clearly better for White, Kanefsck-Maurino, Buenos Aires 1998.

c) 14...♕c7 15 ♗xg7 ♔xg7 16 ♕f4 h6 17 c3?! (the aforementioned plan, 17 ♘g3 c5 18 ♖e2 ♗b7 19 ♕h4, looks much better) 17...dxc3 18 ♘xc3 ♗e6 19 d4 ♖fd8 20 ♖ad1 ♖d7 21 ♖e3 ♖ad8 ∓ Degraeve-Meins, Groningen open 1997.

15 ♕f4 ♗b7 16 ♕h4 f6!? 17 ♗xg7 ♔xg7 18 exf6+ exf6 19 ♖e2 ♕d5

The chances are approximately balanced, Kanefsck-Zarnicki, Mar del Plata 1997.

C32)
5...e5 *(D)*

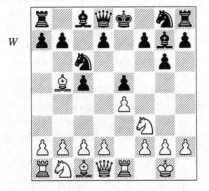

6 ♗xc6
Alternatives:

a) 6 c3 ♘ge7 7 d4 looks like an inferior version of 5 c3 e5 6 d4 since in that line White often does not need to play ♖e1. I suppose White can play quietly with 7 d3 too but it is not really anything that I would recommend.

b) 6 b4!? is a pawn sacrifice that contains a certain amount of venom. There is certainly no hidden agenda here – White plays directly for an attack. Since White obtains a promising game if Black declines the sacrifice, there is little choice for Black:

b1) 6...cxb4 (Kraut regards this as rather dubious, but it has been Black's preferred reply lately; if I should come with a rational explanation, it must be because it seems to maintain better control of the centre) 7 a3 ♘ge7 8 axb4 and Black must now decide whether he dares to take the pawn on b4:

b11) Van der Wiel showed that Black should keep his hands off this pawn: 8...♘xb4?! 9 ♗a3 ♘bc6 10 ♗d6 0-0 11 ♘c3 a6! 12 ♗c4 b6 13 ♘d5 ♗b7, Van der Wiel-Reindermann, Leeuwarden 1993, and now Van der Wiel recommends 14 ♘xe5! ♘xd5!? (14...♘xe5 15 ♘xe7+ ♘xe7 16 ♗xe5 d5 17 exd5 ♘xd5 18 ♕g4 ±; or 14...♘xe5?! 15 ♗xe7) 15 ♗xd5! ♘xe5 16 ♗xb7 and White has a clear, most likely winning, advantage.

b12) 8...0-0 9 ♗b2 d6 10 ♗xc6 ♘xc6 (10...bxc6 11 d4 f6 12 c4 ♗e6 13 c5 dxc5 14 bxc5 ± Barle-Pavlov, Bucharest 1976) 11 b5 ♕b6 12 ♘a3 ♘a5 13 ♗c3 and White is better, Timoshchenko-Arseniev, USSR 1972.

b2) 6...♘xb4 and now:

b21) 7 c3 ♘c6 8 d4 exd4 (8...cxd4 9 cxd4 ♘xd4 10 ♘xd4 exd4 11 ♘d2 ♘e7 12 ♗a3 0-0 13 ♗d6 with compensation) 9 e5 ♘ge7 10 cxd4 cxd4 11 ♗a3 0-0 12 ♘bd2 a6 13 ♗d3 b5 14 ♗d6 ♖e8 15 a4 and White has reasonable play for the pawns, Sigurjonsson-Kroon, Nice OL 1974.

b22) 7 ♗b2 and now:

b221) 7...♕c7 is surprisingly dangerous, e.g. 8 c3 ♘c6 9 d4 d6 10 d5 a6

11 ♘a3! ♔e7 (11...axb5 12 ♘xb5
♕b6 13 ♘xd6+ ♔e7 14 dxc6 ±) 12
dxc6 axb5 13 cxb7 ♕xb7 14 c4 and
White has excellent compensation,
Alexandria-Schul, Kislovodsk 1974.

b222) 7...a6 (also risky but nevertheless Black's best) 8 a3 axb5 9 axb4
♖xa1 10 ♗xa1 cxb4 11 ♗xe5 ♗xe5 12
♘xe5 ♘e7 13 d4, Kapengut-Boris-
enko, USSR 1975, and now 13...d5!?
would have been roughly equal.

Returning to 6 ♗xc6 (D):

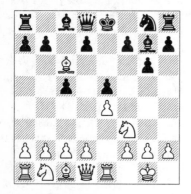

Now we have:
C321: 6...bxc6 48
C322: 6...dxc6 49

C321)
6...bxc6 7 c3

It feels strange that 7 b4!? should be
more recommendable than at the previous move, but it has got a famous
game linked to it since Fischer used it
in his 'return-match' against Spassky.
7...cxb4 8 a3 gives Black a difficult
choice:

a) 8...♘e7 9 ♗b2 d6 10 d4 (this is of
course much more fun, and probably

also better than just regaining the pawn
with 10 axb4) 10...bxa3 11 ♘xa3 0-0
12 dxe5 d5 13 exd5 cxd5 14 c4! dxc4
15 ♘xc4 ♕xd1 16 ♖exd1 ♗g4 17
♖d3 ± Ambrož-Vokač, Czech tt 1994.

b) 8...bxa3?! (Timman had already
cited a reason to reject this, so it is
strange that a top-class player such as
Hübner uses it) 9 ♘xa3 (Timman suggested 9 ♗xa3 d6 10 d4 exd4 11 e5
dxe5 12 ♘xe5 ♗e6 13 ♘d2 ♘e7 14
♘df3 ±) 9...d6 10 d4 exd4 11 e5 dxe5
12 ♘xe5 ♗e6 13 ♕f3 ♘e7 (13...♕d5
14 ♕xd5 cxd5 15 ♘b5 ±) 14 ♘xf7!
♗xf7 15 ♗g5 (incidentally 15 ♖xe7+
♕xe7 16 ♕xc6+ ♔f8 17 ♕xa8+ ♗e8
18 ♗d2 looks even stronger) 15...0-0
16 ♗xe7 ♕d7 17 ♗xf8 ♖xf8 18 ♕d3
± Klundt-Hübner, Bad Wiessee 1997.

c) 8...c5 9 axb4 cxb4 10 d4 exd4 11
♗b2 d6 12 ♘xd4 ♕d7 (there is no
better defence to White's main threat
♘c6; 12...♕b6 is strongly met by 13
♘d2! ♗xd4 14 ♘c4 ♗xf2+ 15 ♔h1
♕c5 16 ♘xd6+ ♔e7 17 ♖f1 ♕xd6 18
♕f3 with a powerful attack for White –
Timman) 13 ♘d2 ♗b7?! (Black is
better advised to develop his kingside;
hence 13...♘e7 has been suggested,
even though after 14 ♘c4 I do not see
a better move than 14...♗b7) 14 ♘c4
♘h6 (14...♘e7 15 ♘b5 ♗xb2 16
♘bxd6+ ♔f8 17 ♘xb2 is also good
for White) 15 ♘f5!? (15 ♘b5 would
be a simpler solution but Fischer goes
for an attack) 15...♗xb2 16 ♘cxd6+
♔f8 17 ♘xh6 and White is better,
Fischer-Spassky, Sveti Stefan (11)
1992.

**7...♘e7 8 d4 cxd4 9 cxd4 exd4 10
♘xd4 0-0 11 ♘c3** (D)

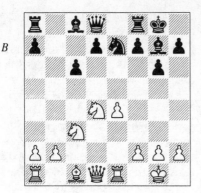

B

11...♖b8

Black would like to play ...d5 but it is not so easy. The immediate 11...d5? is bad in view of 12 exd5 cxd5 13 ♗g5, and the rather passive 11...d6 gives White a nice grip after 12 ♗g5 ♗b7 13 ♕d2 ♖e8 14 ♖ad1 as in Magomedov-Kharlov, USSR Cht (Azov) 1991.

However, an interesting plan, but probably too experimental, was tried in the game Smyslov-Zsu.Polgar, Monaco Women vs Veterans 1994, which went 11...♗b7 12 ♗g5 h6 13 ♗h4 g5 14 ♗g3 d5 15 exd5 ♘xd5, when Black hoped that her active pieces would compensate for the mess the pawns have become. However, Smyslov found the very strong 16 ♘e4!, which illustrated rather well Black's weaknesses (in particular d6, c5 and f5), and he was able to keep an advantage.

So in the end it makes reasonable sense to counter-attack down the b-file so White at least has to prepare developing the bishop.

12 ♘b3

The other idea is to try to take advantage of Black not having moved the d-pawn: 12 e5!? c5 13 ♘b3 ♘c6 14 ♘xc5 ♘xe5 15 ♘5e4 ♗a6 16 ♗g5 f6 17 ♕d5+!? (White goes for a direct refutation of Black's play, but it might have been better simply to retreat the bishop to e3) 17...♔h8 18 ♘xf6!? ♗xf6 19 ♗xf6+ (this gives Black a pretty easy game, but even after the more complicated 19 ♖xe5 ♗xg5 20 ♖xg5 ♖xb2 21 ♘e4, Black has the resourceful 21...♕b6!, when it is White who must be on the alert) 19...♕xf6 20 ♕xe5 ♕xe5 21 ♖xe5 ♖xb2 with the better ending for Black in Girinath-Gufeld, Calcutta 1992.

12...d5 13 ♗e3!

13 ♗g5 is another possibility but the text-move is now regarded as more accurate.

13...♗b7

13...dxe4? 14 ♗c5! ♖b7 15 ♘xe4! ♗xb2 16 ♘d4! ♗xd4! (16...♗xa1 17 ♘f6+ ♔h8 18 ♕xa1 +−) 17 ♗xd4 ♘d5 was seen in Makarychev-Krasenkov, Moscow Tal mem 1992, and now according to Kasparov Black could have been severely punished with 18 ♗c5! ♖e8 19 ♕xd5!! ♕xd5 (19...cxd5? 20 ♘f6+ ♔g7 21 ♖xe8 ♕a5 22 ♗d4 g5 23 ♖g8+ ♔h6 24 h4 gxh4 25 ♗e3#) 20 ♘f6+ ♔g7 21 ♘xe8+ ♔h8 22 ♗d6! +−. However, I do not see anything completely clear after, for example, 22...f6.

14 ♗d4 dxe4 15 ♗xg7 ♔xg7 16 ♘xe4

White may claim a small edge.

C322)

6...dxc6 7 d3 *(D)*

7...♕e7

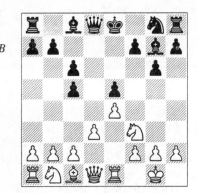

B

Black has a large number of alternatives at this stage, but moving the queen to e7, where it supports the pawns on e5 and c5, and thus prepares a further reinforcement by ...♘f6-d7, is not only a standard move in such positions but also, in my opinion, the most logical move. Others:

a) 7...f6?! is an attempt to be flexible, but it impedes his own bishop, and this suggests that White should prepare the d4 advance. 8 ♗e3 b6 9 a4 a5 10 c3! ♘h6 11 h3 g5!? (11...0-0 12 ♕b3+ ♔h8 13 d4 is very good for White since Black will have trouble with his queenside when the centre opens) 12 ♘a3 ♘f7 13 d4 cxd4 14 cxd4 g4 15 hxg4 ♗xg4 (Black's impetuous g-pawn has served to create counterplay against the centre, but White replies with a nice positional sacrifice) 16 dxe5!? ♕xd1 17 ♖exd1 ♘xe5 18 ♘xe5! ♗xd1 19 ♖xd1 fxe5 20 ♗xb6 0-0 21 ♘c4 ± Damljanović-Ivanisević, Pale 1997. White has only one pawn for the exchange but a couple of black pawns are likely to drop off.

b) 7...♕c7 8 ♗e3 b6 9 a3! ♘f6 10 b4 cxb4 11 axb4 0-0 12 h3! ♘h5 13 ♘c3 ♘f4 14 ♗xf4! exf4 15 ♕d2 h6?! 16 e5! g5 17 d4 ± Shirov-Illescas, Madrid 1996.

c) 7...♘h6!? 8 a3 a5 9 a4 f6 10 ♘a3 ♘f7 11 ♗e3 b6 12 c3 0-0 13 ♘c4?! (White's idea from line 'a' above looks worth repeating: 13 d4 cxd4 14 cxd4 ♗g4 15 dxe5 ♕xd1 16 ♖exd1 ♘xe5 17 ♘xe5 ♗xd1 18 ♖xd1 fxe5 19 ♗xb6 followed by ♘c4 with excellent compensation) 13...♗e6 14 ♕e2 ♗xc4 15 dxc4 ♘h6 16 ♖ed1 ♕e7 17 ♗xh6 ♘xh6 ½-½ Zhang Zhong-B.Lalić, Szeged 1997.

d) 7...♗g4 8 ♗e3 ♕e7 9 ♘bd2 ♘f6 10 a4 a5 11 h3 ♗xf3 12 ♕xf3 ♘d7 13 ♘c4 0-0 14 ♕g3 ♕e6 15 ♗d2 b6 16 ♗c3 ± Van der Wiel-Antunes, Wijk aan Zee 1996.

e) 7...♘e7 8 ♗e3 (8 a3 is probably best met by 8...a5 since in the game Glek-Lemmers, Belgium 1995, White was able to demonstrate an advantage after 8...0-0 9 b4 cxb4 10 axb4 ♗e6 11 ♗e3 b6 12 ♕c1 ♕d6 13 ♖a4!? ♔h8 14 h3 ♘c8 15 ♘c3 ♗d7 16 ♖d1 ♕e7 17 d4!) 8...b6 *(D)* and now:

e1) 9 ♘bd2 f6 10 a3 g5!? 11 b4 ♘g6 12 ♘c4 cxb4 13 axb4 ♗e6 14 ♖a6 0-0 15 ♕a1 ♕b8 16 ♕c3 g4 17 ♘fd2 ♘f4 18 ♕a3 f5!? with counterplay, Ricardi-Petursson, Dubai OL 1986.

e2) 9 ♘c3 0-0 10 a3 ♕d6 11 ♘d2 ♗e6 12 ♘c4 ♕c7 (White is probably slightly better after 12...♗xc4 13 dxc4 ♕xd1 14 ♖exd1 as his minor pieces are superior to their black counterparts) 13 b4 ♖fd8 14 ♕b1 cxb4 15 axb4 ♘c8 16 f3 ♗xc4 17 dxc4 ♘d6 18 ♕b3 b5

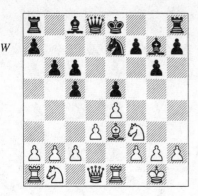

19 cxb5 cxb5 (Black should, according to Becerra Rivero, try 19...♘xb5 20 ♖a6 ♘d4 21 ♕a4, when White is only slightly better) 20 ♘d5 ♕b7 21 ♖ed1 ± Becerra Rivero-Paredes, Albacete 1996.

e3) 9 a4 a5 10 ♘bd2 f6 11 ♘c4 ♗e6 12 ♘fd2 0-0 13 b4!? (it is not entirely clear how good this really is, but it is an instructive way of combating the black fortress on the queenside) 13...axb4 14 a5 bxa5 15 ♗xc5 ♗h6! 16 ♕b1 (Kostiakov suggests that White might have something after 16 ♖a4!? ♗xd2 17 ♘xd2 ♖e8 18 ♕f3 f5 19 ♕g3 and I believe this is about right, though I suspect Black is on the wrong track with his 17th and 18th move; actually it is far from easy to parry White's idea of doubling on the a-file and so threatening ♗xb4) 16...♕c7 17 ♖a4 ♗xd2 18 ♘xd2 ♖fb8 19 ♕a1 ♕d8 20 ♖b1 ♔f7 21 h4!, Anand-Kramnik, Monaco Amber blindfold 1998. Black seems to have consolidated reasonably well but the problem is that it is much easier for White to switch from one flank to the other:

White can generate some attacking chances on the kingside, while Black is tied to the defence of the queenside.

We return to 7...♕e7 *(D)*:

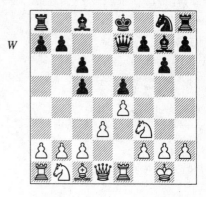

8 ♘bd2 ♘f6

The other option is 8...♘h6 9 ♘c4 (9 a3!?) 9...f6 and now:

a) 10 a4 b6 11 b3 ♘f7 12 ♗b2 ♗g4 13 ♘e3 ♗xf3 14 ♕xf3 ♘g5 15 ♕d1 ♘e6 16 ♘c4 0-0 17 ♕d2 ♖fd8 18 f3 ♕f8 = Kazimdzhanov-Jansen, Vlissingen 1996.

b) 10 b4 cxb4 (10...♗e6?! 11 bxc5 ♗xc4 12 dxc4 ♕xc5 13 ♕d3 ♕e7 14 a4 ♕d7 15 ♕b3 0-0 16 ♗a3 ♖fd8 17 ♖ab1 was better for White in Adorjan-Mednis, Budapest 1978) 11 a3 0-0 12 axb4 ♗e6 13 ♗a3 ♖fd8 14 ♕e2 ♘f7 (Maliutin-Ikonnikov, Lugano 1989) 15 ♘fd2 ±.

9 ♘c4

The other natural continuation is 9 a3 0-0 (9...a5 10 ♘c4 ♘d7 11 a4 0-0 is playable for Black but positions like this are just a lot more pleasant for White) 10 b4 ♗e6 11 bxc5 ♕xc5 12 a4 b5! 13 &b2 ♘h5 14 c3 ♕b6 15 d4 ♖fd8 ∓ Motwani-Lanka, Vienna 1991.

9...♘d7 10 &d2!?

A few games have continued 10 &g5 f6, but I do not see much point in provoking ...f6 in these positions.

The text-move has the idea that White prepares a3 and b4, while ruling out a defence based on ...a5.

10...0-0 11 a3 b6

A better defence might be 11...♘b6 12 ♘a5 ♖d8 13 ♕e2 &g4, with the idea 14 h3 &xf3 15 ♕xf3 c4!.

12 b4 &a6 13 &c3 ♖fd8 14 ♘fd2 ♕e6 15 ♕e2 &f8 16 ♖f1 (D)

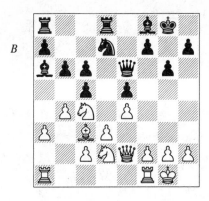

B

White is better, Torre-Timman, Moscow 1981.

2 Rossolimo Variation with 3...e6

1 e4 c5 2 ♘f3 ♘c6 3 ♗b5 e6 *(D)*

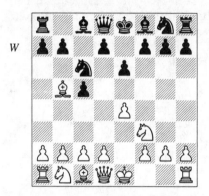

3...e6 is becoming more and more popular. First of all Black intends to develop his king's knight to e7, from where it might continue to g6, controlling the vital squares e5 and f4. Another advantage of having the knight on e7 is that Black can chase the white bishop away from b5 without worrying about doubled pawns after ♗xc6, since Black can recapture with the knight.

White can of course exchange on c6 before Black develops his king's knight, and so saddle Black with doubled c-pawns, but Black's centre is then strengthened and the c-pawns are not really weak unless Black advances his d-pawn prematurely.

However, I should state that even though, by having doubled c-pawns, Black obtains a compact and solid centre, his pawn structure really *is* worse. Therefore White should generally try to keep the position closed.

Conceding the bishop-pair

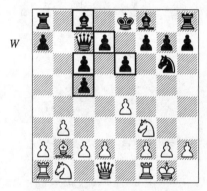

Mortensen – S.B. Hansen
Danish Ch (Tåstrup) 1998

The above position has been reached after 7...♕d8-c7. Another reasonable move would have been 7...f6, preparing to develop the dark-squared bishop. With 7...♕c7 Black prepares ...e5, but it will always be a mistake to try to break out with a move like ...d5 as this exposes the c-pawns to a future attack.

8 d4?

This typical Sicilian move is a mistake here. Black easily neutralizes White's slight initiative, and in the longer term Black will have the better chances due to his bishop-pair.

Better is 8 ♖e1 or 8 e5!? (see more on this in Line A of this chapter).

8...cxd4 9 ♕xd4 f6 10 c4

White prevents Black from suddenly expanding in the centre with ...d5, and prepares to play the cramping c5.

10...c5 11 ♕e3 ♗e7 12 e5? *(D)*

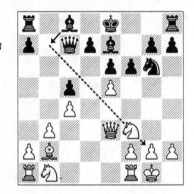

It seems that White is frustrated by the fact that Black has solved his opening problems, and prematurely starts action in the centre. However, this completely exposes his king's position, and Black now develops a strong attack due to his domination of the h1-a8 diagonal.

12...0-0 13 ♘bd2 ♗b7 14 ♖fe1 f5 15 ♖ad1 ♕c6 16 ♖e2?! h6 17 ♘e1?!

This rather artificial way of protecting g2 loses material. White should play ♘f1 on move 16 or 17, but Black

would then have a comfortable position anyway.

17...♗g5 18 ♕g3 ♘f4 19 ♖e3 ♕c8?!

There is absolutely nothing wrong with 19...♘h5 20 ♕h3 ♗xe3; for example 21 fxe3 g6 simply leaves Black an exchange up. With the text-move Black attempts to win the exchange under even more favourable conditions. However, this does not quite succeed.

20 ♘df3 ♘h5 21 ♕h3 ♗xe3 22 ♕xh5

22 fxe3 ♕e8 is Black's idea, threatening 23...g5, but now White at least gets a pawn for the exchange.

22...♗d4 23 ♘xd4 cxd4 24 ♖xd4 f4! 25 ♕g6?

25 ♕g4 ♕c7!? 26 ♖d6 ♗c6 27 ♗c3 ♖f5 28 h4 followed by ♘d3 gives White some compensation.

25...♖f5 26 f3

26 ♖d6!?.

26...♗c6 27 ♕g4 ♖xe5 28 ♘d3 ♖g5 29 ♕xf4 ♕b7

Black went on to convert his material advantage into a win in 37 moves.

Cementing a black pawn weakness on c5

By playing 3...e6 Black more or less signals his intention of advancing his d-pawn to d5. True, this will give Black a strong centre, but he must be very careful when and under which circumstances he advances his d-pawn. When White has played 4 ♗xc6, thereby doubling Black's c-pawns, this can be a very risky operation, as Black can easily end up having these pawns fixed by White playing c4 at some stage. Here is an example:

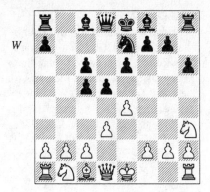

Rogers – V. Milov
Baden 1998

Black has just played 7...d7-d5?!, but should have chosen 7...g6 or 7...e5. The d-pawn's advance leaves Black with a weak pawn on c5. There is actually a close resemblance to the Nimzo-Indian, although White is probably better off here than Black usually is in the Nimzo-Indian.

8 f4!

This is a very good move for several reasons. First of all, White should never fear the liquidation following an exchange on e4. Even though White loses the right to castle after Black captures on d1, Black's horrible c-pawns are a more significant feature in the position. Secondly, it is in accord with White's plan and White is now ready to meet an ...e5 thrust with the space-gaining f5.

8...g6 9 0-0 ♗g7 10 ♘f2 ♗a6 11 ♘a3!

Black should not, of course, be allowed to play ...c4.

11...0-0 12 ♖b1 ♖b8 13 c4!

Cementing the weakness on c5. The mirror thrust (...c5) is also a basic part of Black's strategy in the Nimzo-Indian but comparing the two opening variations White is much more active here.

13...dxc4

I do not really like this but it is probably the best solution. Black intends to keep the position open, so at least his bishops will have something to say. If the position were to become closed, White's knights would be much superior.

14 dxc4 ♕xd1 15 ♖xd1 ♗d4 16 b3 ♖fd8 17 ♗b2 ♗xb2 18 ♖xb2 ♖xd1+ 19 ♘xd1 ♖d8 20 ♘c3

White threatens to win the c5-pawn with ♘a4.

20...e5 21 fxe5 g5 22 ♘ab1

There is nothing very wrong with 22 ♘a4 but White's position is so good that he can afford to spend some time ruling out any chance of Black gaining counterplay.

22...♘g6 23 ♖d2 ♖xd2 24 ♘xd2 ♘xe5 25 ♔f2 ♗c8 26 ♘f3 ♘d3+ 27 ♔e3 ♘b4 28 a3 ♘c2+ 29 ♔d2

I suspect 29 ♔d3 is an easier win; for example, 29...♘a1 (29...♘xa3 cannot be any good) 30 ♘d2 f5 31 ♘d1 fxe4+ 32 ♔c3 eventually winning the knight.

29...♘a1 30 ♘a4 ♘xb3+ 31 ♔c3 ♘c1

31...♘a5 looks a lot safer. White is still much better but Black can put up some resistance.

32 ♘g1! ♗g4 33 h3 ♗d1 34 ♘xc5

34 ♘b2! wins – Rogers.

34...♔f8 35 ♘d7+ ♔e7 36 ♘e5 ♗a4

Black now managed to hold the game. Although White did not win this game, there can be no doubt that Milov will think twice about taking on such a structure in the future.

The Theory of the Rossolimo with 3...e6

1 e4 c5 2 ♘f3 ♘c6 3 ♗b5 e6

Now:

A:	4 ♗xc6	56
B:	4 ♘c3	61
C:	4 0-0	65

Of these moves, my preference is for Lines A and C, but I have chosen to include all three anyway, since Line B is important for transpositional purposes – it may also arise after, for example, 1 e4 c5 2 ♘f3 ♘c6 3 ♘c3 e6 4 ♗b5, and this may be a way to lure someone who usually prefers to meet 3 ♗b5 with 3...g6 into unfamiliar territory. Another possible move-order is 1 e4 c5 2 ♘f3 e6 3 ♘c3 ♘c6 4 ♗b5.

A)

4 ♗xc6

If White wants to make sure of doubling Black's c-pawns, it is essential to make this capture before Black gets the time to play ...♘ge7. The most logical way for White to follow up seems to be a queenside fianchetto. However, White should in general be careful not to open up the position, for then Black's bishops might become superior.

4...bxc6 *(D)*

4...dxc6 is certainly inferior but not as bad as its reputation. White should again choose a queenside fianchetto combined with advancing the pawn to e5, e.g. 5 0-0 ♕c7 6 e5 ♘e7 7 b3 ♘f5 8 ♗b2 ♗e7 9 d3 h5 10 ♘bd2 ♗d7 11 a4 ± Rogers-Vaglio, Dubai OL 1986.

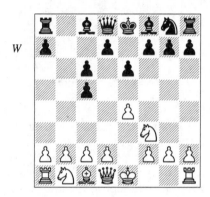

5 b3

It is not completely clear whether White should fianchetto his bishop before or after castling; obviously there are many transpositional possibilities. However, the immediate fianchetto gives White some options of increasing the pressure more rapidly, and even sometimes leaving out castling entirely. Alternatives:

a) 5 d3 is also a natural move, but here White has more difficulties finding a general plan. The best idea is to move the knight from f3 (usually to g5) followed by advancing the f-pawn. Black has several options:

a1) 5...f6!? has worked well in recent games. Black remains rather flexible, with such ideas as ...♘ge7-g6 or sometimes ...♘h6-f7. My suggestion is 6 ♘h4!?, which is aimed against these ideas but is still in line with the general plan. If 6...g6 7 f4 d5, White should probably try 8 c4!? f5 (8...dxe4 9 dxe4 ♕xd1+ 10 ♔xd1 ±) 9 ♘f3 fxe4 (9...dxe4 10 dxe4 ♕xd1+ 11 ♔xd1 fxe4 12 ♘g5 ♘f6 13 ♘c3 is also clearly better for White) 10 dxe4 ♘f6 11 ♘c3 with an unclear position but I venture the assessment that White is to be preferred.

a2) 5...d5 6 0-0 ♘f6 7 ♘c3 ♗e7 (if 7...♗a6, White should continue 8 ♖e1 ♗e7 9 b3 0-0 10 e5 ♘d7 11 ♘a4 with 12 c4 followed by 13 ♗a3, or 12 ♗a3 immediately, coming next – Kraut) 8 ♗g5 0-0 9 e5 ♘d7 10 ♗xe7 ♕xe7 (Lein-Lengyel, Cienfuegos 1972) 11 ♕d2 with the idea of meeting 11...f5 with 12 ♕f4 ±.

a3) 5...♘e7 *(D)* and then:

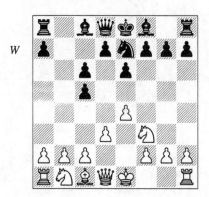

W

a31) 6 0-0 ♘g6 (6...f6 7 ♘h4!) 7 ♘g5!? (this knight sortie is the only

really constructive plan White has; if allowed, he will play ♕h5 and f4 with a dangerous attack) 7...e5 (it would be surprising if Black has time for this, but the alternatives are not really appealing; 7...f6?! 8 ♘h3 is good for White, as he is ready to play f4, and 7...♗e7 8 ♕h5!? ♗xg5 9 ♗xg5 ♕b6 10 ♘d2 also gives White an advantage). Now:

a311) 8 ♕h5 ♕f6! 9 ♘c3 d6 10 ♘xh7?! (this is a little too brave, but on the other hand I find it difficult to believe that White has any compensation after 10 f4!? exf4 11 g3 h6 12 ♘f3 fxg3 13 hxg3 ♗e7) 10...♕d8 11 g3 ♕d7!! (Ma.Tseitlin's suggestion, which appears to be the key move, threatening ...♕h3; after 11...♗e7?! 12 f4 exf4 13 gxf4 ♔d7 14 ♕f5+ ♔e8 15 ♕h5 ♔d7 16 ♕f5+ a draw was agreed in Hennigan-Cherniaev, Gausdal 1995) 12 ♔g2 ♗e7 (Black's king is now ready to flee to the queenside, while, if White does nothing, the pin on the knight on h7 will eventually win a piece) 13 f4 exf4 14 gxf4 ♕g4+ 15 ♕xg4 ♗xg4 16 f5 ♘e5 17 h3 ♗f3+ ∓.

a312) 8 f4!? (Cherniaev's suggestion) 8...♘xf4 (if 8...exf4, 9 ♕h5 is annoying) and now 9 ♗xf4 exf4 10 ♘h3 ♗d6 leads to an unclear position, but there is something to be said for the more brutal 9 ♘xf7!? ♔xf7 10 g3 with a rather messy position, e.g. 10...g5 11 gxf4 exf4 12 ♕h5+ ♔g8 13 ♗xf4 gxf4 14 ♖xf4 ♕e7 15 ♘c3 d6 16 ♘d5 cxd5 17 ♕xd5+ ♕e6 18 ♕xa8 ♗g7 19 ♖af1, when White has the initiative.

a32) 6 ♘h4 (not as good as 6 ♘g5) 6...♘g6 7 ♘xg6 hxg6 8 ♗e3 d5

(8...♕f6!? 9 ♘c3 d5 is also worth considering) 9 ♘d2 ♗d6 10 c3 ♗a6 11 ♕c2 f5!? 12 e5 ♗e7 13 0-0-0 ♔f7 14 ♘f3 g5 15 h3 c4 16 dxc4 ♗xc4 17 ♘d2 ♗e2 18 ♖de1 ♗b5 is unclear, Bologan-Krasenkow, New York 1997.

a33) 6 ♘g5!? and now:

a331) 6...♘g6?! (this does little to interfere with White's plan) 7 f4 ♗e7 8 ♘f3 d5 (8...♕c7 9 g3 d6 10 ♕e2 f5 11 h4 0-0 12 e5! ♘h8 13 b3 ♘f7 14 ♗b2 ♖b8 15 exd6 ♗xd6 16 ♘bd2 with total control, Komliakov-Milanović, Pozarevac 1995) 9 ♕e2 0-0 10 c4! (a common theme in this line – White cements the weak pawn on c5; the following moves are aimed exclusively against this weakness) 10...♖e8 11 0-0 ♖b8 12 ♘c3 ♗f6 13 e5 ♗e7 14 ♘a4 ♗b7 15 b3 d4 16 ♘d2 ♘f8 17 ♘e4 ♘d7 18 ♗a3 ♕a5 19 ♕e1 ♕xe1 20 ♖axe1 and White finally wins the pawn, Rogers-Megibow, US Open 1998.

a332) 6...f6 7 ♘h3 g6 should be met by 8 b3, e.g. 8...♗g7 9 ♗b2 0-0 10 0-0 e5 11 f4 d6 12 fxe5 fxe5 13 ♖xf8+ ♕xf8 14 ♘g5 and White has an edge since Black's centre pawns are chronically weak.

a333) 6...h6 7 ♘h3 g6 (another possibility is 7...e5 8 f4 exf4 9 ♘xf4 g6 10 c4 ♗g7 11 0-0 0-0 12 ♘c3 ♖b8 with fairly even chances, Solomon-Gi.Hernandez, Elista OL 1998; 7...d5 was dealt with in Rogers-Milov, in the introduction to this chapter) 8 f4 ♗g7 9 ♘d2 d6 10 ♘f2 ♖b8 11 c3 ♗a6 12 0-0 0-0 13 ♕c2 f5 = Gi.Hernandez-Minzer, Buenos Aires 1998.

a4) 5...♗e7!? (preventing any ♘g5 ideas) 6 0-0 ♕c7 (Black intends ...e5

with a reasonable position, which explains White's next move) 7 e5 (7 ♘e1!? is not as silly as it looks; White prepares the usual set-up with f4) 7...f6 8 ♗f4 ♕d8! 9 ♘bd2 fxe5 10 ♘xe5 ♘f6 11 ♘e4 (trying to improve on Yandemirov-Filipenko, Lvov 1995 which went 11 ♘dc4 0-0 12 ♗d2 ♕e8 13 f4 d6 14 ♘f3 ♘d5 15 ♘g5 ♘b6 with a good game for Black) 11...0-0 12 ♘xf6+ and now 12...♖xf6?! 13 ♗g5 ♖f5 14 ♗xe7 ♕xe7 15 f4 gave White a slight advantage in Yandemirov-Mukhaev, Tomsk 1998. However, there was no need for Black to concede the bishop-pair. Smirin recommends 12...♗xf6!? 13 ♗g3 d6 14 ♘c4 e5 15 f4 e4! with the better game for Black.

b) 5 0-0 ♘e7 *(D)*.

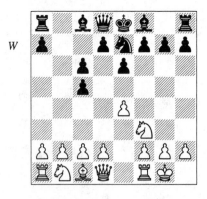

Now, apart from 6 b3 ♘g6 7 ♗b2, which transposes to the main line, White may try:

b1) 6 d3 ♘g6 7 ♘g5!? transposes to line 'a31'.

b2) 6 ♖e1 ♘g6 7 c3 ♗e7 8 d4 0-0 9 ♘bd2 cxd4 10 cxd4 f5! (since he has the bishop-pair, Black logically seeks to open the position) 11 ♘b3 ♗a6 12 ♕c2 fxe4 13 ♖xe4 ♖xf3! (perhaps not strictly necessary, but this thematic sacrifice looks very strong) 14 gxf3 ♕f8 15 ♘c5 ♗xc5 16 dxc5 ♕xf3 17 ♖e3 ♕h5 18 ♖g3 and now, rather than 18...♘h4?! 19 ♗f4!, which gave White some hopes of rescue in Timman-Rogers, Dutch Cht 1998, 18...♖f8!, and only then ...♘h4, is strong.

Returning to 5 b3 *(D)*:

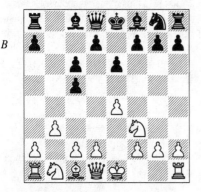

5...♘e7

This is the most sensible move, but Black has a wealth of alternatives:

a) 5...♕f6?! (Black does not achieve anything by provoking White's e-pawn forward) 6 e5! ♕f5 7 0-0 f6 8 ♖e1 fxe5 9 ♖xe5 ♕f6 10 ♘c3 d6 11 ♖e1 ♗e7 12 d4! cxd4 13 ♘xd4 d5 14 ♗b2 ♗d7 15 ♘a4 ± Ehlvest-Vaïsser, Novosibirsk 1993.

b) 5...d5 and now 6 e5 ♗a6 7 d3 c4 8 dxc4 dxc4 9 ♕xd8+ ♖xd8 10 ♗e3 ♖d7 11 ♘bd2 ♗b4! is probably quite playable for Black, but I would recommend 6 d3! with the idea of c4.

c) 5...d6 and here:

c1) 6 0-0 e5 7 ♖e1 ♗e7 8 d3 ♘f6?! (after this White effortlessly gains the advantage by preparing d4; better is 8...f5!) 9 c3! 0-0 10 d4 exd4 11 cxd4 d5 12 exd5 ♘xd5 13 ♗a3 ♘b4 14 ♘c3 ♗g4 15 dxc5 ♗xc5 16 ♘e4 ± Timman-Sveshnikov, Tilburg 1992.

c2) 6 e5! dxe5 7 ♘xe5 and now White would just be a lot better if he could get in ♗b2, so Black tries to stop this:

c21) 7...♕g5 gave White a strong attack in Hraček-Araslamov, Pardubice 1993: 8 ♘f3 ♕xg2 9 ♖g1 ♕h3 10 ♗b2 f6 11 ♕e2 e5 12 ♘a3 ♘e7 (or 12...♗g4 13 ♖g3 ♗xf3 14 ♕xf3 ♕d7 15 0-0-0 ±) 13 0-0-0 ♘g6 14 d4! cxd4 15 ♘xd4 ♗d7 16 ♖g3 ♕h6+ 17 ♔b1 ♗e7 18 ♘db5! cxb5 19 ♖xd7! ±.

c22) 7...♕d4 8 ♘c4 ♕xa1 9 ♘c3 ♗a6 10 0-0 ♗xc4 11 bxc4 ♗d6 12 ♕e2 ♘f6 13 ♗a3 and White is better – Murugan.

d) 5...f6 (this is Black's soundest alternative) 6 0-0 ♘h6 7 d4 (usually this kind of move would not be advisable, but since 7...cxd4 is met by 8 ♗xh6 gxh6 9 ♘xd4 ±, White is in time to exchange bishops and thus get rid of Black's main asset) 7...♘f7 8 ♗a3! cxd4 9 ♗xf8 ♔xf8 10 ♕xd4 (10 ♘xd4 gives Black fewer problems, for example 10...♗b7 11 ♘c3 c5 12 ♘de2 g6 13 ♕d3 ♔g7 14 ♖ad1 ♗c6! = Ehlvest-Sveshnikov, Podolsk 1993) 10...e5 (10...♕b6 11 ♕d2 d6 12 c4 e5 13 ♘c3 ♗e6 14 ♘e1!, intending ♘d3 followed by c5 or ♔h1 and f4, gives White an edge, de la Paz-Lopez, Matanzas 1996) 11 ♕d2 d6 12 c4 g6 13 ♘c3 ♔g7 14

♖ac1 ♗e6 15 ♘e1 ♕e7 16 ♘d3 g5! with approximately equal chances, Yudasin-Sveshnikov, St Petersburg 1997.

6 ♗b2 ♘g6 7 0-0 *(D)*

The alternative is 7 h4 h5, when White should probably choose the calm 8 d3, and only then follow up with 9 e5, for after the immediate 8 e5 Black has the strong pawn sacrifice 8...c4!. German-Milos, Buenos Aires 1997 then continued 9 bxc4 ♖b8 10 ♗c3 c5 11 d3 ♗e7 12 ♘bd2 f5! 13 exf6 gxf6 14 ♕e2 ♔f7 15 0-0 ♗b7 16 ♕e3 ♕c7 17 ♖fe1 ♖bg8 with a strong attack. Note, however, that this idea only works since Black has a target on the kingside, due to the interpolation of the moves h4 and ...h5.

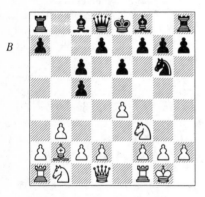

7...♕c7

This flexible move prepares ...e5. There are two other ways to do this:

a) 7...d6 8 e5! ♗a6 9 d3 d5 10 c4 ♗e7 11 ♘c3 ♘f8 12 ♘a4 ♘d7 13 ♖c1 ♘b6 14 ♘c3 0-0 15 ♘e2 ♕b8 16 ♗a3 ♖d8 17 ♕e1 ± de la Paz-Gamboa, Santa Clara 1998.

b) 7...f6 8 e5!? ♗e7 9 d3 0-0 (after 9...♕c7, play is likely to transpose to the main line) 10 ♘bd2 fxe5 11 ♘xe5 ♘xe5 12 ♗xe5 d6 13 ♗g3 g5!? 14 f4 gxf4 15 ♗xf4 e5 16 ♗h6 ♖xf1+ 17 ♕xf1 ♗e6 with approximately equal chances, Gubanov-Cherniaev, St Petersburg 1997.

8 e5

This is the principal continuation. Other options:

a) 8 d4?! cxd4 9 ♕xd4 f6 with a good and solid position for Black, Mortensen-S.B.Hansen, Danish Ch (Tåstrup) 1998. See the introduction to this chapter.

b) 8 ♖e1!? e5 9 c3 ♗d6 10 ♘a3 ♗a6 11 d4 0-0 12 ♕d2 f5!? with an unclear position, Vallejo Pons-Lopez, Cienfuegos 1997.

8...♗e7 9 d3 0-0 10 ♘bd2 f6 *(D)*

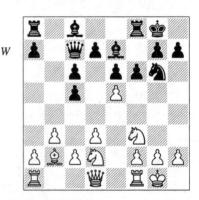

11 exf6

11 ♖e1 fxe5 12 ♘xe5 ♘h8! with the idea of ...d6 is quite promising for Black, while 11 ♘c4 fxe5 12 ♘fxe5 ♘xe5 13 ♗xe5 d6 14 ♗g3 e5 also seems OK.

11...gxf6 12 ♘e4 d5 13 ♘g3 e5 14 ♖e1 ♗d6 15 c4

The position is rather unclear. Black is quite active but must be careful not to expose himself too much, Wach-Löbler, Austrian Cht 1996/7.

B)

4 ♘c3 (D)

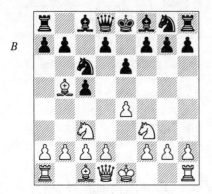

Now we have:

B1: 4...♘d4   61
B2: 4...♘ge7   63

B1)

4...♘d4 5 0-0

It is interesting that White, in general, is not worried about an exchange of his light-squared bishop. White is so far ahead in development that he can quickly generate pressure.

5 ♗d3 is the alternative, but compared to the main line Black does not have to spend a tempo on ...a6. 5...♘e7 6 0-0 ♘ec6 7 b3 g6 (7...♘xf3+ 8 ♕xf3 g6 must be fine for Black) 8 ♘xd4 cxd4 9 ♘e2 ♗g7 10 ♗a3 d6 11 f4 f5? (too loosening; Sveshnikov suggests

11...0-0 12 ♘g3 f5) 12 exf5 exf5 13 ♗c4! d5 14 ♗b5 ♕b6 15 ♖e1! ♔f7 16 ♗xc6 bxc6 17 ♘c1! d3+ (White would be more or less winning if he were allowed to bring his knight to d3) 18 ♔h1 ♗xa1 19 ♖e7+ ♔g8 20 ♖e8+ ♔f7 21 ♖e7+ ♔g8, Gipslis-Sveshnikov, Podolsk 1992, and now, according to Blatny, 22 c3! ♕d8 23 ♕e1 ♗d7 24 ♕e5! would have given White a decisive attack.

Note also that 5 ♘xd4? is wrong due to 5...cxd4 6 ♘e2 ♕g5 with a double attack on the b5-bishop and the g2-pawn. After 7 ♘xd4 ♕c5! 8 c3 e5 White loses a piece for inadequate compensation, so best is 7 a4 ♕xg2 8 ♘g3 ♕h3 9 c3 dxc3 (9...♗d6!?) 10 bxc3 ♘f6, when White can try to claim that his superior development suffices for some kind of compensation, Bukhtin-Kalinichev, Moscow 1978.

5...a6

5...♘e7 transposes to Line B2. 5...♘xb5?! is positionally desirable but Black is a long way from completing his development, and thus White is able to generate pressure rapidly: 6 ♘xb5 ♘f6 7 d4! cxd4 8 ♕xd4 a6 9 ♘c3 d6 10 ♖d1! (this is more accurate than 10 ♗g5 ♗e7 11 ♖fd1, after which Black should play 11...♕c7 rather than 11...0-0?! 12 e5 dxe5 13 ♕h4!? ♕c7 14 ♘e4 ♘d5 15 c4! f6 16 cxd5 exd5! 17 ♖ac1 ♕b8 18 ♖xd5 when Black is on the brink of defeat, Tkachev-Lysenko, Russia 1992) 10...♗e7 (here White can meet 10...♕c7 with 11 ♗f4, for 11...e5 12 ♘xe5 dxe5 13 ♗xe5 gives White a strong, perhaps winning, attack) 11 e5 dxe5 12 ♕xe5

♗d7 13 ♕g3 ± Gurgenidze-Pohla, Pärnu 1967.

6 ♗d3 *(D)*

This clumsy move appears best. After 6 ♗e2 the c3-knight has no useful retreat following an exchange on d4.

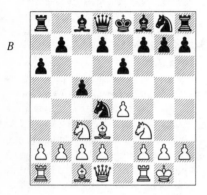

6...♘e7

This is the most natural move, but a peculiar transposition to a main-line Sicilian could occur after 6...♘c6!?. White seems to have nothing better than 7 ♗e2, after which Black can play either 7...♘ge7!? or 7...♘f6 8 d4 cxd4 9 ♘xd4 and then 9...d6 or 9...♕c7 would be a normal Scheveningen or Paulsen variation respectively.

7 ♘xd4 cxd4 8 ♘e2 ♘c6

8...d5 is a major alternative. Then White can play:

a) 9 c3?! dxe4 10 ♗xe4 d3! 11 ♘f4 e5 12 ♘xd3 f5 and Black wins a piece.

b) 9 ♖e1 (with the idea of 10 ♘xd4 since 10...dxe4 can now be met by 11 ♖xe4) 9...♘c6 10 c3 ♗c5 should be fine for Black. It is difficult to see what the rook is doing on e1 when comparing with the main lines.

c) 9 e5 ♘c6 10 f4 ♗d7!? and now 11 a3?! g5! 12 f5? ♕c7 was very good for Black in Speelman-Larsen, New York 1990. Speelman instead recommends 11 ♔h1! intending to answer 11...g5 with 12 c3.

d) 9 exd5 ♕xd5 (after 9...♘xd5 10 c3 dxc3 11 dxc3, 11...g6 12 ♗e4 gives White an edge according to Svidler, but Black does better with 11...♗d6 12 ♘d4 ♕c7 13 ♕h5 ♘f4 14 ♗xf4 ♗xf4, with an equal position, Kraut-Jasnikowski, Bundesliga 1994/5) 10 c3 ♘c6 11 ♕c2 f5 (White was threatening 12 ♗e4, winning a pawn, but an interesting, and positionally better, alternative is 11...♗d6!?; then Brodsky-Markowski, Katowice 1993 continued 12 b3 ♕h5 13 ♘g3 ♕h4 14 ♖e1 0-0, when Black seems to be doing fine) 12 cxd4 b5 13 ♖e1! ♘b4 14 ♕c3 ♘xd3 15 ♕xd3 ♗c5! 16 b3 (after 16 ♘f4 ♕xd4 17 ♕xd4 ♗xd4 18 ♘xe6 ♗xe6 19 ♖xe6+ ♔d7 20 ♖e2 ♖he8 Black is of course doing very well despite his pawn deficit) 16...0-0 17 ♗b2 (Svidler-Zyla, Groningen open 1993) and now according to Svidler Black should play 17...♗d6 18 ♘c3 ♕b7 19 d5 e5 with an unclear game.

9 c3 *(D)*

9...♗c5

Black should rarely exchange on c3 in these positions because after White recaptures with the d-pawn, he has solved his only problem, the development of the dark-squared bishop, and Black will generally be left with either a backward or an isolated d-pawn.

In this respect it makes sense to defend the d4-pawn with ...♗c5. The

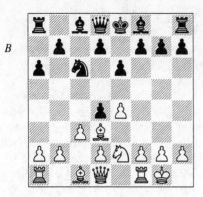

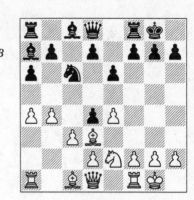

other option is immediately to strike at the centre with 9...d5, viz. 10 cxd4 dxe4 11 ♗xe4 and now:

a) 11...♘xd4 12 ♕a4+ ♘b5 13 d4 ♗d6 14 h3 0-0 15 ♖d1 ♕e7 16 ♕c2 h6 17 ♗e3 gives White a favourable IQP position in view of Black's misplaced knight on b5, A.Sokolov-Skripchenko, Cannes 1998.

b) However, *ECO*'s suggestion of 11...♗e7!? may not be so bad. If White wants to be consistent he should play 12 ♕b3 0-0 13 d5, attempting to hang on to his extra pawn, but 13...exd5 14 ♗xd5 ♘b4 15 ♘c3 ♘xd5 16 ♕xd5 ♕xd5 17 ♘xd5 ♗c5 seems fine for Black even though he is a pawn down. This might not even be the strongest approach; I suspect Black has other possibilities on move 16.

10 b4 ♗a7 11 a4 *(D)*

11 cxd4 should be answered by either 11...♘xb4 or 11...d5!?, but not 11...♘xd4?! 12 ♗b2 ♘xe2+ 13 ♕xe2 0-0 14 e5!, which was very good for White in Ma.Tseitlin-Khenkin, Israeli Ch (Tel-Aviv) 1994.

11...0-0

Black must time the central thrust ...d5 precisely. Here 11...d5 would be wrong due to 12 exd5 ♕xd5 13 b5 ♘e5 14 ♘f4 ♕d7 15 ♗a3 with advantage to White, Kraut-B.Stein, Bundesliga 1989/90.

12 ♗a3 ♘e5 13 ♕c2 d5 14 exd5

According to Gufeld, Black would be doing OK after 14 cxd4 ♘xd3 15 ♕xd3 dxe4 16 ♕xe4 ♕d5.

14...♘xd3 15 ♕xd3 dxc3 16 b5 ♖e8

Now, rather than the over-optimistic 17 d6?, as in Gurgenidze-Dzhindzhi-khashvili, Gori 1971, White should be content with 17 ♘xc3 exd5 18 ♘xd5 ♗e6 19 ♘e7+ ♔h8 20 ♕xd8 ♖exd8 21 bxa6 bxa6 = Gufeld.

B2)

4...♘ge7 *(D)*

5 0-0 a6

Others:

a) 5...♘d4 6 ♘xd4 cxd4 7 ♘e2 a6 would generally lead (after 8 ♗d3) to Line B1, but White might take the opportunity to vary with 8 ♗a4 ♘c6 9 d3 ♗c5. Then:

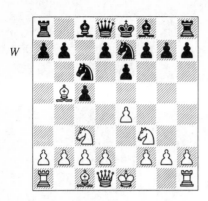

a1) 10 f4 d5 11 ♘g3 dxe4 12 ♕h5!? (12 ♘xe4 is more cautious) 12...♗e7 13 dxe4 g6 14 ♕f3 b5 15 ♗b3 h5!? with an unclear position, Yudasin-Krasenkow, Vilnius Mikenas mem 1997.

a2) 10 c4!? ♖b8 11 ♗f4 d6 12 b4! ♗xb4 13 ♘xd4 ♗d7 14 ♘xc6 bxc6 15 d4 and White is better, W.Watson-Nunn, Kilkenny 1996.

b) 5...♘g6 6 d4 cxd4 7 ♘xd4 and now:

b1) 7...♕c7!? 8 ♗e3 ♗d6 9 g3 a6 10 ♗e2 ♗e7 11 f4 0-0 12 a4 ♘a5?! (12...d6 is better, but White can still try the same plan as in the game, namely 13 h4 followed by h5) 13 h4! h6 14 h5 ♘h8 15 ♕d3 ± Fressinet-Kouatly, French Ch (Méribel) 1998.

b2) 7...♗e7 8 ♗e3 ♕c7 (8...0-0 9 f4 a6 10 ♗xc6 bxc6 11 ♕h5 c5 12 ♘b3 f5 13 ♘xc5 ♕c7 14 ♘b3 fxe4 15 f5 ♕e5 16 g4 led to a complete mess in Tal-Ornstein, Tallinn 1977) 9 ♔h1 a6 10 ♗d3 b5 11 ♘xc6 ♕xc6 12 f4 ♗b7 13 f5 ♘e5 14 ♕h5 ♗f6 15 ♗g5! g6! 16 ♕h4 ♗xg5 17 ♕xg5 gxf5 with an unclear position, Yudasin-V.Milov, Haifa 1995.

6 ♗xc6 ♘xc6 7 d4 cxd4 8 ♘xd4 ♕c7

With this Black prevents ideas with ♘xc6 followed by e5. Alternatives:

a) 8...d6 and now:

a1) 9 ♘xc6 bxc6 10 ♕g4 h5 (or 10...♖b8 11 ♕g3 h5 12 h3 h4 13 ♕d3 ♗e7 14 ♘a4! 0-0 15 c4 and White is better, San Segundo-Karpov, Madrid 1992) 11 ♕e2 h4!? 12 h3 ♗e7 13 b3 0-0 14 ♗b2 ♕c7 15 ♘d1 e5 16 ♘e3 ♗e6 17 ♕h5 g6 18 ♕e2 d5 with approximately equal chances, Zarnicki-Illescas, Buenos Aires 1993.

a2) 9 ♖e1 and then:

a21) 9...♗d7 10 ♘xc6! bxc6 11 e5 d5 (11...dxe5?! 12 ♖xe5 ♗e7 13 ♗f4 0-0 14 ♖e3! ♖a7 15 ♖d3 ± Gipslis-Sorokin, Ostrava 1992) 12 ♕g4! h5 13 ♕g3!? h4 14 ♕g4! h3! 15 g3, Yudasin-Salov, Tilburg 1993, and now Yudasin suggests 15...♕c7!, to prevent ♘e2-f4, but White should be able to retain some advantage with 16 ♗f4 ♖b8 17 ♖ab1 as 17...c5? fails in view of 18 ♘xd5!.

a22) 9...♗e7 10 ♘xc6 bxc6 11 ♕g4 and now Black should tread carefully:

a221) 11...0-0? 12 ♗h6 ♗f6 13 e5! dxe5 14 ♘e4 is too dangerous for Black; White will continue ♖ad1 and perhaps ♗e3-c5.

a222) 11...♔f8 is better, but Yudasin has shown the way for White to continue: 12 b3! d5 13 ♕g3! h5?! 14 ♘a4! h4 15 ♕c3 ♖b8 16 ♗e3 h3 17 g3 ± Yudasin-Greenfeld, Haifa 1995.

a223) 11...g6!? 12 b3!? (12 e5 dxe5 13 ♗h6 f5 14 ♕g3 ♗f6 15 ♖xe5 ♕d6 16 ♖e3 ♕xg3 17 hxg3 ± Gipslis-Kveinys, Ostrava 1992) 12...0-0 13

♗h6 e5?! (probably the wrong plan; Black should try to complicate the game with 13...f5!?) 14 ♕g3 ♖e8 15 ♖ad1 ♗e6 16 ♘a4 ♕c7 17 c4 and White is better, Kuczynski-Cifuentes, Polanica Zdroj 1992.

b) 8...♗e7 9 ♘xc6 bxc6 10 e5!? ♕c7 (10...0-0 11 ♘e4 f6 12 exf6 ♗xf6 13 ♕d6!? ♗e7 14 ♕g3 d5 15 ♗h6 ♖f7 16 ♘g5 was better for White in Gufeld-Furman, Moscow 1970) 11 ♖e1 0-0 12 ♗f4 f5 (more or less forced since White was ready to improve his position substantially with ♕g4 or ♘e4) 13 exf6 ♕xf4 14 fxe7, Yudasin-Lautier, Moscow OL 1994, and now Black has to try 14...♕xf2+ 15 ♔h1 ♖e8, when Yudasin claims 'compensation' with 16 ♘e4 ♕h4 17 ♘d6 ♖xe7 18 ♖f1 but I would not be surprised if there is a forced win for White. Black's pieces are laughably placed, while White's knight on d6 is especially powerful.

9 ♖e1 (D)

9 ♘xc6 is still quite interesting, when 9...bxc6 10 f4!? d5 11 f5! ♗c5+ 12 ♔h1 0-0 13 f6! yielded White a strong attack in Smyslov-Arakhamia, Roquebrune Women vs Veterans 1998.

9...♗d6

9...♗e7 10 ♘xc6 bxc6 11 e5! transposes to note 'b' to Black's 8th move.

10 ♔h1!?

White might also try the more violent 10 ♘d5!? but Black should be able to equalize with 10...exd5 11 exd5+ ♘e5 12 f4 (12 ♘f5? 0-0 13 ♗h6 gxh6 14 ♕h5 ♘g6! and Black consolidates, Timman-Lautier, Horgen 1995) 12...0-0 13 fxe5 ♗xe5 14 ♘f3 d6 15 ♘xe5

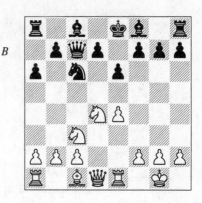

B

dxe5 16 d6 ♕c5+ 17 ♗e3 ♕c6 18 c4 b6! = Lautier.

10...♘xd4 11 ♕xd4 f6!?

11...♗e5 12 ♕d3 b5 is also equal.

12 f4

Or 12 ♗e3 b5 13 ♖ad1 ♗e5 14 ♕d3 ♗b7 with a roughly level position.

12...0-0 13 ♖f1 ♗c5 14 ♕d3 b5

With equality, Vydeslaver-Poluliakhov, Kahovka 1997.

C)

4 0-0 ♘ge7

White has several possibilities here, but we shall concentrate on...

5 b3 (D)

From b2, White's bishop will exert strong pressure against Black's kingside. To neutralize this bishop, Black will be forced to make some kind of concession.

5...a6

There are a number of other options:

a) 5...b6!? 6 ♗b2 ♗b7 7 ♖e1 ♘g6 8 a4 (8 c3!?) 8...f6 9 ♗xc6 ♗xc6 10 d4 cxd4 11 ♘xd4 ♗b4 12 ♗c3 ♗c5 13 ♘xc6 dxc6 14 ♕xd8+ ♖xd8 15 ♘d2

e5 16 ♘f3 ♘f4 17 ♔f1 ♔e7 = Ivano-
vić-Komarov, Yugoslavia 1997.

b) 5...♘d4 (this is not so effective
when White has not played ♘c3) 6
♘xd4 cxd4 7 c3! and now:

b1) 7...♕b6 8 ♘a3 (8 ♕e2 is also
good) 8...♘g6 9 ♗e2 ♗e7!? 10 ♘b5!
(this is much stronger than 10 ♘c4,
the only purpose of which is to threaten
Black's queen; now Black is forced to
clarify the centre) 10...dxc3 11 dxc3?!
(this kind of capture is the normal response but here 11 ♘xc3, with the idea
of d4, is better, and gives White an edge)
11...a6 12 ♘d4 0-0 13 ♗e3 ♕c7 14 c4
b6 15 g3 ♗b7 16 ♗f3 ♘e5!? 17 ♗g2
♘c6 = Golubev-Moroz, Yalta 1996.

b2) 7...♘c6 8 ♗b2 ♗c5 9 b4!? (another plausible approach is 9 ♕h5
dxc3 10 dxc3 ♗e7 11 ♘d2 0-0 12 f4 f5
13 ♔h1 ± Plaskett-Sveshnikov, Sochi
1984) 9...♗b6 10 a4 a6 11 ♗e2 0-0
(Black should probably prefer 11...d5!?
with the idea 12 b5 axb5 13 axb5 ♖xa1
14 ♗xa1 ♘e7 =) 12 b5 dxc3 13 dxc3
axb5 14 axb5 ♖xa1 15 ♗xa1 ♘e5 16
c4 ♕c7 (Pavasović-Podlesnik, Maribor 1996) 17 ♕b3 ±.

b3) 7...a6 8 ♗d3 ♘c6 9 ♗b2 ♗c5
10 cxd4 ♗xd4 11 ♗xd4 ♘xd4 12 ♘c3
d6 13 ♕h5 0-0 14 ♖ae1 ♗d7 15 f4
♗b5 16 ♖e3 g6 17 ♕h6 ± Peng Xiao-
min-Miladinović, Elista OL 1998.

c) 5...♘g6 6 ♗b2 f6 7 ♖e1 ♗e7 8
c3 (8 d4 gives White nothing; Black
equalizes simply with 8...cxd4 9 ♘xd4
♗c5!? 10 ♘xc6 dxc6 11 ♕xd8+ ♔xd8
12 ♗f1 ♔c7 ½-½ Borge-Schandorff,
Danish Ch (Tåstrup) 1998) 8...0-0
(8...♕b6?! 9 ♗f1 ♘ge5 10 ♘a3 ±
Akopian-Kurajica, Ubeda 1996) 9 d4 a6
10 ♗f1 d5 11 ♘bd2 cxd4 12 cxd4 ♗d7
= Timoshenko-Verdikhanov, Nikolaev
Z 1993.

6 ♗xc6

This is the only move that gives
Black any problems. Retreating the
bishop by 6 ♗e2 is too much of a concession: 6...d5 (6...♘g6 7 ♗b2 f6 8 d4
cxd4 9 ♘xd4 ♗c5 is also fine for
Black) 7 exd5 exd5 8 d4 (8 ♖e1 g6 9
♗b2 d4 10 c3 ♗g7 11 cxd4 cxd4 12
♘a3 0-0 = Kreiman-Waitzkin, New
York 1993) 8...♘f5 9 dxc5 ♗xc5 10
♗b2 0-0 11 ♘c3 (Hübner-Masić,
Sombor 1970) 11...♗e6 =.

6...♘xc6 7 ♗b2 *(D)*

Black must now choose carefully
how he is going to develop his kingside, and should take into account the
possibility of White opening the position with d4. He can play this in con-
nection with c4, which leads to a type
of Hedgehog position, or without it,
simply seeking active piece play.

7...b5

An active response, denying White
the opportunity of reaching a Hedgehog, but also postponing the decision

B

of what to do on the kingside. Other approaches:

a) 7...d6 8 d4 cxd4 9 ②xd4 ♗d7 (Black's queen manoeuvre to g6, i.e. 9...♕f6 10 ②a3! ②xd4 11 ♗xd4 ♕g6, is quite common in these positions but I have my doubts about it here, e.g. 12 ②c4! ♕xe4 13 ♖e1 ♕c6 14 ②b6 ♖b8, Kr.Georgiev-Grigorov, Sofia tt 1991, 15 ♕h5 would leave Black looking in vain for a decent move) 10 ♖e1 ♕g5!? (10...♕c7 is normal but this active move has its merits) 11 ②d2 ②xd4 12 ♗xd4 ♗c6 13 ♖e3 e5 14 ♗b6! ♗e7 15 ②c4 ♕g6 16 ♗c7 0-0 17 f3 b5! 18 ②a5 ♗d7 19 ♖d3 ♗h3 20 g3 ♖ac8 21 ♗xd6 ♗xd6 22 ♖xd6 ♕g5 23 ♕d3 f5! with counterplay, Kreiman-Waitzkin, USA 1993.

b) 7...♕c7 and now:

b1) 8 c4 b6 9 ♖e1 ♗b7 10 d4 (the rather unclear sacrifice 10 ②c3 ♗d6 11 ②d5!? exd5 12 exd5+ ②e7 13 ♗xg7 was tried in J.Johansson-L.Schneider, Swedish Ch (Borlange) 1992) 10...cxd4 11 ②xd4 ♗d6 12 ②f3 0-0. So far we have followed the game Yagupov-Filipenko, Rostov on Don 1993. Now

Kraut recommends 13 e5 followed by 14 ②c3 or 14 ②bd2. If White is allowed to follow up with 15 ②e4 he will have promising attacking chances.

b2) 8 d4 cxd4 9 ②xd4 ②xd4 (the alternative 9...♗d6?! 10 ②xc6 dxc6 11 ♕h5 promises White the better chances, as Jansa has proved in a few games) 10 ♕xd4 f6 11 ♗a3 b6 12 ♗xf8 ♖xf8 13 ②d2 ♕c5 14 ♕d3 b5 15 ♖fd1 ♔e7 16 a4 ± Yandemirov-Seliviorstov, Podolsk 1993.

c) 7...f6 8 ②h4 (in many lines where Black adopts a set-up with ...f6 White can exert strong pressure with this move, which, apart from threatening ♕h5+, clears the way for the f-pawn) 8...g6 9 f4 ♕e7 (according to Blatny Black ends up in serious trouble after 9...♗g7 10 f5 exf5 11 exf5 ②e5 12 ②c3! d5 13 d4! cxd4 14 ♕xd4 g5 15 ②f3 ♗xf5 16 ♕xd5 ♕b6+ 17 ②d4 ♖d8 18 ②a4! ♕b4 19 ♕c5 ♕xc5 20 ②xc5 intending ②e6 ±) 10 f5 gxf5 (10...g5? loses to 11 fxe6) 11 exf5 e5? (11...♗g7 is stronger but I would definitely rather be White after 12 ②c3 0-0 13 ♕h5) 12 c4 b5 13 ②c3 ± Golubev-Verdikhanov, Nikolaev Z 1993.

d) 7...d5 8 exd5 ♕xd5 9 ②c3 ♕d7 (9...♕h5 10 ②a4! is good for White – Smirin and Gelfand) 10 ♖e1 b6 (this is more cautious than 10...b5, which gives White a target on the queenside; note also that 10...♗e7? is very bad in view of 11 ②a4!), and now 11 ②e4 ♗b7 yields approximately equal chances. Possibly 11 ②a4 is better, after which Smirin and Gelfand claim a small edge for White if Black plays 11...♖b8.

8 a4 b4 9 d4 cxd4 10 ②xd4 *(D)*

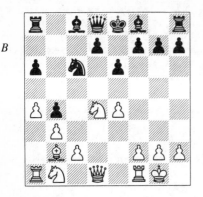

10...♗b7

Or 10...♕f6!? (an important, and quite possibly superior, alternative) 11 ♖a2 ♘xd4 12 ♗xd4:

a) 12...♕g6 13 ♘d2 is good for White:

a1) 13...f6?! 14 ♖e1! ♗b7 15 f3 ♕f7 16 ♘c4 d5 17 exd5 ♗xd5 18 ♕e2! ♖d8 19 ♗b6 ♖c8 20 ♘e3 ♗b7 21 ♖aa1! (preparing to centralize the only inactive piece) 21...e5 22 ♖ad1 ♕e6 23 a5 ♗e7 24 ♖d2 0-0 25 ♖ed1 ± Jansa-Scherbakov, Mlada Boleslav 1994.

a2) 13...a5 14 ♖e1 ♗a6 15 ♘f3! f6 16 c4 ♗e7 17 ♖d2 and again White is controlling everything, Jansa-Kogan, Eupen 1994.

a3) 13...♗b7 is Jansa's suggestion, after which he thinks that 14 f3 d5 15 e5 is slightly better for White.

b) 12...e5! 13 ♗e3 ♗b7 14 ♕d3 ♕g6 15 ♖d1 ♖d8 16 f3 d5 = Hraček-Ye Jiangchuan, Jakarta 1994.

11 ♘d2 *(D)*

Other possibilities for White include:

a) 11 ♖e1 ♖c8 12 ♘d2 ♘xd4 13 ♗xd4 d5 14 e5 ♗e7 15 f4 0-0 16 ♘f3 ♖c6 17 ♖c1 ♕c7 = Thiel-Arakhamia, London 1994.

b) 11 ♘xc6 ♗xc6 12 ♕g4!? h5 13 ♕e2 ♕g5 14 ♘d2 h4 15 h3 ♗c5 16 ♘f3 ♕h5 17 ♖fe1 f6 18 c4! and White is better, Spangenberg-Gi.Hernandez, Matanzas 1993.

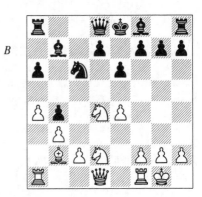

11...♕c7 12 ♖e1 ♘xd4 13 ♗xd4 e5 14 ♗e3! ♗e7 15 ♘c4 0-0 16 ♗b6 ♕c6 17 a5 f6

17...d6?! 18 ♕d2 f5 19 ♕xb4 fxe4 20 ♖ad1 gave White a large advantage in the game Jansa-Boyd, Benasque 1994.

18 ♕g4 d5 19 exd5 ♕xd5

Now White has a pleasant choice between 20 ♘e3 and 20 ♖ad1 with a slight advantage in either case – Jansa.

3 Rossolimo Variation: Other Third Moves

1 e4 c5 2 ♘f3 ♘c6 3 ♗b5 *(D)*

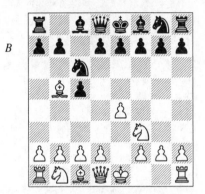

B

In this chapter we shall consider some of the rarer alternatives to the three most common options for Black, which are 3...g6 (Chapter 1), 3...e6 (Chapter 2) and 3...d6 (Chapter 5).

None of the moves encountered here enjoys a very high status but they are played occasionally, and the trick is not to underestimate them. As is the case with most openings when your opponent tries something offbeat, the most practical thing you can do is to look for a good and safe line, rather than instantly searching a refutation. This would certainly be my advice against all of Black's five alternatives we shall analyse in this chapter. Since we are at such an early stage of the game it is hardly likely that White can achieve more than just a solid advantage.

The Theory of Rare Third Moves in the Rossolimo

1 e4 c5 2 ♘f3 ♘c6 3 ♗b5
Now:

A:	3...♘a5	70
B:	3...♘d4	71
C:	3...♘f6	72
D:	3...♕c7	72
E:	3...♕b6	73

Black has a few other strange moves at his disposal, but I will restrict myself to a few cursory observations. 3...a6 is hardly any good since White exchanges on c6 – as Black's most obvious plan is to follow up with ...g6, no matter which way he decides to recapture, White will basically be a tempo up on many lines considered in Chapter 1. 3...b6 is even rarer. White has a pleasant choice between capturing on c6 or simply developing with 0-0 and ♖e1, followed by c3 and d4.

And what is there to say about a move like 3...e5? Consider a Ruy Lopez (1 e4 e5 2 ♘f3 ♘c6 3 ♗b5).

Would Black seriously consider playing 3...c5 if this were legal? Well, probably not, but ...e5 is in fact quite a common move in the Rossolimo. Anyway, the simple 4 0-0 looks good for White. Black's best is 4...♘ge7, as White is threatening to exchange on c6 and capture on e5, but e7 is hardly the best place for the knight in these kind of positions.

A)

3...♘a5 *(D)*

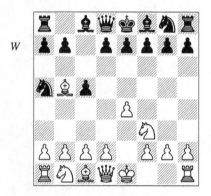

W

It is not unreasonable to raise an eyebrow upon seeing this move for the first time, but it is not as stupid as it looks, and incidentally it has featured in quite a few recent grandmaster games. One can argue that Black is going too far to avoid an exchange of his knight for White's bishop, but White is in no position to exploit this immediately. It is common that Black first develops his queenside, and therefore neglects to develop the kingside for a few moves. Hence the idea of building up a broad centre with c3 and d4

makes most sense to me, as White might have hopes of launching a quick attack, while Black is not ideally organized.

4 c3

Alternatives:

a) 4 ♗e2 b6!? 5 ♘c3 ♗b7 6 d4 cxd4 7 ♘xd4 g6 8 ♗e3 ♗g7 9 0-0 ♘f6 = Jakupović-Kožul, Sarajevo 1998.

b) 4 d4 a6 5 ♗e2 cxd4 6 ♘xd4 and now:

b1) 6...b5 7 0-0 ♗b7 8 ♕d3 e6 9 a4 b4 10 ♘d2 ♕c7 11 f4 ♖c8 12 ♔h1 ♗c5 13 b3 ♘e7 14 ♗b2 0-0 15 ♕g3 f6 16 ♗d3 ♘ac6 17 ♘e2 ♖f7 with a roughly equal position, Prokopchuk-Chernyshov, Pardubice 1997.

b2) 6...♕c7 7 0-0 e6 8 ♕d3 (8 c4!? ♘xc4 9 ♗xc4 ♕xc4 10 ♘c3 ♘f6 11 ♗f4 is suggested by T.Horvath, and looks very promising since ♖c1 is coming next; perhaps Black should not accept the sacrifice, which leads to similar play to the game, except that White might not have to play ♕d3) 8...♘f6 9 c4 b6 10 ♘c3?! (White should be very careful with his move-order here; 10 b3 is worth considering) 10...♗b7 11 b3?! (T.Horvath suggests 11 f3 but Black simply replies 11...♖c8!; then 12 b3 b5! is good for Black) 11...♗b4 12 f3 b5! 13 ♗d2 bxc4 14 bxc4 ♗c5! with the better game for Black, A.Grosar-Kožul, Maribor 1994.

4...a6 5 ♗a4

White would rather have his bishop on the b1-h7 diagonal, and so this retreat is the most common. 5 ♗e2 is also sensible. Then Styrenko-Lysenko, Podolsk 1993 continued 5...d6 (5...d5 6 exd5 ♕xd5 7 d4 would be a good c3

Sicilian for White, but 5...b6!? is possible) 6 d4 cxd4 7 cxd4 g6 8 ♗d2!? ♗d7 9 ♗c3 ♗g7 10 ♕d2 ♘c6 11 d5 ±.

5...b5 *(D)*

5...e6 6 0-0 b5 7 ♗c2 ♗b7 8 d4 cxd4 9 cxd4 ♘f6 10 ♕e2 ♖c8 11 ♗d3 ♗e7 12 ♘c3 d5 13 e5 ♘d7 14 ♗f4 was better for White in Hraček-Minasian, Manila OL 1992.

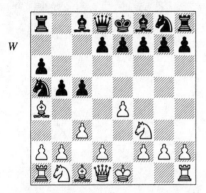

W

6 ♗c2 ♘f6

Black hopes that a quick attack against White's e-pawn will oblige White to weaken his centre. Other options:

a) 6...d5 7 d4! dxe4 8 ♗xe4 ♗b7 9 ♗xb7 ♘xb7 10 0-0 ♘f6 11 ♕e2 e6 12 ♗g5 ♗e7 13 a4 b4 14 dxc5 bxc3 (Zapolskis-Dambrauskas, Cuxhaven 1993) 15 b4! a5 16 c6 ♘d6 17 b5 ± Zapolskis.

b) 6...d6 and then:

b1) 7 0-0 ♘f6 8 d4 cxd4 9 cxd4 e6 10 ♕e2 ♗e7 11 a4 b4 12 ♘bd2 ♕c7 13 ♗d3 ♗b7 14 ♖e1 0-0 15 ♖b1 ♖fc8 16 b3 ± Baci-Aleksić, Croatian Cht (Poreč) 1998.

b2) 7 d4 ♗g4 8 h3 ♗xf3 9 ♕xf3 e5 10 d5 ♘c4 11 h4 h5 12 a4 with a substantial advantage to White, Spangenberg-Paglilla, Villa Martelli 1996.

7 0-0 ♗b7 8 ♖e1 e6

Black is badly off after 8...d5? 9 e5 followed by e6.

9 d4 cxd4 10 ♘xd4! *(D)*

10 cxd4 d5 11 e5 ♘e4 would solve most of Black's problems.

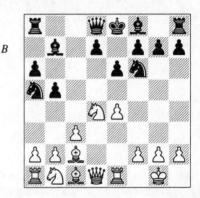

B

10...♗e7 11 e5 ♘d5 12 ♕g4 g6 13 ♗h6 ♕c7 14 ♘d2

White has the better game, Kobelev-Fominykh, Perm 1997.

B)

3...♘d4

As I stated earlier, this kind of move is hardly advisable when White has not developed his knight on c3.

4 ♘xd4 cxd4 5 0-0 g6 6 c3! *(D)*

6...♕b6

6...♗g7 7 cxd4 ♕b6 8 ♘c3 e6 9 ♗e2 ♗xd4 10 ♘b5 ♗g7 11 ♕c2 ± Ribeiro-Costa, Loures 1997.

7 ♗c4 ♗g7 8 cxd4 ♗xd4 9 ♘c3 a6 10 d3 e6 11 ♔h1 ♘e7 12 f4 0-0 13 f5!

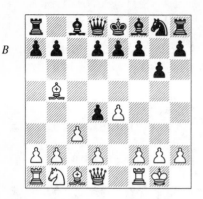

White has a strong attack, Petronić-Gorbatov, Paks 1997.

C)

3...♘f6 4 ♕e2

Alternatives are 4 ♘c3 and 4 e5.

4...g6 5 ♘c3 ♗g7

5...d6?! 6 e5 is very good for White and 5...♘d4?! is also inferior in view of 6 ♘xd4 cxd4 7 e5! dxc3 8 exf6 e6 9 dxc3 ♕xf6 10 ♗e3 and White is better – Dvoretsky.

6 e5 ♘g4 7 ♗xc6 dxc6 8 h3 ♘h6 9 g4! *(D)*

Just in time before the knight joins the game via f5.

9...0-0 10 d3 f5 11 g5 ♘f7 12 ♗f4 ♕a5 13 ♕e3

White is better, Dvoretsky-Simić, USSR-Yugoslavia 1977.

D)

3...♕c7 *(D)*

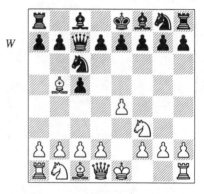

This is one of Black's more respectable options.

4 0-0 ♘f6 5 ♘c3 e6 6 ♖e1 d6

Other moves are inferior:

a) 6...♗e7?! 7 e5 ♘g4 8 ♗xc6 bxc6 9 d4! f5 (9...f6 10 dxc5! ♗xc5 11 ♘e4 ♕b6 12 ♘xc5 ♕xc5 13 ♗e3 ♘xe3 14 ♖xe3 ± Istratescu) 10 h3 ♘h6 11 ♗g5! ♗f8 12 ♗e3! ± Istratescu-Chernyshov, Pardubice 1997.

b) 6...a6?! 7 ♗xc6 ♕xc6 8 d4 cxd4 9 ♘xd4 ♕c4 10 e5 ♘d5 11 ♘e4 ± Rozentalis-B.Kristensen, Copenhagen 1988.

7 e5!

Simpler than the more common 7 d4, although this also gives White an advantage, e.g. 7...cxd4 8 ♘d5!? ♕d8

9 ♘xd4 ♗d7 10 ♗g5 ♖c8 (10...exd5
11 ♗xc6! bxc6 12 exd5+ ♗e7 13
♗xf6 gxf6 14 dxc6 ♗c8 15 ♕f3 ♖b8
16 ♖e3 ♖xb2 17 ♖ae1 ♗e6 18 ♖xe6!
and White wins, Rozentalis-Slekys,
USSR 1988) 11 ♘f5 ♘e5 12 ♘xf6+
gxf6 13 ♘xd6+ ♗xd6 14 ♕xd6 ♗b5
15 ♕xd8+ ♖xd8 16 ♗xf6 ♘f3+! 17
gxf3 ♖g8+ 18 ♔h1 ♖d2 19 ♖e3! ♖xf2
20 ♖d1 ♖f1+ 21 ♖xf1 ♗xf1 22 h4 ±
Ulybin.

**7...dxe5 8 ♘xe5 ♗d7 9 ♘xd7
♕xd7 10 ♕f3 ♖c8 11 d3**

White is slightly better – Istratescu.

E)

3...♕b6 4 ♘c3 e6 5 ♗xc6

It is possible to continue conven-
tionally with 5 0-0 and so on, but then
it is not very easy to get in d4, so this is
best.

5...♕xc6 6 d4

6 0-0 a6 7 ♖e1 ♕c7 8 d4 cxd4 9
♕xd4 ♘e7 10 ♗g5 f6 11 ♗h4 e5 12
♕d3 d6 13 ♘d2 ♗e6 14 ♘f1 g5 15
♗g3 h5 16 f3 g4 17 fxg4 (17 ♖ad1!?)
17...hxg4 18 ♘e3 ♗h6, Spasov-Inkiov,
Bulgarian Ch 1996, 19 ♖ad1 0-0-0 20
♘ed5! gives White a solid advantage.

**6...cxd4 7 ♘xd4 ♕c7 8 0-0 a6 9
♖e1 d6 10 ♗g5** *(D)*

Like in the Moscow Variation with
3...♘d7 (Chapter 6), White has obtained a strong lead in development, at

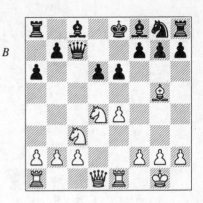

B

the cost of conceding the bishop-pair
to Black.

10...♘f6 11 f4

Another good move is 11 ♕d2 with
the idea 11...♗e7 12 ♘f5! exf5 13
exf5 0-0 14.♖xe7! ♕xe7 15 ♖e1 ♗e6
(much better is 15...♕d7, to meet 16
♗xf6 with 16...♕xf5, when Black has
some chance of defending) 16 ♘d5
♕d8 17 ♗xf6 gxf6 18 ♕h6! +– Arde-
leanu-Bondoc, Romania 1994.

11...h6

11...♗e7 12 e5 gives White an
edge.

**12 ♗xf6 gxf6 13 f5 h5 14 ♔h1
♗d7 15 ♕f3 ♗e7 16 ♕h3 ♕c4 17
♖ad1 ♖c8 18 ♖d3**

Here White has a clear advantage
due to Black's vulnerable centre and
somewhat useless bishops, Ro.Perez-
Re.Gonzalez, Ajeduni 1996.

4 Moscow Variation with 3...♗d7

1 e4 c5 2 ♘f3 d6 3 ♗b5+ ♗d7 *(D)*

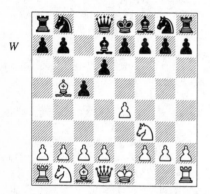

We begin the section on the Moscow Variation with probably the safest line for Black, 3...♗d7.

Following 4 ♗xd7+, Black has a choice of recapturing with the knight or the queen. Both captures provide rapid development for both sides, but in top-level games there is a tendency towards capturing with the queen. Black can then develop his knight on c6, where it plays a greater role in the fight for the centre.

I should explain briefly how the material in this chapter is structured. It is repertoire-based, but for both White and Black. First of all, I recommend that Black plays 3...♗d7 against the Moscow Variation, but rather than recapturing on d7 with the queen, I advocate taking with the knight. Like in the 4...♕xd7 line, White has two main options: to go for a Hedgehog/Maroczy or to continue with c3 and d4.

4...♕xd7 has been very popular lately and White has various ways to play against this, and here I have been rather ruthless in just selecting 5 c4 as my recommendation for White.

Let us, before we begin our theoretical investigation, examine a few general themes. Those that spring to mind are:

1) White plays c3 and d4, and Black replies with ...d5 (usually after a preliminary exchange on d4), obtaining a 'French' structure.

2) White plays d4, but places his c-pawn on c4, thereby obtaining either a Hedgehog or a Maroczy Bind, depending on whether Black plays ...e6 and ...♗e7 or chooses a fianchetto of his king's bishop.

In the Introduction, we looked briefly at these pawn structures. A more thorough investigation is now in order.

The 'French' Structure

The 'French' structure can arise after both 4...♘xd7 and after 4...♕xd7, but it is most commonly reached in the former case. A key position for the

'French' structure is the following, which arises when Black recaptures **4...♘xd7** and play continues **5 0-0 ♘gf6 6 ♕e2 e6 7 c3 ♗e7 8 d4 cxd4 9 cxd4 d5 10 e5 ♘e4** (*D*), which is Line A21:

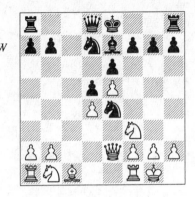

S. Pedersen – Hodgson
Oxford 1998

White has a space advantage in the form of his central pawns d4+e5 vs e6+d5, but Black's structure is the more solid since it presents no obvious target, whereas White must watch his d4-pawn. Another feature that should catch your eye is Black's knight on e4. This knight is so strong that it has to be removed, and White has two ways to do so. One is the immediate challenge by ♘bd2, while the second is to avoid exchanges and play ♘e1, followed by f3.

11 ♘bd2 ♘xd2 12 ♗xd2 0-0 13 ♖ad1

My idea was to reinforce the d-pawn by preparing to defend it with the rook. I hoped thereby to free my minor pieces for some more exciting assignments, such as a kingside attack.

13...♖c8 14 ♘e1 ♕b6 15 ♗e3 ♕a6!

An excellent defensive move. Only Black can be happy with an exchange of queens, even if it is at the cost of doubled a-pawns.

16 ♕xa6

Hodgson said after the game that he had been more afraid of 16 ♕g4. I had rejected this on the simple account that Black would reply 16...f5. Hodgson would of course have played this and had even planned a nice manoeuvre to force an eventual exchange of queens: 17 exf6 ♘xf6 18 ♕h3 ♖c6 19 a3 ♕e2! 20 ♖d2 ♕g4 with a good game for Black.

16...bxa6 (*D*)

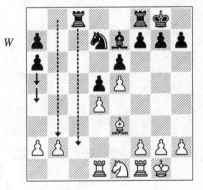

17 ♘d3 a5 18 ♖c1 a4 19 ♗d2?! ♖c4! 20 ♖xc4 dxc4 21 ♘b4 ♖c8 22 ♖c1 ♘b6

Black has much the better ending.

The other main option for White is to retreat the knight to e1, and thus threaten to trap Black's knight with 12 f3 ♘g5 13 h4.

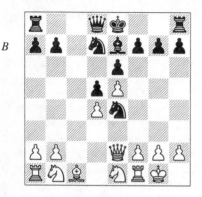

Chekhov – Ftačnik
Bundesliga 1992/3

11...♕b6! 12 ♗e3 f6

This is the correct decision. Since he has a space advantage, White would benefit from a stable centre, which makes moves like 12...h6 and 12...f5 inferior.

13 f3 ♘g5 14 ♘d3 ♘f7 15 ♘c3 0-0 16 ♖fe1 *(D)*

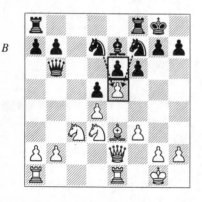

Black has a nice target in White's e-pawn but must be careful that his own pawn on e6 does not become any weaker. Black's route to a good position is a well-timed capture on e5, but Black's next move appears to be premature.

16...fxe5?!

16...♖ac8 is suggested by Chekhov. White would rather not take on f6, but 17 ♗f2 would again pass the ball to Black. 17...fxe5 18 dxe5 ♕a6 19 ♘f4 still looks slightly better for White – note that 19...♖c4 can be met by 20 ♘fxd5!. Also after 17 ♗f2 Black must constantly be alert to ♘xd5 ideas.

17 dxe5 ♕a6 18 ♘f4! ♕xe2

18...♘d8 19 ♕xa6 bxa6 20 ♘d3 ♘c6 21 ♗f2 is only slightly better for White.

19 ♖xe2 ♘d8 20 ♘b5 ♗c5 21 ♘d3 ♗xe3+ 22 ♖xe3

White has a clear advantage due to his more active position. Black has not been quick enough with his pressure against White's pawn on e5, which is now well covered, and the pawn on e6 has become just as weak.

The Hedgehog

For many players, Hedgehog positions look dreadfully passive at first sight, and indeed in many older books such positions were always evaluated as better for White. Today, however, many grandmasters happily play the black side of the Hedgehog, as it has been shown that Black's position is full of hidden dynamism. White must often play with extreme accuracy to avoid over-extending and allowing a

...b5 or ...d5 break. On the other hand, Black should also be careful not to drift into unnecessary passivity, as White is then often able to build up a kingside attack. One such example is the following:

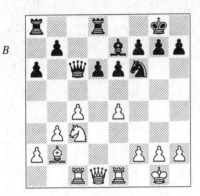

Tkachev – W. Watson
London Lloyds Bank 1993

A fairly typical Hedgehog position has arisen. Black will try to force through ...b5 or ...d5, while White should attempt to prevent these breaks and simultaneously build up a kingside attack.

14...&e8
Preparing ...b5.
15 a4
This leaves a hole on b4, but Black is not in a position to exploit it.
15...&ac8 16 &e2 &d7 17 &cd1 &c5 18 &c2 &c6?
This is really asking for it. 18...b6 19 &e3 &f6 is much better.
19 &e3 &f6?
One mistake is often followed by another one, and this was obviously

Black's intention when playing his previous move.
20 &d5! exd5 21 exd5 &d7 22 &xf6 gxf6 23 &g3+ &h8 24 &xh7+! &xh7 25 &d4 1-0

The key to White's attack succeeding lies in the rook transfer via e3 to g3. Black should seek to prevent this.

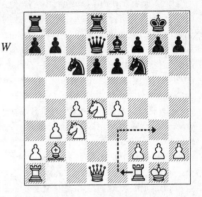

Arkhipov – A. Petrosian
Lippstadt 1993

12 &e1 b6 13 &c1 a6 14 &xc6 &xc6
We have come to the same position as in the previous example but with Black choosing ...b6 rather than ...&e8. I would stress that the best defensive set-up for Black is with the queen on b7. This removes the queen from the c-file and supports ...b5 and ...d5, while also serving the very useful purpose of defending the e7-bishop.
15 &e2 (D)
It is very sensible to remove the queen from the d-file, and from e2 her majesty helps to prevent Black from

playing ...b5. However, Black is not yet threatening ...b5, so it seems odd that nobody has tried the more active 15 ♖e3. White then intends an attacking formation with ♕e2, ♖g3 and f4. Black must be very careful but with accurate play his chances do look fine. We consider the position after 15 ♖e3 ♕b7 in the next example.

15 a4 was tried in Oratovsky-Shmuter, Rishon le Zion 1995, but Black got into some trouble with 15...♖ac8 16 ♖e3 ♕b7 17 ♖g3 ♘e8 (Black has delayed the freeing ...♘d7-c5 manoeuvre for too long, and thus must go in for this passive set-up) 18 ♕e2 ♗f6 19 f4 g6 20 ♖d1, with a very promising game for White. Black needs to be more accurate, though, and 15...♕b7! is the best move in this respect. Having seen the above variations you have probably already guessed that the key defence after 16 ♖e3 is 16...♘d7!. Black is ready to play ...♗f6, and has sufficient counterplay.

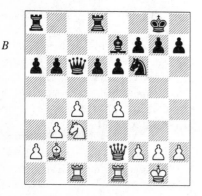

15...♕b7 16 ♖c2 ♖ab8
Preparing ...b5.

17 a4 ♘d7
Here comes the knight.
18 ♗a3 ♖bc8 19 ♖d1 ♘c5
Black has plenty of counterplay.

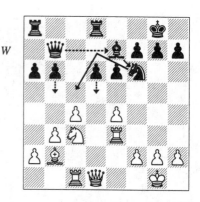

Black's last move was 15...♕c6-b7. I have already explained the purpose of this move, and feel that Black cannot play it soon enough. Sometimes one single misstep means that Black is not in time with his counterplay. Another useful defensive idea to know about is that if Black can provoke White into playing a4, the manoeuvre ...♘d7-c5 is enough to disturb White's attack. Retreating the knight also vacates f6 for the bishop.

16 ♕e2
If 16 ♖g3, Black gets counterplay with 16...b5!.
16...♖ac8
Black needs first to provoke White into playing a4, and then to manoeuvre his knight around to c5.
17 a4
Again Black is ready to counter 17 ♖g3 with 17...b5, for if 18 cxb5 axb5 19 ♘xb5, Black has 19...♖xc1+ 20

♗xc1 ♘xe4 21 ♖e3 d5 with a good game.

17...♘d7 18 ♖d1

If 18 ♖g3 here, 18...♗f6 comes in helpful.

18...♘c5

Black has good counterplay, since if White plays 19 b4, Black retreats his knight and suddenly the c4-pawn, or even the b4-pawn, becomes a target.

The Maroczy Bind

The Maroczy Bind occurs when White places his c-pawn on c4 and follows up with d4, and Black replies by taking it, followed by a fianchetto of his dark-squared bishop. A very interesting strategic struggle arises and both sides must be well familiar with the key ideas to play these positions accurately.

Look at the following position:

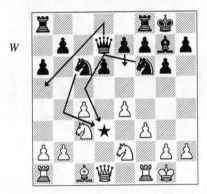

Rublevsky – Gelfand
Polanica Zdroj 1998

This position has occurred in many games, and seems like a good starting point for a discussion of the Maroczy Bind structure. White enjoys a small space advantage due to his c4- and e4-pawns, opposed to Black's on d6 and e7. However, the positional cost is the weakening of White's dark squares. Hence we often see Black employ a strategy based on play on the dark squares, with the manoeuvres ...♕d8-a5, ...♘d7-c5 and ...♘b4 aiming at the d3-square. However, Black needs to prepare this with ...e6 in order to control the d5-square and this gives White a target in the form of the d6-pawn.

12 a4

This move is essential in White's attempt to maintain his space advantage. His ideal formation would be something like ♗e3/g5, ♕d2, ♖fd1, ♖ab1 and b3, but after the immediate 12 ♗e3, Black can play 12...♘e5 13 b3 b5 with a good game.

12...♕d8

12...♕c7 is an interesting alternative. Black wants to initiate the plan ...e6 and ...♘d7-c5 without placing the queen on a5. After 13 ♔h1 e6 14 ♗g5 ♘d7 15 b3 ♘c5 16 ♖b1 ♖ac8, Ponomariov-Shipov, Lubniewice ECC 1998 continued 17 ♕d2 ♘a5! 18 ♘c1, when the tactic 18...♘axb3! 19 ♘xb3 ♘xb3 20 ♖xb3 ♕xc4 21 ♖fb1 ♗xc3 22 ♕xd6 ♗g7 23 ♖xb7 ♕xa4 netted Black a pawn. Instead, 17 b4 ♘d7 18 b5 ♘ce5 19 ♗e7 is critical, but Black is doing fine after 19...♖fe8 20 ♗xd6 ♕xc4 21 ♖b4 ♕d3. Hence White need to be more precise, and while 17 ♕c2 allows 17...♘b4, the right move is 17 ♘a2!. Even though it looks rather strange to decentralize the knight in this way, Black is a long way from being able to execute ...b5 or ...d5, and White is ready for his ideal set-up with ♕d2 and ♖fd1.

13 ♗e3

13 ♔h1 is also possible.

13...♕a5 14 ♔h1 ♖fd8 *(D)*

Now Black intends ...e6 followed by ...♘d7-c5, but White effectively puts a stop to this with his next move. After 14...♘d7 15 ♖b1, 15...♘c5 16 ♘d5 is also good for White, while 15...♘b4 is met by 16 ♕d2 – Gelfand and Khuzman.

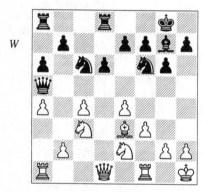

15 ♘d5! ♘xd5 16 exd5 ♘e5 17 b3! ♘d7 18 ♗d4

The transformation of the position has yielded White excellent long-term chances due to his queenside majority and the semi-open e-file. Black must therefore play actively.

18...♘f6

18...♗xd4 19 ♘xd4 is very good for White, who prevents Black's counter-thrusts ...b5 and ...e6 and has chances of building up a kingside attack.

19 ♕d3

19 ♗c3 ♕c7 20 a5 ♖e8 21 ♗d4, as suggested by Gelfand and Khuzman, may be an even simpler path to an advantage.

19...♖e8 20 ♘c3 e6 21 dxe6 fxe6 22 ♖ad1

White is still slightly better but Black has succeeded in mixing things up a little and actually went on to win the game.

The Theory of the Moscow Variation with 3...♗d7

1 e4 c5 2 ♘f3 d6 3 ♗b5+ ♗d7 4 ♗xd7+

There are a few alternatives to this logical exchange, but none of them promises anything for White:

a) 4 ♕e2 and then:

a1) 4...♘f6 5 ♗xd7+ (5 e5 dxe5 6 ♘xe5 e6! is equal according to Timman) 5...♕xd7 (5...♘bxd7 6 0-0 e6 transposes to Line A2) 6 e5 dxe5 7 ♘xe5 ♕e6! 8 ♘a3 ♘fd7 9 ♘ac4 ♘xe5 10 ♘xe5 f6 11 ♘c4 ♕xe2+ 12 ♔xe2 ♘c6 = Timman-Ivanchuk, Amsterdam 1994.

a2) 4...♗xb5 5 ♕xb5+ ♕d7 6 ♕xd7+ ♘xd7 leads to an equal endgame.

b) 4 a4 ♘f6 5 d3 ♘c6 (this must be quite a good version of Chapter 5 for Black) 6 0-0 g6 7 ♖e1 ♗g7 8 ♗xc6 ♗xc6 9 e5 dxe5 10 ♘xe5 ♖c8 11 ♘c3 0-0 12 ♘xc6 ♖xc6 13 ♕f3 ♕d7 14 a5 ♖d8 = Becerra Rivero-Ki.Georgiev, Erevan OL 1996.

Now we have:

A: **4...♘xd7**   81
B: **4...♕xd7**   86

The second option is the more common in practice, but I am recommending Line A for Black.

A)
4...♘xd7 *(D)*

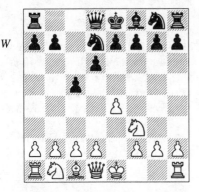

5 0-0

White might also immediately go for a Hedgehog or Maroczy Bind with 5 c4. Black usually chooses a Hedgehog formation, which seems the more logical when Black does not have a knight on c6. Here are a couple of examples after 5 c4 ♘gf6 6 ♘c3:

a) 6...e6 7 0-0 ♗e7 8 d4 cxd4 9 ♘xd4 0-0 10 b3 a6 11 ♗b2 ♖e8 12 ♕e2 ♗f8 13 ♖ad1 ♕a5 14 f4 ♖ad8 with a roughly equal position, Sedina-Novikov, Nova Gorica 1997.

b) 6...g6 7 0-0 ♗g7 8 d4 cxd4 9 ♘xd4 0-0 10 b3 a6 11 ♗e3 e6 12 ♖c1 ♖c8 13 ♕e2 ♖e8 14 ♖fd1 d5! and Black has equalized, Nevednichy-Sorokin, Bled 1992.

5...♘gf6

We shall now deal with two options for White:
A1: 6 ♖e1   81
A2: 6 ♕e2   82

A1)
6 ♖e1 e6 *(D)*

6...g6 7 c3 ♗g7 8 d4 0-0 9 h3 e6 10 ♘bd2 ♕c7 11 b3 ♖fd8 12 ♗b2 ♖ac8 13 ♕e2 gave White an edge in Gdanski-Sax, Budapest 1993.

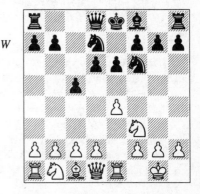

7 c3

Unless White tries the idea of c3 and d4, the game will most likely evolve into a roughly equal Hedgehog position:

a) 7 c4 ♘e5 8 d3 ♗e7 9 b3 0-0 10 ♗b2 ♘c6 11 d4 cxd4 12 ♘xd4 ♘xd4!? 13 ♕xd4 ♕a5 14 ♘c3 a6 15 a3 ♖fd8 16 h3 ♖ac8 17 ♖ad1 ♘e8 18 ♕e3 ♗f6 19 f4 h6!? with approximately equal chances, Antonio-Ricardi, Elista OL 1998.

b) 7 d4 cxd4 8 ♕xd4 ♗e7 9 c4 0-0 10 ♘c3 ♘g4!? (the more intricate 10...a6 is of course also perfectly playable, and has been tried many times) 11 h3 (Kraut suggests 11 ♕d3!? with an equal position) 11...♘ge5 12 ♘xe5 dxe5! 13 ♕d1 ♖c8 14 b3 a6 15 ♖e3 ♕c7 and Black has a good game, Westerinen-Bator, Jyväskylä 1994.

c) 7 b3 ♗e7 8 ♗b2 0-0 9 c4 a6 (9...e5!?) 10 d4 cxd4 11 ♘xd4 ♕c7 12 ♘c3 ♖fe8 13 ♕d2 ♗f8 14 ♖ad1 ♖ac8 15 ♕g5 h6 16 ♕h4 ♕c5 = Akopian-Vaïsser, Novosibirsk 1993.

7...♗e7 8 d4 0-0!?

8...cxd4 9 cxd4 d5 10 e5 ♘e4 11 ♘bd2 ♘xd2 gives White an interesting choice:

a) 12 ♘xd2!? 0-0 13 ♕g4 ♕b6 14 ♘f3 (Kraut-Tolnai, Dortmund 1986) and now, according to Kraut, Black should play 14...♖fc8 with an unclear position.

b) 12 ♗xd2 0-0 13 ♖c1 ♘b8!? 14 ♕b3 ♕d7 15 ♗b4 ♗xb4 16 ♕xb4 ♘c6 17 ♕a3 ♖ac8 = Leko-Yudasin, Leon 1993.

9 e5

9 ♗g5 ♖c8 10 ♕b3 ♘b6 11 dxc5 ♖xc5 12 ♘bd2 ♘g4 13 ♗xe7 ♕xe7 14 h3 ♘e5 15 ♘xe5 ♖xe5 16 a4 ♕c7 17 a5 ♘d7 18 ♕a3 d5! = B.Larsen-Pelletier, Zurich 1998.

9...♘e8

Black does best to keep the centre fluid. After 9...dxe5 10 dxe5 ♘d5, White gets a good position with 11 ♕e2 followed by c4.

10 exd6

White does not have to resolve the tension immediately and can, for example, play 10 ♕e2 ♖c8 (10...d5 is maybe better, when after 11 ♘bd2 cxd4 12 cxd4 ♖c8 13 ♘f1 ♖c6!? the

position is about equal) 11 exd6 ♗xd6 (Black needs to take with the bishop since after 11...♘xd6, 12 d5! really is strong) 12 ♗g5 ♕c7 13 ♘a3 a6 14 ♘c4 cxd4 15 ♘xd6 ♘xd6, Szmetan-Tal, Termas de Rio Hondo 1987, when Tal recommends 16 ♗e7 ♖fe8 17 ♗xd6 ♕xd6 18 ♘xd4 with an edge for White.

10...♘xd6

It is preferable to activate the knight rather than taking with the bishop. Ideally Black wants to give White an isolated pawn on d4, blockade it, and then play ...♘f5 to attack it. All this serves to explain White's next move.

11 d5 exd5 12 ♕xd5 ♖c8 13 ♗f4 ♘b6 14 ♕d1 ♖e8

The position is equal, Short-Tiviakov, Linares 1995.

A2)

6 ♕e2 e6 *(D)*

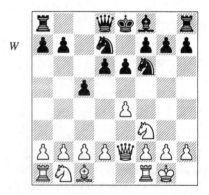

We shall examine White's two most important moves in detail:

A21)

7 c3 ♗e7 8 d4 cxd4

After 8...0-0 we have:

a) 9 e5 ♘e8 10 dxc5 ♘xc5 11 ♖d1 ♕c7 12 exd6 ♘xd6 13 ♗f4 ♖ad8 14 c4?! (this looks a little odd as White develops his knight on a3 anyway; 14 ♘a3 is better) 14...♗f6 15 ♘a3 ♕c6 16 ♗e5 ♕e4! = Wahls-Serper, Adelaide jr Wch 1988.

b) 9 ♖d1 cxd4 10 cxd4 and then:

b1) 10...d5 11 e5 ♘e4 12 ♘e1 is an improved version of the main line for White, since Black does not have the same counterplay:

b11) In Arkhipov-Leko, Lippstadt 1993, Black struggled on to a draw with 12...h6 13 ♘d3 ♘b8 14 ♕g4 ♔h8 15 ♘f4 ♘c6 16 ♘c3 ♘xc3 17 bxc3 ♗g5 18 ♖d3 ♗xf4 19 ♗xf4 ♘e7 20 ♖h3 ♔h7, etc., but I would much prefer White's attacking prospects.

b12) 12...f5 13 f3 ♘g5 14 ♘d3 ♖c8 15 ♘c3 ♘b6 16 ♗e3 ♘c4 17 ♗f2 ♘f7 18 ♖ac1 ♕d7 19 b3 ♘a5 20 ♘c5! ♗xc5 21 dxc5 and White has the advantage, Zhang Zhong-Lin Weiguo, Beijing 1997.

b2) 10...♘b6 11 ♘c3 ♕c7 (11...♖c8 12 ♖d3 ♕c7 13 ♗g5 h6 14 ♗xf6 ♗xf6 15 ♖ad1 ♗e7 = Chekhov-Panchenko, Russian Cht (Podolsk) 1992) 12 ♗g5 h6 13 ♗h4 ♖fc8 14 ♖ac1 ♕d8 15 ♖c2 (15 d5!? may give White an edge) 15...d5 16 e5 ♘e8 17 ♗xe7 ♕xe7 18 ♖dc1 ♖c6 = Torre-Polugaevsky, Biel 1989.

9 cxd4 d5 10 e5 ♘e4 *(D)*

11 ♘e1

The alternative is 11 ♘bd2 ♘xd2 12 ♗xd2 0-0:

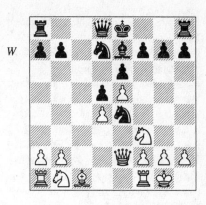

a) 13 ♖ad1 ♖c8 14 ♘e1 ♕b6 15 ♗e3 ♕a6 16 ♕xa6 bxa6 ∓ S.Pedersen-Hodgson, Oxford 1998.

b) 13 ♕b5 ♘b6 14 ♗a5 ♕d7! 15 ♕xd7 ♘xd7 16 ♖fc1 ♖fc8 was equal in Zo.Varga-Tolnai, Hungarian Ch (Lillafüred) 1999.

c) 13 ♕d3 h6 14 ♖ae1 ♕b6 15 ♗c3 ♖fc8 16 ♗e3 a5 17 ♘e1 ♕a6 18 ♕d1 ♖c4 19 ♖g3 and White has reasonable prospects of building up an attack, Dreev-Kengis, Pavlodar 1987.

11...♕b6!

This is an important intermediate move. Alternative moves are clearly inferior:

a) 11...f5?! 12 exf6 ♗xf6 13 ♘c3! ♗xd4 14 ♘xe4 dxe4 15 ♕xe4 ♘c5 16 ♕g4 ± Timman-Khenkin, Tilburg 1994.

b) 11...h6?! 12 f3 ♘g5 13 ♘c3 ♕b6 14 f4 ♘h7 15 ♗e3 ± Kalegin-Tolnai, Balatonbereny 1994.

12 ♗e3 f6

Seeking to destabilize the centre, which is logical since Black is short of space. 12...f5 13 f3 ♘g5 14 ♘c3 0-0 15 ♘d3 ♘f7 16 ♔h1 ♖ac8 17 ♖g1 gave White an edge in Ricardi-A.Hoffman, Buenos Aires 1995.

13 f3 ♘g5 14 ♘d3 0-0 15 ♘c3 ♘f7

This looks very sensible, increasing the pressure against the e5-pawn. Nevertheless, Black has tried a few other moves:

a) 15...♖ac8 16 ♗f2 ♕a6 17 ♖fe1 fxe5 18 dxe5!? (18 ♘xe5 ♘xe5 19 ♕xe5 ♖xf3 20 ♘xd5 ♗f6 21 ♘xf6+ gxf6 22 ♕e2 ♕xe2 23 ♖xe2 ♖f4 is roughly equal, Lechtynsky-Donchev, Bratislava 1983) 18...♖c4 is claimed by Lechtynsky to be clearly better for Black, but White has the very interesting possibility 19 h4!? ♘f7 20 ♘xd5 exd5 21 e6.

b) 15...♕a6 and then:

b1) 16 ♗f2 fxe5 17 dxe5 ♘f7 18 ♖fe1 ♘h6! (a very fine move, preventing ♘f4 and avoiding any ♘xd5 ideas) 19 ♖ad1 ♖ac8 20 ♘c1 ♕xe2 21 ♘1xe2 ♗b4! (I like this move very much, as it shows a good understanding of the position; Black's knights will simply turn out much superior to White's knight and bishop) 22 a3 (22 ♗xa7 b6 embarrasses the bishop) 22...♗xc3 23 ♘xc3 a6 and Black is better, Zhang Zhong-Kudrin, Beijing 1998.

b2) 16 ♖ae1 ♖ae8 17 ♗f2 fxe5 18 dxe5 ♘f7 19 f4 (19 ♘xd5 exd5 20 e6 ♗f6 21 exf7+ ♔xf7 22 ♕d2 may be worth trying) 19...♘h6 20 ♖c1 ♖c8 21 ♖c2 ♖c6 22 ♖fc1 ♕a5 23 a3 a6 24 ♘a2 ♕b5 25 ♖ab4 ♖c4 ∓ Shaked-de Firmian, Bermuda 1997.

16 ♖fe1 fxe5?!

16...♖ac8 is suggested by Chekhov as an improvement but 17 ♗f2 fxe5 18

dxe5 ♕a6 19 ♘f4 still looks slightly better for White.

17 dxe5 ♕a6 18 ♘f4! ♕xe2 19 ♖xe2 ♘d8 20 ♘b5 ♗c5 21 ♘d3 ♗xe3+ 22 ♖xe3

White is clearly better, Chekhov-Ftačnik, Bundesliga 1992/3.

A22)

7 b3 *(D)*

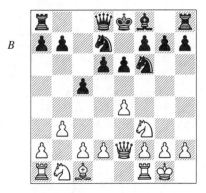

7...♗e7

Black might also change his strategy and play 7...g6:

a) 8 d4 cxd4 9 ♘xd4 ♗g7 10 ♗a3 ♕b6 11 ♘c3 a6 (11...♕xd4? 12 ♘b5 ♕b6 13 ♘xd6+ ♔d8 14 ♘xf7+ ♔c7 15 ♘xh8 ♖xh8 16 ♖ad1 ± Ftačnik) 12 ♖ad1 0-0 = Kramnik-Gelfand, Sanghi Nagar FIDE Ct (1) 1994.

b) 8 c3!? (as Black has changed his strategy, it is very reasonable for White to modify his plan too; going for c3 and d4 is very reasonable when Black has played ...g6) 8...♗g7 9 d4 0-0 10 ♘bd2 ♕c7 11 ♗b2 ♖fc8 (11...cxd4 12 cxd4 ♖fc8 13 e5 dxe5 14 dxe5 ♘d5 15 ♘c4 gave White the advantage in

Ulybin-Zagrebelny, Russia Cup 1997) 12 ♖fe1 a6 13 e5 ♘e8 14 h4 b5 15 h5 ♕b7 16 hxg6 hxg6 17 ♕d3 and White is better, Rublevsky-Neverov, St Petersburg 1996.

8 ♗b2 0-0 9 c4

After 9 d4 cxd4 10 ♘xd4, Polugaevsky suggests 10...♘e5 =, but Black also seems to do quite well with 10...♘c5 11 ♘d2 ♕b6 12 ♖ad1 ♕a6 13 ♕xa6 ♘xa6 14 ♖fe1 ½-½ Nunn-Ribli, Thessaloniki OL 1984.

9...a6

Black will need to play this move sooner or later but the question is whether it is worth spending a tempo on it here. Alternatives:

a) 9...e5 10 ♘c3 leads to a further branch:

a1) 10...♘e8 11 ♘e1! ♘c7 12 ♘c2 ♘e6 13 ♘e3 (it is worth noting that even though Black seems to be controlling the d4-square just as well as White controls the d5-square, White can always remove a black knight from d4, whereas it is harder for Black to evict a white knight from d5, as that requires an exchange of all the knights) and now:

a11) 13...♗g5?! 14 g3! ♘f6 15 ♕d3! (preparing ♘e2 followed by f4) 15...♕d7!? 16 ♘cd5! ♗xe3 (16...♘xd5 17 cxd5 ♘d4 18 f4 exf4 19 gxf4 ♗f6 20 ♔g2, with the idea of h3 and ♘g4 or ♖ae1 and ♘f5, gives White a clear advantage – Yudasin) 17 ♘xf6+ gxf6 18 fxe3 ± Yudasin-Shirov, Ljubljana 1995.

a12) 13...♘f6 is better, preparing to exchange a set of knights if White hops in on d5.

a2) 10...g6 11 a3 ♘h5 12 g3 ♘g7 13 b4 b6 14 ♘d5 f5 15 exf5 ♘xf5 16 bxc5 bxc5 17 ♗c3 ♘f6 18 ♘xf6+ ♗xf6 19 ♕e4 ± Kamsky-Alterman, Tilburg 1993.

a3) 10...♘b8 is better; Black keeps one knight with contact to the d5-square while preparing to manoeuvre the other around to d4. Rublevsky-Rashkovsky, Elista 1994 witnessed an interesting idea, with White in the first place avoiding knight exchanges: 11 d3 (11 ♘e1 ♘c6 12 ♘d5 ♘xd5 13 cxd5 had been the normal continuation) 11...♘c6 12 ♘d2 ♘d4 13 ♕d1 a6 14 f4 exf4 15 ♖xf4 b5 16 ♖f1 ♖b8 17 ♘f3 ♘e6 18 ♕d2 ±.

b) 9...♖e8 10 d4 cxd4 11 ♘xd4 ♕b6 12 ♖d1 ♘c5 13 ♘c3 ♖ad8 14 ♖ab1 ♗f8 15 ♕f3 a6 16 ♖d2 d5! and the complications turn out fine for Black, Tal-Geller, USSR Ch 1979.

10 d4 cxd4 11 ♘xd4 *(D)*

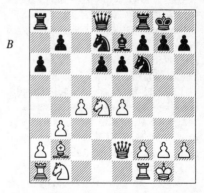

11...♕b6

Depriving White of his most natural continuation, ♘c3. White could just defend the d4-knight with 12 ♖d1 and then play ♘c3 next move, but White would rather have his queen's rook on d1, keeping the rook on f1 to support an advance of the f-pawn.

Other options:

a) 11...♖c8 12 ♘c3 ♕a5 13 ♖ad1 ♕h5 14 f3 ♖fe8 15 ♔h1 ♗f8 16 ♕e1!? ♕a5 17 f4 e5 18 fxe5 ♕xe5 19 ♕f2 ♕h5 20 ♘f5 ♘c5 21 ♕f3 ♕xf3 22 gxf3 ± Adams-Kengis, Århus 1997.

b) 11...♕a5 12 ♘c3 ♖fc8 13 ♖ad1 (13 ♖ac1!?) 13...♘e8 14 ♔h1 ♗f6 15 f4 b5!? with counterplay, Marciano-Relange, Belfort 1997.

12 ♔h1

White stubbornly attempts to keep his rook on f1, but at the same time neglects his development. Other options:

a) 12 ♘c2 ♖ac8 13 ♘c3 ♖fe8 14 ♔h1 ♕c5 15 ♖ac1 ♕h5 16 ♕xh5 ♘xh5 with approximately equal chances, Adams-Tiviakov, New York PCA Ct (12) 1994.

b) 12 ♖d1 ♖fe8 13 ♘c3 ♗f8 14 ♘f3 ♖ac8 15 ♘a4 ♕c6 16 e5 dxe5 17 ♘xe5 ♘xe5 18 ♗xe5 b5 19 ♗xf6 gxf6 20 ♘b2 ♖ed8 ∓ K.Berg-Van Wely, Leeuwarden 1993.

12...♕c5 13 f4

13 ♘d2 ♕h5 14 f3 ♖fe8 15 g4?! ♕g5 16 ♖g1 (Sadler mentions 16 f4!? ♕xg4 17 ♖f3 with some compensation) 16...♘e5 17 ♖af1 ♘g6 ∓ Plaskett-Sadler, Hastings 1998/9.

13...♖fe8 14 ♘f3

White consistently avoids putting his knight on d2, but this allows Black a break on the queenside.

14...b5 15 e5 ♘g4 16 ♘d4 dxe5 17 ♘xe6 fxe6 18 ♕xg4 ♗f6 19 fxe5

19 ♘c3!?.

19...♗xe5 20 ♘c3

The position is unclear, Ricardi-Wolff, Buenos Aires 1997.

B)

4...♕xd7

White can now choose between two plans. One is to go for a Maroczy Bind or Hedgehog by playing c4 and d4; the other is the classical build-up of the centre with c3 followed by d4. The former possibility is my unequivocal recommendation, so we shall here only discuss...

5 c4 *(D)*

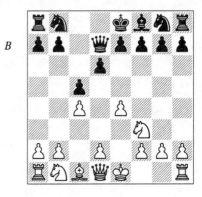

5...♘c6

Alternatives:

a) 5...♕g4?! has now been condemned as being too risky. Black grabs a pawn but at the cost of wasting a lot of time with his queen. 6 0-0 ♕xe4 7 d4! cxd4 (7...♘f6 8 ♘c3 ♕f5 9 ♕b3 b6 10 dxc5 ♕xc5 11 ♗e3 ± Ostojić-Quinteros, Torremolinos 1974) and then:

a1) 8 ♘xd4 ♘f6 9 ♖e1 ♕g4 10 ♕a4+ ♕d7 11 ♘b5 ♘c6 12 ♘1c3 e5

13 ♗g5 ♗e7 14 ♖ad1 and White is better, Aagaard-Josephsen, Lyngby 1995.

a2) 8 ♖e1 ♕g4 (8...♕c6 9 ♘xd4 ♕xc4 10 ♘a3 ♕c8 11 ♗f4 ♕d7 12 ♘ab5 ± Browne-Quinteros, Wijk aan Zee 1974) 9 ♘a3!? a6 (according to Peptan and Stoica Black should play 9...♘c6 10 ♘b5 0-0-0 11 h3 ♕d7 but White still has great compensation after 12 ♘fxd4) 10 c5! (Peptan-Madl, Kishinev 1998 continued with the less clear, albeit quite sensible, 10 ♕b3) 10...dxc5 11 ♘c4 ♕g6 12 ♘fe5 ♕f5 13 g4! ♕f6 14 ♗g5! ♕xg5 15 ♕f3 ± Peptan and Stoica.

b) 5...e5 is the ultra-solid choice. Usually one would avoid such a move as it makes Black's bishop more 'bad'. However, in reality, Black's bishop is not so much worse than its white counterpart. Admittedly, White's bishop has a little more scope but it is being fairly well hampered by Black's pawns, and if White becomes ambitious, he will inevitably have to open up the game, thereby also opening lines for Black's bishop. 6 ♘c3 ♘c6 7 d3 (it is quite interesting that Rublevsky chose to delay this in a recent game, and instead opted for 7 0-0 g6 8 a3 ♗g7 9 b4 ♘ge7 10 bxc5 dxc5 11 d3 0-0 12 ♘d5 with just an edge, Rublevsky-Brestian, Elista OL 1998) 7...g6 8 ♘d5 ♗g7 9 0-0 ♘ge7 10 ♗d2 0-0 11 ♖b1 ♘xd5 12 cxd5 ♘d4 13 b4 f5 14 bxc5 dxc5 15 ♘xd4 exd4?! (15...cxd4 is safer) 16 ♕b3 b6 17 f4 fxe4 18 dxe4 ♖ac8 19 ♕c4 ♔h8 20 a4 and White is better, Shaked-Kaidanov, USA Ch (Parsippany) 1996.

Returning to 5...♘c6 *(D)*:

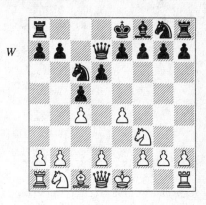

Now:
B1:	**6 ♘c3**	87
B2:	**6 d4**	91

B1)
6 ♘c3
We already have another branch:
B11:	**6...♘e5**	87
B12:	**6...g6**	89

6...♘f6 7 d4 cxd4 8 ♘xd4 transposes to Line B2, while 6...e6 is likely to lead to variations considered in Line B22.

B11)
6...♘e5 *(D)*
7 ♘xe5
In my opinion this move is rather underrated. Black will get good play along the d-file if White plays slowly, but with active play it is possible to subject Black to some unpleasantness. Alternatives:

a) 7 d3 is the sort of thing Black hopes for, since White's basic plan has

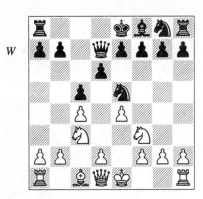

been put on hold for the time being. 7...e6 8 0-0 ♘e7 (8...♘f6 9 h3 ♗e7 10 ♗e3 0-0 11 b3 a6 12 a4! ♘g6 13 d4 ♕c7 14 ♕c2 ♖ad8 15 ♖ad1 cxd4 16 ♘xd4 gave White an edge in Relange-Mir.Marković, Sabac 1998) 9 ♘e1 g6 10 f4 (or 10 ♘c2 ♗g7 11 ♗e3 0-0 12 f4 ♘5c6 13 d4 cxd4 14 ♘xd4 f5 15 exf5 ♘xf5 ½-½ Sax-Kasparov, Tilburg 1989) 10...♘5c6 11 ♘f3 ♗g7 12 ♗e3 ♘d4 (preventing d4) 13 ♗xd4 cxd4 14 ♘e2 ♘c6 15 ♖b1 a5 16 a3, Dolmatov-Khasin, Volgograd 1974, and now Kraut claims that Black can equalize with 16...0-0 17 b4 axb4 18 axb4 e5.

b) 7 d4!? gives Black a very difficult choice:

b1) 7...♘xc4? 8 dxc5 dxc5 9 ♕e2 is just horrible for Black, who will suffer seriously for his lagging development.

b2) 7...cxd4 8 ♕xd4 ♘c6 9 ♕d2 ♘f6 10 0-0 g6 11 b3 ♗g7 12 ♗b2 0-0 13 ♖fe1 ♘g4 14 ♖ad1 ♖ad8 15 h3 ♘ge5 16 ♘h2!? ♘b4 17 ♕e2 g5 18 ♘d5 ♘xd5 19 exd5 ± Belikov-Golubev, Moscow 1996.

b3) 7...♘xf3+ 8 gxf3 cxd4 9 ♕xd4 e6 10 ♗e3 ♘e7 11 0-0-0 and now:

b31) 11...♘c6 12 ♕d2 ♖d8 (the alternative 12...♘e5 13 ♕e2 ♕c6 14 b3 is probably good for White, for he is ready to push the knight away from e5 with f4) 13 ♖hg1 ♕c8 14 f4 favoured White in Rublevsky-Becerra Rivero, Lucerne Wcht 1997.

b32) I suggest 11...♖c8!? as an improvement for Black, intending ...♘c6-e5. While 12 ♕xa7 ♖xc4 does not look too intimidating, 12 b3 b5! highlights the unpleasant aspect for White of having his king on c1 opposed to a rook on c8.

7...dxe5 8 ♕h5! *(D)*

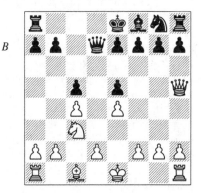

If Black is allowed some peace he will soon obtain promising play against White's backward d-pawn, so White has to follow up very energetically.

8...♕d4

This forces White's queen back from its active post at h5 but Black's own queen also soon has to retreat.

8...♕d6 is the more solid approach. Then White has got nothing from 9

♘b5, e.g. 9...♕b8 10 0-0 a6 (10...e6?! is risky due to 11 f4 exf4 12 d4!; Komliakov-Lipman, Moscow 1989 continued 12...♘f6 13 ♕e5 ♘d7 14 ♕xb8+ ♖xb8 15 ♗xf4 ±) 11 ♘c3 e6 12 d3 ♘f6 13 ♕e2 ♘d7 = Titov-Rashkovsky, Moscow 1991. However, I would like to draw your attention towards the interesting, albeit as yet untested 9 f4!? exf4 10 d4!?. It seems to me that there is a lot of unexplored territory here.

9 ♕e2 e6 10 d3 ♕d7 *(D)*

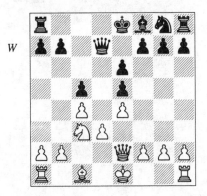

11 f4!

This is much better than 11 0-0 ♘e7 12 f4 after which Black got quite a decent position with 12...exf4 13 ♗xf4 ♘g6 14 ♗g3 ♗e7 15 e5 0-0 16 ♔h1 ♖ad8 in Nevednichy-Mi.Tseitlin, Bucharest 1993.

11...♘e7

White's idea is designed to prevent the defensive method outlined in the Nevednichy-Mi.Tseitlin game above, since here 11...exf4 12 ♗xf4 ♘e7 would be too slow in view of the reply 13 ♘b5!.

12 fxe5 ♘g6 13 ♗e3 ♘xe5 14 0-0-0 ♘c6 15 ♕f2 b6 16 ♖hf1 ♖d8 17 d4! cxd4 18 ♗xd4 ♕b7 19 ♘b5

White has a very strong attack, Oral-Barbero, Basle 1999.

B12)
6...g6 7 d4 *(D)*

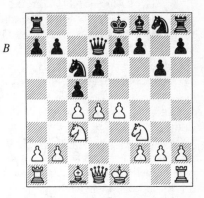

7...♗g7!?

Some move-order subtleties come into play here; the alternative is to exchange on d4 first, and then to play ...♗g7. If White answers the text-move with 8 ♗e3, then Black will reply 8...cxd4 9 ♘xd4, reaching the same position as after 7...cxd4 8 ♘xd4 ♗g7 9 ♗e3, but having avoided 9 ♘de2, which is currently regarded as somewhat better for White (9...♘f6 10 0-0 is Line B23). However, 7...♗g7 also gives White an extra option, which we take to be the main line of this section.

Let us, then, briefly look at 7...cxd4 8 ♘xd4 ♗g7 9 ♗e3 ♘f6 10 f3 0-0 11 0-0. Black now has two plans:

1) Preparing a ...b5 break, beginning with ...a6 and playing either rook

to c8. This might force White to weaken himself with a4, which would give Black the opportunity to settle his knights on c5 and b4.

2) Preparing a ...d5 break, initiated by the moves ...♖fd8 and ...e6.

Hence we consider:

a) 11...♖ac8 12 b3 ♖fd8 13 ♕d2 e6 14 ♖ac1 (14 ♖ad1 might be preferable, when White is in a better position to answer 14...d5 with 15 exd5 exd5 16 c5) 14...d5 15 exd5 exd5 16 c5? (Black has no worries after 16 ♘xc6 bxc6 but this is still White's best choice) 16...♘xd4! (16...♖e8 has also been played, for example in Gelfand-Shirov, Wijk aan Zee blitz 1998, but the text-move is better) 17 ♗xd4 ♘e4! 18 fxe4 dxe4 (it is surprising that Shirov, who is such a sharp tactician, missed this nice idea, even in a blitz game) 19 ♘xe4 ♕xd4+ 20 ♕xd4 ♗xd4+ 21 ♔h1. Kraut now claims that Black is clearly better, and while I would not disagree, I feel that a few accurate moves are needed to display it, and the right starter seems to be 21...♗e5! with the intention of following up with ...f5.

b) 11...♖fc8 12 b3 ♕d8 (12...a6 13 ♘xc6 ♕xc6 14 a4 ♘g4! 15 ♗d4 ♘e3 16 ♗xe3 ♗xc3 = Kuijf-Van den Doel, Wijk aan Zee 1998) 13 ♕d2 ♘d7 14 ♘de2 a6 15 ♖ab1 ♖ab8 16 a4 ♘c5 17 ♖fd1 ♘b4 18 ♘d4 ♕d7 19 ♔h1 b6 20 ♘d5 ♘xd5 21 exd5 ♗xd4! 22 ♗xd4 b5 with a roughly equal position, Oratovsky-Ilinčić, ECC 1998.

c) 11...a6 12 a4 e6 13 ♘de2 ♕c7 14 ♖c1 ♘d7 15 b3 ♘c5 16 ♖b1 ♖ac8 17 ♔h1 ♖fd8 18 ♗g5 ♖e8 19 ♗f4

♗e5 and also here is Black doing well, Zubarev-Savchenko, Donetsk Z 1998.

d) 11...♖fd8 12 ♕d2 e6 13 ♖ad1 d5 (on the face of it I would prefer 13...♘e5 14 b3 d5) 14 ♘xc6 bxc6 15 ♗g5 ♕c7 16 cxd5 cxd5 17 exd5 exd5 18 ♕f2 ♕b7 and Black seems to have enough counterplay to compensate for his weak d-pawn, Morozevich-Sadler, Elista OL 1998.

8 d5 ♗xc3+!? 9 bxc3 ♘a5 *(D)*

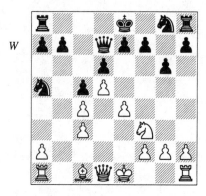

The whole point of Black's play has been to give White doubled c-pawns. The nature of the position is similar to some Nimzo-Indian lines and is indeed a very modern interpretation of such positions. If Black succeeds in keeping the position closed White will inevitably experience problems with his c4-pawn.

10 ♘d2

Shirov had rejected this on the grounds that it was unnecessary to protect the pawn immediately, but since he was forced to do so anyway, the text-move seems the most flexible. Shirov-Kasparov, Erevan OL 1996 proceeded 10 0-0 f6! (10...♘xc4 11 ♕e2 ♘e5 12 ♘xe5 dxe5 13 f4 gives White a dangerous initiative according to Shirov) 11 ♘d2 b6 12 ♕e2?! ♕a4 13 f4 ♘h6 14 e5 0-0-0 and Black is close to standing better.

10...f6

Black copies Kasparov's plan, but 10...e5 is also interesting, even though after 11 dxe6 ♕xe6 12 ♕a4+ ♘c6 13 ♖b1 0-0-0 14 0-0 ♘ge7 15 ♖e1 ♖d7 16 ♘f1 White retained a small advantage in Ponomariov-Bologan, Belfort 1998.

11 f4 0-0-0?!

While this, strictly speaking, might not be a mistake in itself, it definitely looks like Black is committing his king prematurely. I would instead suggest 11...♘h6, by analogy with Kasparov's plan. Then after 12 0-0 ♘f7 13 a4 b6 Black can still choose whether to castle queenside or kingside.

12 0-0 b6 13 a4

13 ♕e2 is met by 13...♕a4!.

13...♗b7

In Rublevsky-Ehlvest, Polanica Zdroj 1997, Black played 13...♘h6?, failing to take White's idea of 14 ♘b3! into account. Black could not then stop White opening lines on the queenside: 14...♘f7 (both 14...♘xc4 15 ♕e2 and 14...♘b7 15 a5 are clearly very good for White, while Black would also rapidly get into trouble with 14...♘xb3 15 ♕xb3 f5 16 a5 bxa5 17 ♖xa5 fxe4 18 ♕a2 ± Ftačnik) 15 ♘xa5 bxa5 16 ♕b3 ♕b7 17 ♕c2 ♕d7 18 ♖b1 ♔c7 19 e5! (White cannot break through immediately on the b-file, but with this nice sacrifice he finds another, very

instructive, way forward) 19...fxe5 (after 19...dxe5? the c-pawn is too weak) 20 f5! gxf5 21 ♖xf5. Now Black has the almost impossible task of covering the b- and f-files simultaneously while White will find it a lot easier to switch from side to side.

14 ♘b3 ♘xb3 15 ♕xb3 a5 16 ♖b1 ♕c7 17 ♖f2 ♔a7 18 ♖fb2 ♖b8 (D)

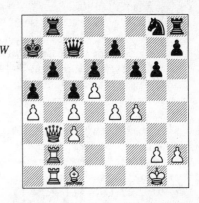

Ftačnik thinks that Black has chances of holding the position and while this does contain a grain of truth, it certainly looks like an uphill struggle to me. For starters, I do not see how Black develops after 19 ♕d1. 19...♘h6 is the most natural, but 20 e5! fxe5 21 fxe5 ♘f7 22 e6 ♘e5 23 ♗h6! ♘xc4 24 ♖f2 is terribly annoying.

B2)

6 d4 cxd4

Or 6...♕g4?! 7 d5! (if 7 0-0, then 7...cxd4 is fully playable) 7...♕xe4+ 8 ♗e3 ♘d4 9 ♕a4+ b5 10 ♕a6 ♘c2+ and now Stean-Geller, Moscow 1975 continued 11 ♔d2 ♕d3+! 12 ♔c1 ♖b8

(12...♘b4? 13 ♕xb5+ ♔d8 14 ♘e1)
13 ♕xa7 ♖d8 14 ♕b7 ♘xa1 15 ♕c6+
♖d7 16 ♕c8+ ½-½. Later Polugaevsky pointed out that Black would be
in trouble after the more accurate 11
♔d1! and this was verified by Baklan-
Ftačnik, Bundesliga 1998/9: 11...♖d8
12 ♕xb5+ ♖d7 13 ♘bd2 ♕g6 14 ♖c1
♘xe3+ 15 fxe3 ♘f6 16 b4! ♘e4
(Black is in dire straits after 16...cxb4
17 c5!, e.g. 17...♕xg2 18 ♖g1 ♕h3 19
♖g3 ♕f5 20 ♖g5 ♕h3 21 cxd6 and
wins, or 17...♘xd5 18 c6!) 17 ♘xe4
♕xe4 (17...♕xg2 18 ♘ed2 ♕xh1+ 19
♔c2 ♕g2 20 bxc5 and White's attack
crashes through) 18 bxc5 ±.

7 ♘xd4 ♘f6

7...e6 or 7...g6 will most likely
transpose to Line B22 or Line B23,
but one independent line is worth
mentioning: 7...g6 8 0-0 ♗g7 9 ♘e2!?
♘e5 10 ♘bc3 ♘xc4 11 b3 ♘b6 12 a4
♕d8 13 ♗e3 ♘f6 14 ♖c1 0-0 15 h3 (I
find it hard to believe that White's
compensation really is sufficient but
Black's knight on b6 is misplaced and
right now Black cannot make use of
his extra pawn) 15...♘bd7 16 g4!?
♘e5 17 f4 ♘c6 18 f5 with some compensation, Morozevich-Topalov, Pamplona 1995/6.

8 ♘c3 (D)

Now we shall look at:

B21: 8...♕g4　　92
B22: 8...e6　　93
B23: 8...g6　　95

B21)

8...♕g4 9 ♕xg4

9 0-0 constitutes no threat since
Black can simplify with 9...♕xd1 10

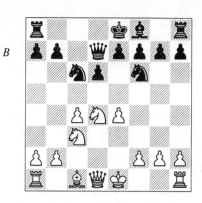

♖xd1 ♘xd4 11 ♖xd4 ♖c8 12 b3 g6 13
♖d1 ♗g7 14 ♗e3 ♘g4 15 ♗d4 ♗xd4
16 ♖xd4 ♘e5 17 f4 ♘c6 18 ♖d2 0-0
and a draw was soon agreed in the
game Leko-Maksimenko, Brønshøj
1995.

9...♘xg4 10 ♘xc6 bxc6 (D)

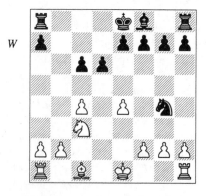

11 ♗f4!

If Black were allowed time to develop, he would have no problems.
With the text-move, White intends h3
and 0-0-0, perhaps combined with an
e5 break, which would compromise
Black's pawn structure somewhat.

Instead Milov-Savon, Simferopol 1992 continued 11 b3 g6 12 ♗b2 ♗g7 13 h3 ♘e5 14 0-0-0 ♘d7 15 ♘a4 ♗xb2+ 16 ♔xb2 c5 =.

11...g5!

This aggressive move seems the only solution to Black's opening problems. Lutz analyses a wealth of alternatives:

a) 11...e6 12 h3 ♘f6 13 0-0-0 ±.

b) 11...f6 12 h3 ♘e5 13 ♗xe5 fxe5 14 c5! ±.

c) 11...♘f6 12 0-0-0 ♘d7 13 ♖he1 (13 ♗e3?! g6 14 f4 ♗g7 15 ♔c2 f5! 16 ♗d4 ♗xd4 17 ♖xd4 0-0-0 18 ♖e1 ♖he8 ½-½ Baklan-Lutz, Bundesliga 1997/8) 13...g6 14 ♘a4 ♘b6 15 ♘xb6 axb6 16 e5 and now 16...dxe5 17 ♗xe5 ♗h6+ 18 ♔b1 leaves White better, but Atalik claims that Black equalizes with 16...♔d7!.

d) 11...g6 12 h3 ♘f6 13 e5 ± Atalik.

e) 11...e5 12 ♗g3 ±.

12 ♗xg5 ♘e5 (D)

Black's counterplay lies on the g-file, and therefore it makes sense to clear the g-file by removing the knight.

Goldin considers 12...♗g7!? but White seems to consolidate with accurate play, viz. 13 ♔e2 and then:

a) 13...♗xc3 14 bxc3 ♘e5 (or 14...♖g8 15 f4! ♘e5 16 c5 f6 17 ♗xf6! exf6 18 fxe5 dxe5 19 g3 ±) 15 c5 ♖g8 16 ♗f4 and Black does not have compensation for the pawn.

b) 13...♘e5 14 c5 ±.

c) 13...♖b8 14 ♖ab1 ♖b4 15 f3 ♘e5 16 c5 ±.

13 b3 ♖g8 14 ♗h4 ♖g4

14...♖xg2?! 15 ♗g3 ♗g7 16 ♔f1 ♖xg3 17 hxg3 turns out favourably for

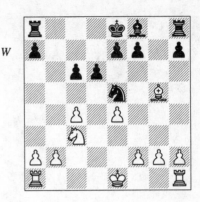

White. Atalik's main line then runs 17...♘d3! 18 ♖d1 ♘b2 19 ♖c1 ♘d3 20 ♖xh7 ♗f6 21 ♘e2 ♘xc1 22 ♘xc1, which he continues even further but it is clear that White has a large advantage.

15 ♗g3 ♗g7 16 ♔d2 ♘g6 17 f3 ♖g5

So far we have followed Baklan-Atalik, Yugoslavia 1998. Now Atalik analyses...

18 f4! ♖g4 19 ♖af1 h5 20 ♘d1 ♗h6 21 ♘f2 ♗xf4+ 22 ♔e2 ♖g5 23 ♘h3 ♖xg3 24 hxg3 ♗xg3 25 ♘g5 ♘f4+ 26 ♔d2 h4 27 ♖f3 ♖d8

Black has some compensation.

B22)

8...e6 (D)

With this move, Black will try to direct the game into a Hedgehog type of position. This set-up is extremely solid and usually provides chances for both sides, with some quite interesting strategic play in view.

9 0-0 ♗e7 10 b3

It is basically a matter of taste whether the bishop is developed on b2

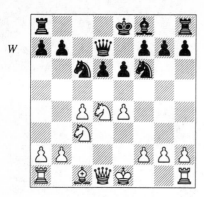

W

or on e3. On b2 the bishop points against Black's kingside, and thus this is usually followed by an attempt to build up a kingside attack, which, of course, needs to be supported by firm control of the centre.

After 10 ♗e3 play might continue 10...0-0 11 ♕e2 (there are other ways for White to arrange his pieces but this does look like the most sensible, freeing d1 for a rook and supporting the c4-pawn). Now Black's choice of move also seems like a matter of taste:

a) 11...a6 12 ♖ad1 ♖fc8 13 b3 ♕c7 14 f4 ♕a5 15 ♘xc6 ♖xc6 16 ♗d4 ♘d7 (16...e5? 17 ♘d5 ±) 17 ♖d3 ♖e8 18 ♘d5!? ♕d8 19 ♘xe7+ ♕xe7 20 ♖fd1 e5! = Gubanov-Nepomnishay, St Petersburg Ch 1997.

b) 11...♖fd8 12 ♖fd1 ♖ac8 (Black would like to play 12...d5? but is not quite ready for it: 13 ♘c2 ♘b4 14 exd5 ♘xc2 15 ♕xc2 ± Kraut-Moingt, Wilhelmsfeld 1985) 13 ♘b3 (13 ♖ac1 transposes to line 'd2') 13...b6 14 f4 ♕b7 15 ♗f2 a6 16 ♖ac1 ♖b8 17 a4 ♘d7 with equality, Korchnoi-Ki.Georgiev, Biel 1992.

c) 11...b6 12 ♖ad1 ♖ad8 13 f4 ♖fe8 14 ♔h1 (Bologan-Tisdall, Gausdal 1991) 14...♕b7 with approximately equal chances.

d) 11...♖ac8 and now:

d1) 12 ♖ad1 a6 13 b3 ♕c7 14 f4 ♕a5 15 ♘xc6 bxc6 (15...♖xc6 16 ♗d4, with the idea 16...♘d7 17 ♘d5 ♕d8 18 ♘xe7+ ♕xe7 19 e5, is slightly better for White) 16 ♗d2 ♕b6+ 17 ♔h1 ♖cd8 18 f5 exf5 19 ♖xf5 ♘d7 20 ♘a4 ♕b7 21 ♗c3 ± Shaked-Alterman, Wijk aan Zee 1998.

d2) 12 ♖ac1 a6 (12...♖fd8 13 ♖fd1 b6 14 f3 ♕b7 15 b3 ♘e5 = Drei-Cvitan, Biel 1995) 13 ♖fd1 ♘xd4 14 ♗xd4 ♕c6 15 b3 e5 16 ♗e3 ♘xe4 17 ♘d5 ♗d8 18 ♘b4 ♕c7 19 ♕d3 f5 20 f3 f4 21 ♕xe4 fxe3 22 ♘d5 ♕a5 23 ♖c2 b5! and it is unclear whether White can make any real use of his magnificent knight on d5, Benjamin-D.Gurevich, Toronto 1998.

10...0-0 11 ♗b2 ♖fd8

This type of position was discussed in some detail in the introduction to this chapter.

The game Panchenko-Tseshkovsky, Sochi 1980 continued 11...a6 12 ♖c1 ♖fd8 13 ♘xc6 ♕xc6 14 ♕e2 (14 ♖e1 transposes to the main line, and looks like a better chance of achieving an advantage) 14...b6 15 ♖fd1 ♕b7 (Black has obtained his more or less ideal defensive formation) 16 e5 dxe5 17 ♕xe5 ♘e8! with an equal game.

12 ♖e1 *(D)*

12...a6

12...♖ac8 could easily lead to the same position, but with the text-move Black introduces the idea of a ...b5

break immediately. Let us, however, take a brief look at 12...♖ac8:

a) 13 ♖c1 b6 14 ♘xc6 ♕xc6 15 ♕f3 a6 16 ♕g3 ♕b7 17 a4 ♘h5 18 ♕f3 ♘f6 ½-½ Smirin-Wojtkiewicz, Antwerp 1994.

b) 13 ♕d2 b6 14 ♖ad1 a6 15 ♘xc6 ♕xc6 16 ♕e2 ♗f8 17 ♖d3 ♘d7 = Tkachev-Lutz, Wijk aan Zee 1995.

13 ♘xc6

13 ♘a4?! ♖ab8 14 ♖c1 b5 15 ♘xc6 ♕xc6 16 cxb5 ♕xb5 17 ♕c2 d5 = Hjartarson-W.Watson, Brighton 1982.

13...♕xc6 14 ♖c1 b6

14...♕e8 15 a4 ♖ac8 16 ♕e2 ♘d7 17 ♖cd1 ♘c5 18 ♕c2 ♕c6? 19 ♖e3 ♗f6? 20 ♘d5! exd5 21 exd5 ♕d7 22 ♗xf6 gxf6 23 ♖g3+ ♔h8 24 ♕xh7+ ♔xh7 25 ♖d4 1-0 Tkachev-W.Watson, London Lloyds Bank 1993.

15 a4

15 ♕e2 ♕b7 16 ♖c2 ♖ab8 17 a4 ♘d7 18 ♗a3 ♖bc8 = Arkhipov-A.Petrosian, Lippstadt 1993.

15...♖ac8

15...♕b7!.

16 ♖e3 ♕b7 17 ♖g3 ♘e8 18 ♕e2 ♗f6 19 f4 g6 20 ♖d1

White is better, Oratovsky-Shmuter, Rishon le Zion 1995.

B23)
8...g6 9 0-0 ♗g7 *(D)*

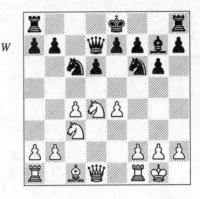

10 ♘de2

10 ♗e3 is not good in view of 10...♘g4, but 10 ♘c2 is a worthy alternative. 10...0-0 and then:

a) 11 ♖e1 a6 12 ♗d2 ♘e5 13 ♕e2 ♖fc8 14 ♘a3 ♕c6 15 ♖ac1 e6 16 b3 ♕c5 17 ♘ab1 ♘fd7 18 ♖ed1 ♕c7 19 ♗e3 ♘c5 20 f4 ♘c6 = Mohr-Sutovsky, Dresden Z 1998.

b) 11 f3 e6 12 ♗g5 ♖ad8 13 ♕d2 d5 14 cxd5 exd5 15 ♗h6 dxe4 16 ♕xd7 ♖xd7 17 ♗xg7 ♔xg7 18 fxe4 ♖d2 19 ♖f2 ♖fd8 20 ♖af1 with approximately equal chances, Marciano-Gallagher, Biel 1998.

c) 11 ♕e2 a6 12 ♗d2 ♖ab8 13 ♖ac1 b5 14 cxb5 axb5 15 ♘d5 e6 = Tkachev-Gelfand, Groningen FIDE KO Wch 1997.

10...0-0 11 f3 a6

Another idea is 11...♖fc8 but it is not clear that Black can do any better than transposing to note 'a' to Black's 12th move, viz. 12 ♗e3 ♕d8 13 b3 (13 ♖c1 a6 14 ♘f4 ♖ab8 15 ♕e2 ♘d7 16 ♖fd1 ± Kr.Georgiev-Ftačnik, Warsaw Z 1987) 13...a6 14 a4, etc.

12 a4 *(D)*

Note that White has to play this preparatory move. 12 ♗e3 would permit 12...♘e5 13 b3 b5 with a good game for Black. For more detailed explanation of the key ideas in this position see the introduction to this chapter.

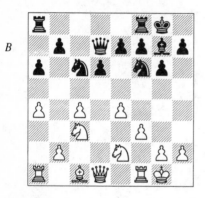

12...♕d8

Alternatives:

a) 12...♖fc8 13 b3 ♕d8 and now White can try:

a1) 14 ♔h1 ♘d7 15 ♗g5 ♕a5 16 ♕d2 ♘c5 17 ♖ab1 e6 18 ♖fd1 ♖ab8 19 ♗h4! ± Kramnik-Gelfand, Sanghi Nagar FIDE Ct (3) 1994.

a2) 14 ♗e3 ♘d7 15 ♖b1 ♘c5 16 ♕d2 ♖ab8 17 ♖fd1 ♕f8 18 ♘f4 ± Andersson-Donner, Wijk aan Zee 1973.

b) 12...♕c7 13 ♔h1 e6 (13...♕b6!? is an interesting idea, transposing to note 'b' to White's 13th move) 14 ♗g5 (Shipov suggests 14 ♗f4!?) 14...♘d7

15 b3 ♘c5 (15...♕a5) 16 ♖b1 ♖ac8!? (16...♖fe8 17 ♕d2 ♘b4 18 ♖fd1 ♘cd3 19 ♗h4 ♕b6 20 ♘a2 d5! is also satisfactory for Black, Rublevsky-Ki.Georgiev, Yugoslavia 1997) 17 ♕d2 (17 b4 ♘d7 18 b5 is critical but Black seems to be in good shape after 18...♘ce5 19 ♗e7 ♖fe8 20 ♗xd6 ♕xc4 21 ♖b4 ♕d3; perhaps the strange-looking 17 ♘a2 is White's best) 17...♘a5! 18 ♘c1 ♘axb3 19 ♘xb3 ♘xb3 20 ♖xb3 ♕xc4 21 ♖fb1 ♗xc3 22 ♕xd6 ♗g7! 23 ♖xb7 ♕xa4 24 h3 a5 ∓ Ponomariov-Shipov, Lubniewice ECC 1998.

13 ♗e3

White does not have to commit his bishop to the e3-square, and might instead play 13 ♔h1. Then Black has tried:

a) 13...♘d7 14 ♖b1!? ♕a5 15 ♘d5 e6 16 b4 ♕d8 17 ♘e3 ♕c7 18 ♗b2 a5 19 ♗xg7 ♔xg7 20 b5 ♘b4 and Black is doing fine, Rublevsky-Khuzman, Erevan OL 1996.

b) 13...♕b6!? 14 ♖b1 ♕c5 15 b3 e6 16 ♗f4 ♖ad8 17 ♕c1 ♘d7 18 ♗g5 ♗f6 19 ♗e3 ♕a5 20 f4 ♗g7 with a roughly equal position, Glek-Khuzman, Bonnevoie ECC 1998.

13...♕a5 14 ♔h1 *(D)*

A very useful prophylactic move. Others:

a) 14 ♘d5 and now 14...♘xd5 15 exd5 ♘e5 16 b3 ♕b4 17 ♘d4 looks slightly better for White, but Black might try 14...♘d7 intending to chase the knight away from d5 by ...e6.

b) 14 ♖c1 ♘d7 15 b3 ♘c5 16 ♘a2 (16 ♘d5 e6 17 b4 ♘xb4 18 ♘xb4 ♕xb4 19 ♕xd6 ♖fc8 is fine for Black) 16...♖ac8 17 ♖b1 (17 b4? ♘xb4 18

♗d2 ♘cd3! holds more than well for Black) 17...b5! 18 cxb5 axb5 19 axb5 ♕xb5 = Kramnik-Gelfand, Sanghi Nagar FIDE Ct (7) 1994.

c) 14 ♖b1!? ♘e5 15 b3 ♖fd8 16 ♔h1 (Lutz recommends 16 ♕d2! e6 17 ♖fd1, while 16 ♘d5 is another alternative) 16...e6 17 ♕d4 ♕c7 18 ♖fd1 ♕e7 19 ♕d2 ♕c7 20 ♖bc1 ♖ac8 with roughly equal play, Komliakov-Lutz, Moscow OL 1994.

15...♘d7 16 b4!.
16 exd5 ♘e5 17 b3! *(D)*

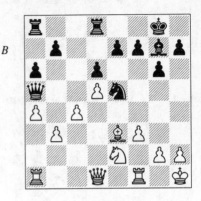

17...♘d7 18 ♗d4 ♘f6 19 ♕d3

19 ♗c3 ♕c7 20 a5 ♖e8 21 ♗d4, as suggested by Gelfand and Khuzman, looks even better.

19...♖e8 20 ♘c3 e6 21 dxe6 fxe6 22 ♖ad1

White is slightly better but must play accurately to maintain his advantage, Rublevsky-Gelfand, Polanica Zdroj 1998.

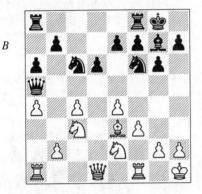

14...♖fd8 15 ♘d5! ♘xd5

5 Moscow Variation with 3...♞c6

1 e4 c5 2 ♞f3 d6 3 ♗b5+ ♞c6 *(D)*

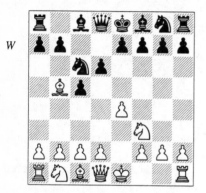

The variation with 3...♞c6 remains quite popular for Black. One important point about this line is that it can also arise via 2...♞c6 3 ♗b5 d6.

The lines discussed in this chapter are quite solid for Black, but probably offer him more serious winning prospects than 3...♗d7. On the other hand, White should not be too unhappy with this since his chances of obtaining a real opening advantage are likewise better than against 3...♗d7.

I am recommending that White plays the main lines, i.e. proceeding with 4 0-0, and after 4...♗d7 5 c3 ♞f6 6 ♖e1 a6, I have decided to examine all three of White's main possibilities, 7 ♗xc6!?, 7 ♗a4 and 7 ♗f1.

Sacrificial options

The line 7 ♗xc6!? ♗xc6 8 d4 is extremely dangerous for Black if he does not know what to do. There is no real alternative to capturing the pawn on e4, but Black needs to decide whether to throw in a preliminary pawn exchange on d4 – it is probably best not to. 8...♗xe4 9 ♗g5 leads to the following position *(D)*:

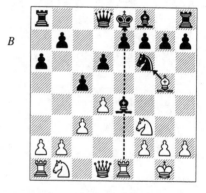

White has a strong initiative for the pawn, but has yet to prove that it is really worth it. Black has found some satisfactory defences but there is no doubt that White has good practical chances. 9...♗d5 seems to be the best way to minimize White's initiative, while simultaneously holding on to the extra pawn.

Ruy Lopez similarities

The other main lines, 7 ♗a4 and 7 ♗f1, often lead to closed positions reminiscent of the Ruy Lopez.

In such positions, White would like to transfer his queen's knight to e3 and maybe then play c4, depending on what Black does in the meantime. If White can prevent counterplay on the queenside, he will usually end up with fairly good chances of a successful kingside attack, but right now White's greatest asset is his space advantage.

What to do with the two bishops?

Quite often White manages to obtain the bishop-pair, but what should he do with them? White has a space advantage, but Black's position is very solid. Here (*see next diagram*) is how a game between two of the world's best players evolved:

12 d4 cxd4 13 cxd4 ♖c8 14 ♕b3

This is the most unpleasant, as it creates a direct threat against Black's b-pawn and vacates d1 for a rook.

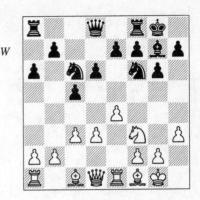

Adams – Tiviakov
Groningen FIDE KO Wch 1997

14...♖c7 15 ♗f4 ♘d7 16 ♖ad1 ♕b8 17 h4!?

White has a space advantage, the two bishops and good control of the centre, and by threatening a kingside attack, he forces Black to do something.

17...e5 18 dxe5 dxe5 19 ♗e3

White has not done anything amazingly creative, but nevertheless he has obtained quite a substantial advantage. He can simply double on the d-file; it is obvious that White's two bishops are much superior to Black's knights, which lack space.

The Theory of the Moscow Variation with 3...♘c6

1 e4 c5 2 ♘f3 d6 3 ♗b5+ ♘c6 4 0-0 ♗d7

An occasional try here is 4...♗g4 but this early bishop excursion proves rather risky. White continues 5 h3 ♗h5 6 c3 and then:

a) 6...♕b6 7 ♘a3 a6 8 ♗a4 ♕c7 9 d4 b5 10 ♘xb5! axb5 11 ♗xb5 0-0-0 12 b4! (this is the point of White's sacrifice; Black's kingside is completely undeveloped, while White is crashing through on the queenside) 12...♗xf3 13 gxf3 ♘b8 14 ♕a4 c4 15 d5! ♘f6 16 ♗e3 ± Adams-Tiviakov, New York PCA Ct (2) 1994.

b) 6...a6 7 ♗xc6+ bxc6 8 d4 cxd4 9 cxd4 ♘f6 10 ♗g5 ± Van der Wiel-Larsen, Brussels 1987.

5 c3 *(D)*

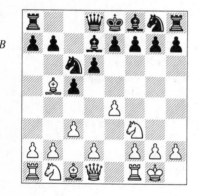

B

5...♘f6

5...a6 has recently gained in popularity. While it often transposes to the main lines, Black is now certain to avoid Line C. White has two possibilities:

a) 6 ♗xc6 ♗xc6 7 ♖e1 e6 (7...♘f6 8 d4 transposes to Line A) 8 d4 cxd4 9 cxd4 d5 10 ♘e5 dxe4 11 ♘xc6 bxc6 12 ♘c3 ♘f6 (12...f5 13 f3!?) 13 ♕a4 ♕b6 14 ♗e3 (14 ♗g5!?) 14...♘d5 15 ♖ac1 ♖c8 16 ♘xe4 ♕b5 17 ♕d1 ♗e7

18 ♕g4 g6 = Moreno-Kharlov, Ubeda 1999.

b) 6 ♗a4 and now 6...♘f6 7 ♖e1 transposes to Line B, while 6...b5 7 ♗c2 e5 8 h3 ♘f6 9 d4 ♗e7 10 d5 looks like a good version of this line since White does not need to play ♖e1.

6 ♖e1 a6 *(D)*

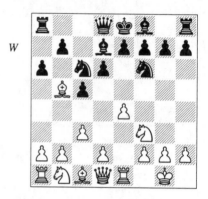

W

We shall now look at:

A: 7 ♗xc6!? 100
B: 7 ♗a4 106
C: 7 ♗f1 109

A)

7 ♗xc6!? ♗xc6 8 d4

This move involves a pawn sacrifice but is the only way to justify giving up the bishop-pair. Black must accept the sacrifice; otherwise White's space advantage will give him the advantage.

8...♗xe4

It is not totally clear who benefits from a preliminary exchange of the c-pawns. 8...cxd4 9 cxd4 ♗xe4 and now:

a) 10 ♗g5 ♗xf3 (10...d5 11 ♘c3 e6 12 ♘xe4 dxe4 13 ♖xe4 ♗e7 14

♗xf6 ♗xf6 15 d5! ± Maksiutov-Yagupov, Orel 1992) 11 ♕xf3 ♖a5 12 ♘c3!? (more dangerous than 12 ♗d2 ♕b6 13 ♘c3 e6 14 ♗g5 ♗e7 15 ♗xf6 ♗xf6 16 ♘d5 ♕d8 17 ♘xf6+ ♕xf6 18 ♕xb7 0-0 = Alterman) 12...♕xg5 13 ♕xb7 ♖d8 14 ♕c6+ ♖d7 15 d5 (15 ♕c8+ ♖d8 16 ♕c6+ ♖d7 17 ♕c8+ is an instant perpetual check) 15...e6! 16 dxe6 (16 ♖xe6+?! fxe6 17 dxe6 ♗e7 18 exd7+ ♔f7 favours Black) 16...fxe6 17 ♖xe6+ ♗e7 *(D)* and now:

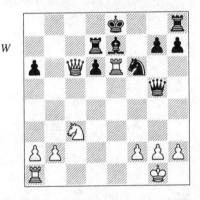

W

a1) 18 ♕c8+ ♖d8 (18...♔f7? 19 ♖xf6+ ±) 19 ♕b7 ♖d7 ½-½ Smirin-Alterman, Israel 1995.

a2) 18 ♖ae1 0-0 19 h4 is more ambitious, but Black should have no worries. 19...♕xh4! 20 g3 (20 ♖xe7 ♖xe7! 21 ♖xe7 ♕f4 ∓) 20...♕h3 21 ♖xe7 ♘g4 22 ♕d5+ ♔h8 23 ♕h1 ♕xh1+ 24 ♔xh1 ♘xf2+ 25 ♔g2 ♖xe7 26 ♖xe7 h6 27 ♖d7 and White is probably active enough to secure the draw, but certainly nothing more, Borisenko-Shabanov, Yaroslavl 1995.

b) 10 ♘c3 ♗xf3 (10...♗c6 11 d5 ♗d7 12 ♗g5 looks dangerous for Black; Pedzich-Wojtcieszyn, Polish Cht (Lubniewice) 1998 went 12...♗g4 13 ♗xf6 gxf6 14 ♘e4 ♗g7 15 h3 ♗c8 16 ♘d4 with compensation) 11 ♕xf3 e6 12 ♕xb7 ♕c8 and now:

b1) 13 ♕xc8+ ♖xc8 14 d5 ♔d7 = Stripunsky.

b2) 13 ♕b3 ♗e7 14 d5 e5 15 ♗g5 (15 ♘a4 ♖b8 16 ♘b6 ♗g4 17 f3 ♕h4 18 ♗e3 0-0 = Shabanov-Stripunsky, Karvina 1993/4) 15...0-0 16 ♘e4 ♖b8 (16...♘xe4 17 ♗xe7 ♖e8 18 ♖xe4 ♖xe7 19 ♖c4 ♕b7 20 ♖b4, intending ♖b6-c6, is slightly better for White – Stripunsky) 17 ♕a3 ♘xd5 18 ♗xe7 ♘xe7 19 ♘xd6 ♕e6 with an equal position, Zaitsev-Stripunsky, Bucharest 1994.

b3) 13 ♕f3 (the queen seems more useful on the kingside) 13...♗e7 14 d5 (Black's defensive resources look adequate after 14 ♕g3 0-0 15 ♗h6 ♘e8 16 ♘d5 ♗d8!, with the idea 17 ♖ac1 ♕b7 18 ♘f4 ♔h8, when White's attack is repelled) 14...e5 15 ♗g5 0-0 16 ♘e4 (16 ♖ac1 ♕d7 17 ♗xf6 ♗xf6 18 ♘e4 ♗e7 with the idea of ...f5 should be all right for Black) 16...♘xd5 (16...♘xe4 17 ♗xe7 ♖e8 18 ♕xe4 ♖xe7 19 ♖ec1 ♕b7 20 b3 ♖c8 21 ♖c6 is good for White, who will take control of the c-file or obtain a monster passed pawn on c6) 17 ♘xd6 ♕e6!? (17...♗xd6 18 ♕xd5 ♕b8 19 ♖ad1 ♗c7 20 b3 ±) 18 ♖ad1! ♕xd6 19 ♗xe7 (19 ♖xd5 ♕b4 20 ♖e4 ♕b7 21 ♖dxe5 ♗xg5 22 ♖xg5 ♕xb2 =) 19...♕xe7 20 ♖xd5 f6! 21 ♖ed1 ♖ad8 with equality, Smirin-Alterman, Struga Z 1995.

9 ♗g5 *(D)*

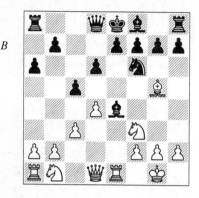

B

Black can now try to defend in various ways, the most popular (and best) being:

A1: 9...d5   102
A2: 9...&d5   104

Others are less explored, e.g.:

a) 9...&f5!? 10 ♘bd2 e6 11 dxc5 dxc5 12 ♕a4+ b5 13 ♕f4 &e7 14 &xf6 gxf6 15 ♘e4 &xe4 16 ♕xe4 0-0 17 a4 with compensation, Brynell-Åström, Swedish Ch (Ronneby) 1998.

b) 9...&xb1 10 ♖xb1 e6 11 &xf6 gxf6 (Yusupov claims an advantage for White after 11...♕xf6?! 12 dxc5 dxc5 13 ♕a4+ b5 14 ♕e4) 12 d5 ♕d7 13 b4 0-0-0 14 ♕d3 &g7 15 ♘d2 exd5 16 ♕xd5 f5 17 ♘c4 and White has a strong attack, Yusupov-Timoshchenko, USSR 1978.

c) 9...&g6 and now:

c1) 10 d5 ♕d7 11 c4 ♘e4! 12 &h4 h6 13 ♕b3 &f5 14 ♘c3 ♘xc3 15 ♕xc3 ♖g8 16 ♖ad1 g5 17 &g3 &g7 18 ♕a3 &f6 and Black has survived the opening with an extra pawn and a good position, Berg-Kristiansen, Aalborg 1995.

c2) 10 ♘bd2 e6 (10...d5 transposes to Line A1) 11 d5 e5 12 ♘c4 &e7 13 ♘fxe5! 0-0 (13...dxe5 14 d6) 14 ♘xg6 hxg6 15 a4 ± Kraut.

d) 9...&c6 10 c4!? (White can also try 10 &xf6 gxf6 11 d5 &d7 and then 12 ♘h4 or 12 ♘bd2) 10...cxd4 11 &xf6 gxf6 12 ♘xd4 ♖g8 13 ♘xc6 bxc6 14 ♘c3 &h6 15 ♕f3 ♔f8 16 ♖ad1 ♕d7 17 h3 ♖b8 18 b3 ♖g6 19 ♘e2! c5 20 ♘g3 and White's more harmonious pieces and better pawn structure compensate for the pawn minus, Ulybin-Dvoirys, Cheliabinsk 1991.

A1)
9...d5 *(D)*

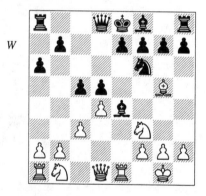

W

10 ♘bd2

An important alternative is to take back the pawn with 10 dxc5, and after 10...e6, to hold on to it with 11 b4. Then a few games have proceeded with 11...&e7 (11...&xf3 12 ♕xf3 &e7 13 ♘d2 0-0 is maybe not so bad since White cannot get his ideal set-up) 12 ♘bd2 &xf3 13 ♘xf3 0-0, when White has tried:

a) Soltis-Browne, USA Ch 1983 was agreed drawn after 14 a4. According to Browne, Black's best reply is 14...a5.

b) 14 ♕d4 ♖e8 15 a3!? (with this move White intends at some stage to play c4, thereby creating a 3 vs 2 scenario on the queenside, and hopefully a slight advantage) 15...♘d7 16 ♗xe7 ♖xe7 17 c4 dxc4 18 ♕xc4 ♖c8 19 ♖ad1 ♕e8 20 ♕e2 and White is better, Damljanović-Dzhandzhgava, Panormo Z 1998.

10...♗xf3

Black hopes to win some time for his development, but there is a drawback to this too: White's queen is activated at f3. Alternatives:

a) 10...♗g6 11 dxc5 (11 ♕b3!? c4 12 ♕xb7 ♕c8 13 ♕b6 e6 14 b3 cxb3 15 axb3 ♗e7 16 c4 ± Zaitsev-Epishin, Podolsk 1992) 11...e6 12 ♕a4+ (a set-up with 12 b4 is still perfectly feasible but not quite as direct as the text-move) 12...♕d7 13 ♕h4 ♗xc5 (White also gets a large advantage after 13...♖g8 14 ♘e5 ♕b5 15 b4 ♕a4 16 ♗xf6 gxf6 17 ♕xf6 ♗e7 18 ♕f4, Zarnicki-Norri, Parana 1993) 14 ♘e5 ♕e7 15 ♘b3 (15 ♘g4 ♘xg4!) 15...♗a7 16 ♕a4+!? b5 17 ♕h4 ♖c8 18 a4 and White is better, Maier-Howell, Groningen 1988.

b) 10...e6 11 ♘xe4 dxe4 12 ♖xe4 ♗e7 13 ♗xf6 gxf6 14 ♕e2! 0-0 15 ♖d1 f5 16 ♖e3 ♗f6 17 dxc5 ♕c7 18 ♘d4 ♔h8 19 b4 ♖g8 20 ♘f3 ± Borisenko-Yaakkimeinen, Russia 1995.

11 ♕xf3 cxd4

White regains his pawn after this, but it is probably best since Black gets some counterplay in return. Worse is

11...e6 12 ♗xf6 gxf6 (12...♕xf6?! 13 ♕xd5 ♕e7 14 ♕e5 cxd4 15 cxd4 ♕d6 16 ♕e4 ♕b4 17 ♘f3 ± Georgadze-Tal, USSR Ch (Tbilisi) 1978) 13 c4! ♗h6 14 ♖ad1 ♗xd2 15 ♖xd2 dxc4 16 ♕f4!? (16 ♖ed1 is another good move; all White's major pieces are ready to attack, while Black still needs to castle and coordinate his pieces) 16...♕a5 17 dxc5 ♖d8 18 ♖de2 ♔e7 19 ♕xc4 ± Kalegin-Kalinichev, Katowice 1990.

12 ♗xf6 gxf6 13 ♕xf6

White can play even more energetically with 13 c4!?, whereafter Ulybin suggests 13...♖g8 14 cxd5 ♖g5 with an unclear game but I would definitely prefer White after 15 d6!. For example, 15...e5 16 ♕xb7 ♖b8 17 ♕xa6 ±.

13...♖g8 *(D)*

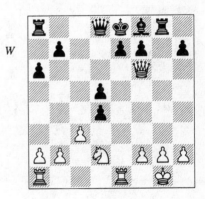

14 ♕xd4

14 cxd4!? is quite an interesting idea. This certainly discourages Black from castling queenside, and thus leave Black struggling to find a safe place for his king. Borisenko analyses 14...♖g6 15 ♕h8! e6 16 ♘f3 ♖g7 17 ♖ac1 ♕f6 18 ♔f1 after which he likes

White. I am not sure that I agree with that; first of all, I would not feel secure with the white queen so short of squares. 18...♖d8 looks like a good move, planning ...♕g6, ...♖g8 and ...♗d6.

14...♕d7 15 ♖ad1

15 ♘f3 is not advisable in view of 15...♕g4!, while the alternative 15 ♘f1 0-0-0 16 ♖ad1 e6 17 ♘g3 ♕c7 was roughly equal in Lanc-Hraček, Stare Mesto 1992.

15...0-0-0 16 ♕d3

Yudasin also mentions 16 ♕a7!? ♕c7 17 ♘f3 e6 18 ♘e5 ♖g7 with an unclear position. Black is intending ...♗c5.

16...♕g4 17 g3 h5

Black seems to have good counterplay, Ulybin-Yudasin, USSR Ch (Moscow) 1991.

A2)

9...♗d5 *(D)*

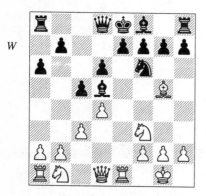

This is the most popular in practice. Black stubbornly tries to hold on to his extra pawn while simultaneously trying to keep White's initiative to a minimum.

10 ♘bd2

Now White is ready to kick the bishop away from d5 by playing c4, but it is worth taking a look at the immediate 10 c4!?. With a second pawn sacrifice White does nothing to reveal his intentions but simply opens the position completely, preparing for the onslaught. Black must be very careful:

a) 10...♗xf3 is often mistakenly chosen as the safe option but it seems that White has the better chances after 11 ♕xf3:

a1) 11...e6 12 ♗xf6 gxf6 13 dxc5 dxc5 14 ♘c3 ♗e7 15 ♕xb7 ♖c8 16 ♕f3 ± Rogers-Nikolaidis, Agios Nikolaos 1995.

a2) 11...cxd4 12 ♕xb7 ♕c8 13 ♕f3 e6 (13...♘d7 14 ♘d2 ♘e5 15 ♕e4 h6 16 ♗f4 ±) 14 ♗xf6 gxf6 15 ♘d2 ♗e7 16 ♘b3! ± Damaso-Grivas, Erevan OL 1996.

b) 10...♗xc4 11 ♘c3 (11 ♗xf6 gxf6 12 d5 ♗b5 13 ♘c3 is also interesting) 11...e6 12 ♗xf6 ♕xf6 (12...gxf6 13 d5 e5 14 ♘h4 ♗b5 15 ♘e4 ♗d7 16 ♕h5 is also unclear, Martinović-Anand, Groningen 1989) 13 dxc5 0-0-0! 14 ♕a4 with a messy position, Taulbut-Kupreichik, Hastings 1981/2.

10...e6

The alternatives all look inferior:

a) 10...b5!? 11 c4!? (11 b3 is another idea) 11...bxc4 (11...♗xc4?! 12 ♘xc4 bxc4 13 dxc5 dxc5 14 ♕a4+ ♕d7 15 ♕xc4 ±) 12 dxc5 e6 13 ♖c1 ♗xf3 and now Kraut analyses:

a1) 14 ♕xf3 d5 15 ♘xc4 dxc4 16 ♕c6+ ♔e7 and White seems to have nothing better than a perpetual check with 17 ♕b7+ ♚e8 18 ♕c6+.

a2) 14 ♘xf3 dxc5 (not 14...d5?! 15 ♘e5 ♗xc5? 16 ♕a4+ ♚f8 17 ♗xf6 ±) 15 ♕a4+ ♕d7 16 ♕xc4 ♗e7 gives White compensation but probably not more.

b) 10...c4 11 b3 b5 12 bxc4 bxc4 with two promising options for White:

b1) 13 ♘f1 e6 (13...♖c8 14 ♘e3 ♗a8 15 d5 ♕a5 16 ♗xf6 gxf6 17 ♖b1 ± Lyrberg-Bator, Stockholm 1992) 14 ♗xf6! gxf6 (14...♕xf6? 15 ♕a4+) 15 ♘e3 ♕a5? (Black has to try 15...♗xf3 16 ♕xf3 ♗e7 but White's attack looks very strong after 17 d5!) 16 ♘d2! ± Fette-Ruban, Miskolc/Tapolca 1990.

b2) 13 ♘h4!? ♕d7 (13...e6 14 ♘f5) 14 ♖b1 and now:

b21) 14...h6 15 ♗xf6 gxf6 16 ♕h5 ♕c6 (16...♗e6 17 ♕f3 ♖c8 18 d5 ♗g4 19 ♕xf6 ± Cifuentes) 17 ♖b6! ♕xb6 18 ♕xd5 ♖d8 19 ♘f5 and White's attack looks too strong, Ricardi-Cifuentes, Buenos Aires 1991.

b22) Later an improvement was found for Black, namely 14...♘g8!?. Elburg-Hendriks, corr 1993-4 continued 15 ♕e2 h6 16 ♗e3 g5 17 ♘hf3 ♖c8 and Black was doing quite well, but 15 ♖b6 looks more annoying.

c) 10...cxd4 11 ♘xd4 ♕d7 12 ♗xf6 gxf6 13 ♕h5! e5 14 c4 (14 ♘e4!?) 14...♗c6 (Oratovsky suggests 14...♗e6 as a better defence, for example 15 ♘e4 ♗e7 16 ♘xe6 ♕xe6 17 ♖ad1 0-0-0 18 ♘c3! ±) 15 ♘xc6! bxc6 16 c5! ♕e6 (16...d5 17 ♖xe5+ fxe5 18 ♕xe5+ ♕e7 19 ♕xh8 ±) 17 cxd6 ♗xd6 18 ♘e4 ± Oratovsky-Yudasin, Israel 1993.

11 c4 ♗xf3 12 ♕xf3 cxd4 13 ♗xf6

13 ♕xb7 ♕c8 14 ♕f3 ♗e7 15 ♘b3 h6! 16 ♗h4 0-0 did not give Black any problems in H.Pedersen-Sher, Farum 1993.

13...gxf6 14 ♕xb7 *(D)*

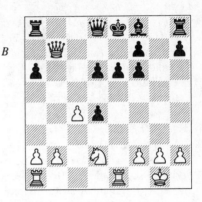

14...♗g7

It is not entirely clear how White should respond to 14...♕c8. In de la Riva-A.David, Andorra Z 1998 Black was more or less OK after 15 ♕d5 ♗e7 16 ♕xd4 ♕c6 17 ♘e4 ♖g8 18 g3 ♖g6. Perhaps 15 ♕e4 ♗g7 16 ♘f3 is best.

15 ♕c6+

15 ♖xe6+? fxe6 16 ♕xg7 ♖f8 is not quite sufficient for White.

15...♚e7 16 ♕e4!?

There have been different opinions about how White should strengthen his position. Here is a brief summary of what else has appeared in practice:

a) 16 ♘b3 f5 17 ♖ad1 ♕c8 18 ♕f3 ♕xc4 19 ♖c1 (19 ♕b7+ ♚f6 20 ♖xd4 ♕b5 21 ♕c7 ♖hd8 22 ♖xd6 ♖ac8 should also be OK for Black) 19...♕b4 20 ♖c7+ ♚f6 21 ♖f1 does not look too convincing, Wells-Grivas, Kopavogur 1994.

b) 16 ♕d5 ♕b6 17 ♘f3 ♖he8 18 ♖ad1 ♕c5 19 ♕xd4 ♕xd4 20 ♘xd4 ♔d7 21 ♖e3 f5 22 ♖ed3 ♖ec8 23 b3 ♔e7 = Vazquez-Vasquez, Santa Clara 1998.

c) 16 ♘f3 f5 17 ♖ad1 ♕c8 18 ♕d5 ♔d7 (18...♗e5!?) 19 ♕a5 ♕c5 and Black was doing fine in Romanishin-Sosonko, Reggio Emilia 1985/6.

16...♕b6 17 ♘f3 ♖hc8

Black might consider 17...♖hd8!? to support a ...d5 advance. Then 18 ♕xh7 ♔f8 is rather unclear.

18 ♕xh7 ♔f8 19 b3

This position occurred in Kalegin-Tiviakov, USSR 1988. Black could not resist the temptation to increase the scope of his bishop by 19...f5?! but was worse after 20 ♘g5 ♕d8 21 ♕h5 ♕e7 22 ♖ad1 ♖c5 23 f4. Instead Black should have returned to the plan of ...d5 and therefore chosen 19...♖d8 with a roughly equal position.

B)

7 ♗a4 *(D)*

We shall now consider:

B1: 7...b5　　106
B2: 7...c4　　108

B1)

7...b5 8 ♗c2 e5

Black decides to steer the game into positions similar to the Ruy Lopez. Alternatives:

a) 8...c4 9 b3 e5 transposes to Line B2.

b) 8...♗g4 9 h3 ♗xf3 10 ♕xf3 g6 (10...♘d7 11 d3 g6 12 ♗b3 e6 13 ♕d1 ♗g7 14 ♗e3 0-0 15 ♘d2 ♘b6 16 a3 ± Svidler-Tiviakov, Russian Ch 1998) 11 a4 ♖b8 (11...♗g7?! 12 axb5 axb5 13 e5! ♖xa1 14 exf6 ♗xf6 15 ♕xf6 0-0 16 ♕f3 ± W.Watson-Kharlov, Cologne 1993) 12 axb5 axb5 13 ♘a3 ♘d7 14 ♕e2 ♕b6 15 ♗d3 c4 16 ♗c2 ♗g7 17 d3 cxd3 18 ♗xd3 b4 19 ♗e3 ♕d8 20 ♘b5 bxc3 21 bxc3 ± Minasian-Tiviakov, Linares 1999.

9 h3 *(D)*

A useful precaution against ...♗g4, which would be annoying if White played 9 d4 immediately, viz. 9...cxd4 10 cxd4 ♗g4 11 ♗e3 (after 11 d5 ♘d4 12 ♘bd2, 12...♘xc2 13 ♕xc2 ♗e7 14 a4 bxa4 15 ♖xa4 0-0 16 ♕d3 a5 looked fine for Black in Typek-Kuczynski, Lubniewice 1995, while Black could also sharpen the game with 12...♖c8 13 ♗d3 ♘h5!?) 11...exd4 12 ♗xd4 ♘xd4 13 ♕xd4 ♗xf3 14 gxf3 ♗e7 with a roughly equal position, Shabanov-Ruban, Kursk 1987.

Another idea is to start with 9 a4 and see how Black responds:

a) 9...b4?! seems to be to White's advantage:

a1) White can even continue 10 d4!?, with the idea 10...cxd4 11 cxd4 ♗g4 12 ♗e3 exd4 13 ♗xd4 ♗xf3 14 gxf3, and now if Black takes on d4 as in the line above, White will have a target on b4, so it is probably better to develop but then White keeps the bishop-pair, i.e. 14...♗e7 15 ♗e3 0-0 16 ♘d2 and White has an edge.

a2) 10 h3 still seems sensible. For example, 10...♗e7 11 d4 bxc3 12 bxc3 cxd4 13 cxd4 ♖c8 14 ♘bd2! ♕c7 15 ♗a3! ± Mi.Tseitlin-Dvoirys, Cappelle la Grande 1994.

b) 9...♗e7 is more solid. 10 axb5 axb5 11 ♖xa8 ♕xa8 12 ♘a3 ♕b7 ½-½ Ye Jiangchuan-Tiviakov, Tan Chin Nam 1998. The game is about level.

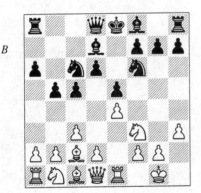

B

9...♗e7

This is the most common; others:

a) 9...♖c8 (aimed against d4, but...) 10 d4!? cxd4 11 cxd4 exd4 12 ♗b3 ♗e7 (12...♕b6 13 ♘g5 ♘e5 14 ♗f4 is also good for White) 13 ♘xd4 0-0 14 ♘c3 and White is better.

b) 9...g6 10 d4 ♗g7 11 dxc5 dxc5 12 a4 ♖b8 13 axb5 axb5 14 ♗e3 ♕e7

15 ♘bd2 0-0 16 ♘b3 c4 17 ♘c5 ♗c8 18 b4 ♖d8 19 ♕c1 ± Zhang Zhong-Ehlvest, Beijing 1998.

10 d4 0-0

Kraut suggests 10...♕c7 with the idea 11 d5 ♘d8 but it does not look like the knight is better on d8 than on a5.

11 d5 ♘a5 *(D)*

11...♘b8?! is clearly worse; after 12 a4 bxa4 13 ♗xa4 White has a distinct advantage, Bukhtin-Gik, USSR 1968.

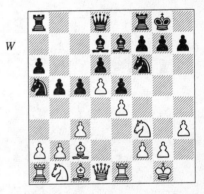

W

12 b3!?

Alternatives:

a) 12 ♘xe5 dxe5 13 d6 ♗c6 14 dxe7 ♕xe7 15 ♘d2 ♘b7 16 ♕e2 ♘d6 ½-½ Zhang Zhong-Tiviakov, Beijing 1998.

b) 12 ♘bd2 and now 12...g6 13 b4 ♘b7 14 ♖b1 a5 15 a3 gave White an edge in Savon-Beliavsky, Leningrad 1975, but Black is fine after 12...c4!.

12...♕c7 13 ♘bd2

White is in fact a tempo down on a line in the Chigorin Variation of the Ruy Lopez, i.e. 1 e4 e5 2 ♘f3 ♘c6 3

♗b5 a6 4 ♗a4 ♘f6 5 0-0 ♗e7 6 ♖e1
b5 7 ♗b3 d6 8 c3 0-0 9 h3 ♘a5 10 ♗c2
c5 11 d4 ♕c7 12 ♘bd2 ♘c6 13 d5
♘a5 14 b3 ♗d7. This line is considered slightly better for White, but with
an extra move I suspect Black should
be fine. A possible continuation:
**13...♖fb8 14 ♘f1 ♘b7 15 c4 bxc4
16 bxc4 ♘a5 17 ♘e3 ♗f8**
The game is roughly equal.

B2)
7...c4 *(D)*

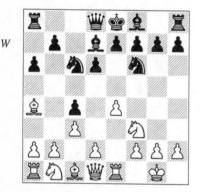

8 d4
White basically has two plans here.
One is introduced by the text-move:
advancing the d-pawn and permitting
Black to capture it *en passant*. This often leads to a Hedgehog or Maroczy
position, while the other plan is to attack Black's c-pawn with b3. This
means that the bishop has to be retreated first, viz. 8 ♗c2 and then:

a) **8...e5** and now:

a1) 9 d3 (inconsistent with White's
plan, but justified because Black has
weakened his d-pawn) 9...cxd3 10

♕xd3 ♗e7 11 ♗g5 ♗e6 12 ♗xf6
♗xf6 13 ♖d1 ♕b6 14 ♘bd2 ♕xb2 15
♗b3 0-0 16 ♗xe6 fxe6 17 a4 favours
White, Shaposhnikov-Se.Ivanov, St
Petersburg Ch 1998.

a2) 9 b3 b5 10 ♕e2 ♖c8 11 b4!
(this was suggested by Dokhoian as an
improvement on Rozentalis-Dokhoian,
Bad Godesberg 1994 which went 11
d3 cxb3 12 axb3 b4 =) 11...♘e7 12 a4
♘g6 13 d3 ♕c7 14 axb5 axb5 15 dxc4
bxc4 16 ♗e3 ♗e7 17 ♘bd2 0-0 18
♖a7 ♕b8 19 ♖ea1 ± Zhang Zhong-Ye
Jiangchuan, Beijing 1998.

b) 8...♖c8 9 b3 b5 10 ♕e2 ♘e5 11
♘xe5 dxe5 12 bxc4 bxc4 13 ♘a3 ♕c7
14 d3 cxd3 15 ♗xd3 e6 16 ♖b1 ♗c5
with roughly equal chances, Zhang
Zhong-Grivas, Elista OL 1998. If
White takes on a6, Black will gain
counterplay on the a-file after ...♖a8.

c) 8...♗g4 9 h3 (9 b3 cxb3 10 axb3
e6 11 d4 ♗e7 12 ♘bd2 0-0 13 ♗b2 b5
14 c4 bxc4 15 bxc4 ♘d7 16 h3 ♗h5
17 ♗a4 ± Manik-Babula, Olomouc
1998) 9...♗h5 10 b3 (10 d4 cxd3 11
♕xd3 ♗xf3 12 ♕xf3 g6 13 ♘d2 ♗g7
14 ♘c4 ♘d7 15 ♗g5 ♘de5 16 ♘xe5
♘xe5 17 ♕e2 0-0 18 ♗b3 b5 19 ♖ad1
♕c7 = Magem-Babula, Elista OL
1998) 10...cxb3 11 axb3 e6 12 d4 d5
13 e5 ♘d7 14 ♘bd2 b5 15 ♘f1 ♗xf3
16 ♕xf3 b4 with counterplay, Jansa-
Hraček, Prague 1994.

8...cxd3 9 ♗g5
The reason for delaying the recapture on d3 is that White wants to avoid
a Maroczy structure; for example, 9
♕xd3 g6! gives Black a satisfactory
position. Zaitsev-Timoshenko, Bucharest 1993 continued 10 ♗xc6 ♗xc6

11 c4 ♗g7 12 ♘c3 0-0 13 ♗d2 ♘d7 14 b4 b5!, and Black had at least equalized.

9...e6

In Timman-Alterman, Belgrade ECC 1999, Black stubbornly played for a set-up with ...g6, beginning with 9...♘g4, and after 10 ♕xd3 ♘ge5 11 ♘xe5 ♘xe5 12 ♗xd7+ ♕xd7 13 ♕d2 g6 he achieved his aim but White was nevertheless able to generate some pressure following 14 f4 ♘c6 15 c4 h6 16 ♗h4 ♕g4 17 ♗g3 h5 18 ♘c3 h4 19 h3! ♕h5 20 ♗f2 ♗g7 21 ♘d5 0-0 22 ♖ad1. However, Black's 15th to 18th moves look a little too ambitious. 15...♗g7 would be a much more sensible move, even though I would still prefer White since he can continue 16 ♘c3 followed by ♘d5.

10 ♕xd3 *(D)*

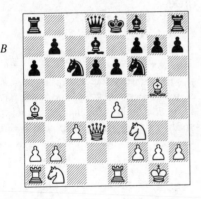

10...♗e7

10...♘e5!? is a feasible alternative. After 11 ♘xe5 ♗xa4, Bronstein-Timman, Rio de Janeiro IZ 1979 continued 12 ♘c4 ♗c6 13 ♘bd2 b5 14 ♘e3 ♗e7 =. Perhaps White ought to

try 12 ♘g4!? as a better chance for an advantage.

11 ♘bd2

In the great Mikhail Tal's last ever tournament game, he preferred to double Black's pawns, and even give up both his bishops for Black's knights, with 11 ♗xf6 gxf6 12 ♗xc6 ♗xc6 (12...bxc6 13 c4 c5 14 ♘c3 0-0 15 ♖ad1 ♖a7 16 ♘d2 ♔h8 17 ♖e3 ♖g8 18 ♖g3 ♖g6 19 f4 ♕g8 20 ♘f1 ♗c6 21 ♕e2 looked slightly better for White in Minasian-Grivas, Panorma Z 1998) 13 c4 0-0 14 ♘c3 ♔h8 15 ♖ad1 ♖g8 16 ♕e3 ♕f8! 17 ♘d4 ♖c8 with an approximately equal position, Tal-Akopian, Barcelona 1992. Compared to 12...bxc6, here Black has dynamic possibilities with ...b5.

11...♕c7

Black can also try 11...♘e5!?, which closely resembles 10...♘e5!? above. Now Nijboer-Akopian, Wijk aan Zee 1993 continued 12 ♘xe5 ♗xa4 13 ♘ec4 ♕c7 14 ♗xf6 gxf6 15 ♘e3 0-0-0!? 16 c4 ♖hg8 17 b3 ♗d7 18 b4 ♔b8 19 a4 ♖c8 20 ♖eb1 d5!? 21 exd5 ♕e5 with an unclear game.

12 ♖ad1 ♖d8 13 ♘f1 0-0

Chances are approximately equal, L.Bronstein-Polugaevsky, Rio Hondo 1987. White has slightly more space but Black's position is rock solid and he will have a good position if he manages a ...d5 break.

C)

7 ♗f1 ♗g4 *(D)*

White would obviously like to play d4, so Black takes steps towards meeting this advance. Others:

a) 7...e6 is too passive, and allows White an advantage, e.g. 8 d4 cxd4 9 cxd4 ♗e7 10 ♘c3 0-0 11 ♗f4 d5 12 e5 ♘e8 13 ♖c1 b5 14 ♗d3, as in Torre-Apol, Nice OL 1974.

b) The other main option is 7...e5, with these possibilities for White:

b1) 8 d4 cxd4 9 cxd4 ♗g4 transposes to Line C1.

b2) 8 h3 ♗e7 (8...h6?! 9 d4 ♕c7 10 a4 g6 11 ♘a3 ♗g7 12 dxc5 dxc5 13 ♘c4 ♖b8 14 b4!? cxb4 15 cxb4 ♗e6 16 ♘d6+ ♔e7 17 ♗a3! ± Andersson-Portisch, Skopje OL 1972) 9 d4 ♕c7 10 ♘a3 b5 11 ♘c2 ♘a5 12 ♗g5 ± Ciocaltea-Kertesz, Romania 1970.

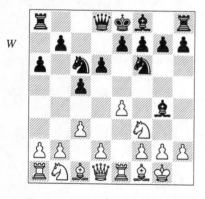

White has three main options:
C1: 8 d4   110
C2: 8 h3   112
C3: 8 d3   112

C1)

8 d4 cxd4 9 cxd4 e5

This position often arises via the move-order 7...e5 8 d4 cxd4 9 cxd4 ♗g4. It makes sense to fight for the centre in this way, and to me it seems that Black has much more influence here than, for example, after 9...d5 10 e5. Others:

a) 9...♗xf3 10 gxf3 d5 11 ♘c3 e6 12 ♗g5 (this, together with White's next couple of moves, is an immediate attempt to refute Black's set-up, but there might be something said for the quieter 12 ♗e3) 12...♗e7 13 ♗xf6 ♗xf6 14 exd5 ♘xd4 15 ♖e4 ♘f5! 16 dxe6 0-0 17 exf7+ ♔h8, and in view of White's tripled f-pawns and the opposite-coloured bishops, Black has plenty of compensation for two pawns – analysis by Morozevich.

b) 9...d5 and then:

b1) 10 exd5 ♘xd5 11 ♘c3 e6 12 h3 ♗xf3 13 ♕xf3 ♗b4 (13...♗e7 is solid and good) 14 ♕g3 0-0 15 ♗h6 ♕f6 16 ♗g5 ♕g6 17 ♗d3 f5 18 ♗c4 ± Seeman-Lautier, Pärnu Keres mem 1998.

b2) 10 e5 and here:

b21) 10...♘d7 11 ♗e3 e6 12 a3 ♗e7 13 ♘bd2 0-0 14 ♗d3 ♘h5! 15 ♕b1 ♗g6 16 ♗xg6 hxg6 (16...fxg6!? is not such a bad idea either; Black has counterplay on the f-file, and White has to decide what to do against Black's space-gaining idea ...g5, ...♖f7 and ...♘f8-g6) 17 ♕d3 b5 18 ♖ec1 ♖c8 19 ♖c2 ♘b6 = Kuczynski-Hraček, Bundesliga 1994/5.

b22) 10...♘g8!? (this idea is becoming more and more popular; Black is willing to spend a few more moves with his knight in order to put it somewhere more active than d7) 11 ♗e3 e6 12 a3! (if 12 ♘bd2, Black will play 12...♗b4, and possibly even exchange it for the knight) 12...♘ge7 13 ♘bd2

♘f5 14 ♗d3 ♗e7 (14...♘fxd4? 15 ♗xd4 ♘xd4 16 ♕a4+ +−) 15 ♕b1 ♕d7 16 b4 ♗h5 (Morozevich-Petursson, London Lloyds Bank 1994) 17 h3! ♗xf3 (17...0-0 18 g4 ♘xe3 19 ♗xh7+ ♔h8 20 ♖xe3 ±) 18 ♘xf3 ± Morozevich.

Returning to the position after 9...e5 (D):

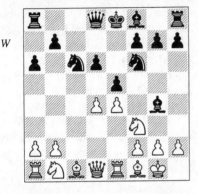

10 d5

White may also try not to concede the d4-square so easily, and thus opt for 10 ♗e3, but Black should be able to equalize without too many problems, e.g. 10...exd4 (10...♗xf3 11 gxf3 exd4 12 ♗xd4 ♗e7 13 ♘c3 ♘xd4 14 ♕xd4 0-0 = Khachian-Dvoirys, Cappelle la Grande 1996) 11 ♗xd4 ♗e7 12 ♗c3 0-0 13 h3 ♗h5 14 g4! (according to Tal, White must play actively; otherwise he will be worse, e.g. 14 ♘bd2 d5! ∓) 14...♗g6 15 ♘h4, Romanishin-Tal, USSR 1975, and now Tal analyses 15...d5! 16 ♘xg6 (16 e5 ♘e4 17 ♘xg6 fxg6 is very good for Black) 16...hxg6 17 exd5 (or 17 ♗xf6 ♗xf6 18 exd5 ♗xb2 19 dxc6 bxc6 20 ♘a3 ∓) 17...♘xd5 18 ♗g2 ♘f4 19 ♕xd8 ♗xd8 20 ♘d2 =.

10...♘d4 11 ♗e3

11 ♘bd2 ♖c8 12 ♗d3 ♘h5! is certainly not a problem for Black.

11...♘xf3+

Worse is 11...♗xf3. For example, 12 gxf3 g6 13 f4 ♘h5 14 ♘d2 ♗g7 15 fxe5 dxe5 16 ♘f3 ♘xf3+ 17 ♕xf3 0-0 18 ♗h3 and White's bishop-pair begins to tell, Kotronias-Kuijf, Wijk aan Zee 1992.

12 gxf3 ♗d7! (D)

This is much better than 12...♗h5, when the bishop is only hidden away on the kingside. An example is Glek-Bosch, Netherlands 1995: 13 ♘d2 ♗e7 14 ♘c4 0-0 15 ♗h3 ±.

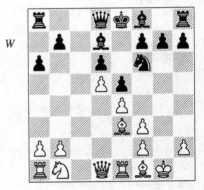

13 ♕b3 b5 14 ♘c3 ♗e7 15 a4 0-0! 16 axb5 axb5 17 ♗xb5 ♖b8 18 ♕c4 ♗xb5 19 ♘xb5 ♘h5!

Van den Doel-Grivas, Athens 1997. Despite being a pawn down, Black has a good position. He is ready to start an attack on the kingside, while White will find it difficult to do anything without surrendering the b-pawn.

C2)

8 h3 ♗xf3

If 8...♗h5, White should indeed take the opportunity to play 9 d4!. After 9...cxd4 10 cxd4, Black can reply in three ways:

a) 10...d5 11 e5 ♘d7 12 e6! is good for White.

b) 10...e5 11 g4 ♗g6 12 d5 ♘b8 13 ♘c3 ♘bd7 14 ♗d3 also gives White an edge.

c) 10...♗xf3 11 gxf3 g6 12 d5! ♘b8 13 ♕b3! ♗g7!? (13...♕c7 14 ♗e3 ♘bd7 15 ♖c1 ♕b8 16 ♘a3 ♗g7 17 ♘c4 0-0 18 ♘a5 ± Glek) 14 ♕xb7 ♘bd7 15 ♕b3 0-0 16 ♘c3 does not give Black quite enough for the pawn, Glek-Hraček, Bundesliga 1995/6.

9 ♕xf3 g6

9...e5 10 ♘a3 ♗e7 11 ♘c4 0-0 12 ♘e3 ♘e8 13 g3 ± Degraeve-Belkhodja, French Cht (Mulhouse) 1998.

10 ♕d1

Preparing d4. Alternatives:

a) 10 ♖d1 d5 11 exd5 ♕xd5 12 ♕xd5 ♘xd5 13 d4 cxd4 14 cxd4 ♗g7 15 ♘c3 ♖d8 = Tal-Kupreichik, USSR Ch (Moscow) 1976.

b) 10 d3 ♗g7 11 ♗e3 ♘d7 12 ♘d2 0-0 13 ♕d1 b5 14 a3 e5 15 a4 ♕c7 16 ♗e2 ♖fd8 17 h4 ♘b6 18 axb5 axb5 19 ♖xa8 ♖xa8 = Kharlov-Brodsky, Russia Cup 1998.

c) 10 ♘a3!? ♗g7 11 ♘c2 ♘d7 12 ♕d1 ♕b6 13 b3 0-0 14 ♗b2 a5 15 ♘e3 ± Glek-Janssen, Vlissingen 1998.

10...♗h6

The other way to prevent d4 is 10...♕b6!? and even though it looks like the queen only exposes itself to an attack from White's knight, Black gets

reasonable counterplay: 11 ♘a3 ♗g7 12 ♘c4 ♕c7 13 d3 (13 d4?! is premature in view of 13...cxd4 14 cxd4 d5) 13...0-0 14 ♗g5 b5 15 ♘e3 e6 16 ♖c1 ♖fc8 17 a3 ♖ab8 with approximately equal chances, Timman-Petursson, Reykjavik 1987.

11 ♘a3

11 a3 0-0 12 b4 ♘d7 13 ♗b2 b5 (afterwards Dorfman considered 13...♗g7 a lot safer) 14 a4 bxa4 15 bxc5 ♘xc5 16 d4 ♕b8! 17 ♗a3 ♘b3 18 ♖a2 ♖d8 with chances for both sides, Gurgenidze-Dorfman, USSR 1978.

11...0-0 12 ♘c2 e5 13 d4 ♗xc1 14 ♖xc1 ♕e7 15 dxc5 dxc5 16 ♘e3! ♖ad8 17 ♕f3

Glek-Bosch, Wijk aan Zee 1999. White has a slight advantage since his bishop will dominate a black knight in any forthcoming ending.

C3)

8 d3 *(D)*

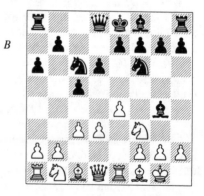

We have already seen a few ways for White to implement a d4 thrust. Now we turn our attention towards a rather different approach. Rather than trying to force through d4 immediately, White remains more flexible and intends first to complete his development. Another theme which sometimes occurs is an attack on the kingside, following h3, g4 and ♘h4. Black's two main options are now:

C31: 8...g6 113
C32: 8...e6 114

C31)

8...g6 9 ♘bd2 ♗g7

Petursson's favourite 9...♗h6!?, with the idea of exchanging the dark-squared bishops, is also interesting. 10 h3 ♗xf3 11 ♘xf3 ♗xc1 12 ♖xc1 (12 ♕xc1 e5 13 ♕h6 ♘d7 14 d4 ♕f6 was approximately equal in Van der Wiel-Petursson, Wijk aan Zee 1990) 12...0-0 13 d4 e5 14 ♕d2 ♔g7 15 ♗c4 ♕e7 16 ♗d5 ♖ac8 17 dxc5 dxc5 18 ♖cd1 b5 19 ♕e3 ♘b8! (improving on Short-Petursson, Wijk aan Zee 1990, which went 19...♘a5 20 b3 with an edge for White due to Black's rather uncomfortable knight on a5) 20 ♕g5 ♖fe8! = Brynell-Petursson, Malmö 1993.

10 h3 ♗xf3

10...♗d7 was seen in Anand-Khalifman, Groningen FIDE KO Wch 1997 and since it was played by such a strong player as Khalifman, one has to view it with some respect. But is it really worth spending two tempi (maybe only one since White plays d2-d3-d4) luring White's knight to d2? The game went 11 d4 cxd4 12 cxd4 ♖c8 13 d5!? ♘b4 14 ♘c4 b5 15 ♘e3 a5 16 a3 ♘a6 17 e5 dxe5 18 ♘xe5 0-0 19 a4 with a clear advantage for White.

11 ♘xf3 0-0 12 d4

12 ♗g5 ♖c8 13 ♕d2 b5 14 a3 ♕b6 15 b4 ♘d7 16 ♖ad1 ♕b7 17 d4 cxd4 18 cxd4 ♘b6 19 ♗h6 ± Glek-Babula, Stare Mesto 1992.

12...cxd4 13 cxd4 ♖c8 *(D)*

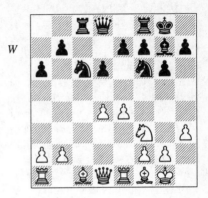

14 ♕b3

White has tried a few other moves but this appears to be the most awkward for Black.

a) 14 a3 e6 (Sveshnikov suggests 14...♕b6!, which also looks good) 15 ♗g5 h6 16 ♗h4 ♕b6 17 ♕d2 d5 is equal, Smirin-Anand, Moscow PCA rpd 1994.

b) 14 d5 ♘b4 15 ♖e2 a5 16 ♗g5 h6 17 ♗f4 = Wahls-Akopian, Adelaide jr Wch 1988.

14...♖c7

14...♘d7 15 ♗e3 b5 16 a4 ♘a5 17 ♕b4 ♘c4 18 axb5 axb5 19 ♗g5 gives White an advantage, Ghinda-Groszpeter, Bucharest 1980, but Adams suggests 14...♘a5. This is probably best, and after 15 ♕b4 Black might even consider 15...d5 16 e5 ♘e4.

15 ♗f4

Har-Zvi suggests 15 e5!? dxe5 16 dxe5 ♘d5 17 ♗g5 ♕d7 18 ♖ad1 with an edge.

15...♘d7 16 ♖ad1

Adams-Tiviakov, Groningen FIDE KO Wch 1997. White is slightly better due to his bishop-pair and good control of the centre.

C32)
8...e6 9 ♘bd2

In Sutovsky-Tiviakov, Isle of Man 1998, White went for the direct 9 h3 ♗h5 10 g4 ♗g6 11 ♘h4 ♗e7 (both 11...♘d7!? and 11...d5!? are worth investigating – compare with the main line) 12 f4 ♘d7 13 ♘g2 h6 14 f5 ♗h7 15 ♘f4 exf5 16 gxf5 ♗g5 17 ♖e2!? ♘f6 18 ♖g2 0-0 19 ♕e1 with promising attacking chances.

9...♗e7 10 h3 ♗h5 *(D)*

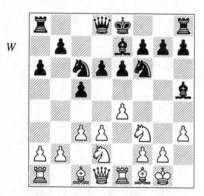

11 g4!?

This seems critical. If White can get in ♘h4 and f4, the attack will be rolling. On the other hand, if the attack fails White will have fatally weakened his kingside. Quieter options:

a) 11 ♕c2 d5 12 ♘h2 ♕c7 13 g3 0-0 14 ♘df3 b5 15 e5 ♘d7 16 ♗f4 b4 with roughly equal chances, A.Sokolov-Volzhin, Russian Ch (Elista) 1996.

b) 11 a3 d5 12 g4 ♗g6 13 ♘h4 (surprisingly, White has been doing very well with this, even though in the main line, after 12...d5!?, White can transpose to this position with 13 a3) 13...dxe4 (13...♕c7!?, as suggested by Christiansen, actually looks more logical, trying to keep the position closed for a while) 14 ♘xg6 hxg6 15 ♘xe4 and now:

b1) 15...♘xe4 16 ♖xe4 ♕d7 17 ♗f4 0-0 18 ♕e2 ♗d6 19 ♖xd6 ♕xd6 20 ♖e1 ± Christiansen-Khalifman, Munich 1992.

b2) 15...♕c7 16 f4 ♘xe4 17 ♖xe4 g5 18 ♕e2 0-0-0 19 fxg5 g6 20 b4 and White is better, McDonald-Grivas, Hampstead 1998.

11...♗g6 12 ♘h4 d5!?

Black might find a more peaceful life in 12...♘d7:

a) 13 ♘xg6 hxg6 14 ♘b3!? (this is not as stupid as it looks; it is not so easy to find a sensible plan for Black) 14...e5 15 d4 cxd4 (15...♗g5 16 dxc5 dxc5 17 ♗xg5 ♕xg5 18 ♕d6 ♕e7 19 ♕c7! ±) 16 cxd4 ♗g5 17 d5 ♘a7 18 ♗xg5 ♕xg5 19 ♘a5 ♖b8 20 ♖c1 ♕d8 21 b4 0-0 22 ♖e3! ± Grosar-R.Sergeev, Pula Echt 1997.

b) 13 ♘g2 h5 (13...e5 14 ♘f3 h5 15 g5 ♘f8 16 ♘gh4 ± Campora-Spangenberg, Buenos Aires 1995) 14 f4 hxg4 15 hxg4 ♗h7 16 ♘f3 g5 17 f5 ♘de5 18 ♘xe5 ♘xe5 19 ♘e3 favoured White in B.Larsen-S.B.Hansen, Danish Ch (Esbjerg) 1997.

13 f4

13 a3 transposes to note 'b' to White's 11th move, but an entirely new idea was introduced in Van den Doel-McDonald, London 1998: 13 ♘xg6!? hxg6 14 e5 ♘d7 15 ♘f3 ♕c7 16 ♗f4 b5 (I believe Black should be doing OK around here) 17 ♗g3 a5 (17...♘b6!?) 18 a4 b4 19 c4 ♘b6 20 cxd5!? ♘xd5 21 ♘d2 0-0 22 ♘b3 and White was better.

13...dxe4 14 dxe4 *(D)*

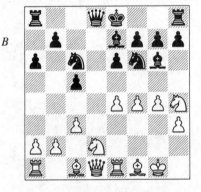

14...♘d7!

14...♘xe4? 15 ♘xg6 and 14...♗xe4? 15 g5 are both disastrous for Black,

but initially it was thought that 14...c4 was the way to create counterplay. However, after 15 f5!? (Zeziulkin suggests another sensible approach: 15 ♘xg6!? hxg6 16 ♘xc4 ♕xd1 17 ♖xd1 ♘xe4 18 ♗g2 ♗c5+ 19 ♔e3 ♗xe3+ 20 ♘xe3 ♘f6 21 ♘c4 ♔e7 and White is slightly better since his bishop is much stronger than either of Black's knights) 15...♘xg4 16 ♕xg4 (not 16 ♘xg6? ♕b6+) 16...♗xh4 17 ♘xc4! (17 fxg6 hxg6 18 ♘xc4!? ♗xe1 19 ♗g5 is also dangerous for Black) 17...♗xe1, Motwani-Zeziulkin, Györ 1990, Zeziulkin recommends 18 fxg6! ♗h4 19 gxf7+ ♔f8 20 ♗f4 ♗e7 21 e5 ♔xf7 22 ♗g2 with a strong attack for White.

15 ♘xg6

In Arkhipov-Dokhoian, Münster 1993, Black seized the initiative after 15 ♘hf3?! h5 16 f5 ♗h7 17 ♘c4 hxg4 18 hxg4 ♕c7 19 ♕d2 b5! 20 ♘e3 ♘de5 21 ♘xe5 ♘xe5 but 15 ♘g2!? might be White's best move.

15...hxg6 16 ♘f3 ♕c7 17 ♕e2 0-0-0 18 ♗d2 e5 19 f5 gxf5 20 exf5

The position is unclear – analysis by Dokhoian.

6 Moscow Variation with 3...♘d7

1 e4 c5 2 ♘f3 d6 3 ♗b5+ ♘d7 *(D)*

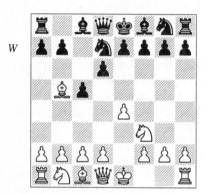

The 3...♘d7 line has had a small boost in the late 1990s – maybe because many people find the 3...♗d7 line too boring, and 3...♘c6 is not too entertaining either. Another reason is the fact that Joe Gallagher recommended it in his excellent book *Beating the Anti-Sicilians*.

While 3...♘d7 certainly appeals to the fighting player, it is, however, a lot riskier than 3...♗d7 and 3...♘c6. Black must play with great care in order to avoid some early pitfalls, and thus it may not be to everybody's liking. My recommendation is 4 d4, immediately trying to open the position, and thus exploiting Black's rather cramped position.

Black takes his share of space

Basically, Black has two ways of playing the 3...♘d7 line. One is to exchange on d4 and then to play ...e5, thereby claiming some space in the centre. While this is a rather solid option, it does leave Black's d-pawn backward, though this scenario is known from several lines of the Open Sicilian.

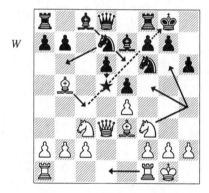

This is a well-known position and one which, in my opinion, is slightly in White's favour. As long as White can prevent Black from breaking out with ...d5, he will always enjoy a positional plus in the form of Black's backward d-pawn. Hence White should strengthen his position with ♗c4 and ♖fd1, and possibly even try to gain the bishop-pair with ♘h4 followed by either ♘f5 or ♘g6.

Black gains the bishop-pair

Black can rather easily 'win' the bishop-pair but this is usually at the cost of space and development.

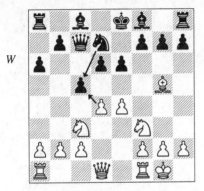

The big question is whether White should exchange on c5, thereby diverting Black's knight away from the centre, or let Black exchange on d4. Let us first take a look at the former option (*see following diagram*):

With the rook on e1, exerting pressure down the e-file towards the black king, Black must be constantly on the alert, watching out for ♘d5. This is a common theme in the Sicilian, and one that occurs quite often in this particular line. Therefore Black chose first to chase the bishop away from g5.

10...f6 11 ♗h4 b5!?

11...♗e7 is a more solid option.

12 ♘d4 b4 13 ♘d5 exd5 14 ♕h5+ ♕f7 15 exd5+ ♗e7 16 ♕e2

White's pressure on the e-file is rather uncomfortable, which explains

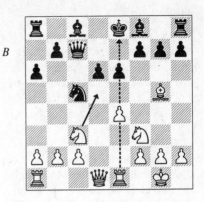

Ricardi – Gallagher
Benidorm 1991

Black's very wise decision just to return the piece.

16...0-0!? 17 ♕xe7 ♕xd5 18 ♖ad1 ♗b7 19 ♘f3 ♕xa2

The position is unclear.

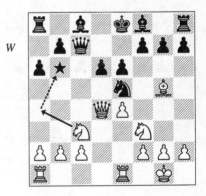

P.H. Nielsen – S. Pedersen
Copenhagen 1998

Black has just played 10...♘d7-e5. Not being aware of the theory here, I thought I was doing reasonably well.

White would rather not exchange on e5, which would just open lines for Black's dark-squared bishop and eliminate one of Black's weaknesses (the pawn on d6). Checking up on the position after the game, it turned out that Kasparov had played exactly the same position as Black against Ljubojević.

11 ♘a4!

A very nasty surprise, and it occurred to me that Black should probably have left the knight on d7 for a while. 11 ♖ad1 was played in the Ljubojević-Kasparov game, but the textmove, highlighting the weakness on b6, is much stronger.

11...h6

Black gains nothing from exchanging on f3, but 11...f6 12 ♗d2 ♗e7 is better.

12 ♘b6 ♖b8 13 ♗d2! *(D)*

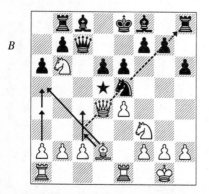

After this excellent move, I did not have much confidence about the future course of the game. Black's position is severely cramped and there is no realistic hope of him ever getting the chance to break out with ...d5,

while White has some very annoying threats like ♗a5, or just strengthening the position with a4-a5, c4 and ♗c3.

The Theory of the Moscow Variation with 3...♘d7

1 e4 c5 2 ♘f3 d6 3 ♗b5+ ♘d7 4 d4 ♘f6 5 ♘c3 *(D)*

I am not going to waste too much time on 5 0-0 except to say that after 5...a6 6 ♗xd7+ ♘xd7 White can play 7 ♘c3, transposing to the main lines, or 7 c4, after which Black should be doing fine with 7...cxd4 8 ♕xd4 ♕b6.

5 e5 is another possibility, but this apparently aggressive line is not really a problem for Black, and thus I will restrict myself to showing two sensible options for Black:

a) 5...♕a5+ 6 ♘c3 ♘e4 7 ♗d2 ♘xc3 8 ♗xd7+ ♗xd7 9 ♗xc3 ♕a6!. It is essential to prevent White from castling since if White got the chance to bring his rooks into the game, he would obtain a strong attack due to his lead in development. However, after this strong retreat chances are approximately balanced:

a1) 10 ♕d2 0-0-0 11 a3 ♗c6 12 ♕e3 dxe5 (12...cxd4!?) 13 dxe5 ♕c4 14 ♖d1 ♕e4 and Black reaches a comfortable ending, O'Donnell-Tukmakov, Toronto 1990.

a2) 10 d5 ♕c4!? (10...♗g4 and 10...♗f5 are other good moves) 11 ♕d2 ♕e4+ 12 ♔f1 ♗h3!? 13 ♕d1 ♗g4 14 exd6 0-0-0! 15 h3 ♗h5 16 ♕e2 ♕xe2+ 17 ♔xe2 ♖xd6 18 ♖hd1

e6 19 dxe6 ♖xe6+ 20 ♔f1 f6 21 ♖e1
♖xe1+ 22 ♖xe1 ♗d6 and Black is
slightly better since in an open position like this Black's bishops are superior to White's combination of knight
and bishop, Arkhipov-Lau, Lippstadt
1993.

b) 5...cxd4!? (the above lines all
appear fine for Black but this might be
an even simpler equalizing method for
him) and now:

b1) 6 ♕xd4 dxe5 7 ♘xe5 a6 8
♗xd7+ ♗xd7 9 0-0 ♗f5 and Black is
already doing very well, Kengis-Lau-
tier, Erevan OL 1996.

b2) 6 exf6 ♕a5+ 7 ♘bd2 ♕xb5 8
fxe7 ♗xe7 9 ♘xd4 ♕d5 10 ♘2f3 ♘e5
11 h3 0-0 (11...♕c4!?) 12 0-0 ♗f6 13
c3 h6 14 ♗f4 b6 15 ♕b3 ♕c5 16 ♘d2
♗b7 = Fernandez Garcia-Dorfman,
Barcelona 1993.

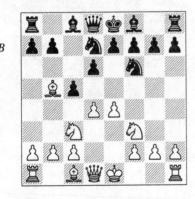

B

Black has two major options:
A: 5...cxd4 119
B: 5...a6 123

A)
5...cxd4 6 ♕xd4 e5

There are a number of other moves
available to Black, but all of them are
slightly passive and give White the
more active position:

a) 6...e6 7 ♗g5 and now:

a1) 7...♗e7 8 e5! dxe5 9 ♘xe5 is
unpleasant. Black's best seems to be
9...0-0 10 ♘xd7 ♘xd7 11 ♗xe7 ♕xe7
12 0-0-0 ♘f6 13 ♖he1 (Polugaevsky)
but White is obviously better. 9...h6?!
is worse: 10 ♗xf6 ♗xf6 11 0-0-0 0-0
12 ♗xd7 ♗xd7 13 ♘e4 ♗xe5 14 ♕xe5
♕e7 15 ♕c7 ± Vasiukov-Beliavsky,
Vilnius 1975.

a2) 7...a6 8 ♗xd7+ ♗xd7 9 0-0-0
♗e7 10 e5!? (White tries to make maximum use of his lead in development;
10 ♖he1 is another natural move)
10...dxe5 11 ♘xe5 ♗c6 12 ♘xc6 bxc6
13 ♗xf6 ♗xf6 14 ♕c5 and now rather
than 14...♕c8? 15 ♘e4 ♗e7 16 ♘d6+
♗xd6 17 ♖xd6, Gurgenidze-Gufeld,
Tbilisi 1969, Black ought to try
14...♕c7. White can reply 15 ♘d5!?
exd5 16 ♖he1+ ♔d7 17 ♖xd5+, hoping
for 17...♔c8?! 18 ♖d6 ♔b7 19 ♖xf6
gxf6 20 ♖e7, but after 17...cxd5 18
♕xd5+ ♔c8 19 ♕xa8+ ♕b8 I think
White should take a perpetual with 20
♕c6+. Instead, White's best is probably still 15 ♘e4, since after 15...♕f4+
16 ♕e3 ♕xe3+ 17 fxe3 White has a
tiny edge in any sort of endgame.

b) 6...a6 7 ♗xd7+ ♗xd7 8 ♗g5 h6
9 ♗xf6 gxf6 10 ♘d5! and then:

b1) 10...♖g8 11 0-0!? ♖c8 (not
11...♗h3 12 ♘h4 ♖g4? 13 ♘b6 ♖xh4
14 gxh3 and White wins – Ulybin and
Lysenko) 12 c4 ♗h3 13 ♘e1, with the
idea ♔h1, f4 and ♘f3, gives White the
advantage – Ulybin and Lysenko.

b2) 10...♗g7!? 11 ♘b6 ♖b8 12 ♘xd7 ♕xd7 and now, instead of 13 ♘h4 e6 14 0-0-0 ♔e7 15 f4 ♖hc8 = Lipovsky-Browne, Winnipeg 1974, Razuvaev and Matsukevich suggest 13 h4!? as a possible improvement.

b3) 10...♖c8 11 0-0-0 ♕a5 12 ♘b6 ♖c5 13 ♘xd7 ♔xd7 14 ♔b1 ± Ulybin-Istratescu, Moscow OL 1994.

c) 6...g6 7 ♗g5 ♗g7 8 e5 (8 0-0-0 0-0 9 e5! dxe5 10 ♘xe5 is a more accurate move-order) 8...dxe5 9 ♘xe5 (D) and now:

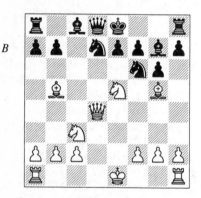

c1) 9...0-0 10 0-0-0 ♕a5 11 ♘c4! (better than 11 ♘xd7 ♗xd7! 12 ♗xf6 ♗xf6 13 ♕xd7 ♗xc3 14 bxc3 ♖ad8 15 ♕xe7 ♖xd1+ 16 ♖xd1 ♕xb5 = Radulov-Ljubojević, Poiana Brasov 1973). There are now two not very encouraging options for Black:

c11) 11...♕b4 12 ♕h4 ♘b6 13 ♘xb6 ♕xh4 14 ♗xh4 axb6 15 a3 ± Stean-Dueball, Germany 1974.

c12) 11...♕c7 12 ♖he1 ♕xh2 13 ♖xe7 (also good is 13 ♖h1 ♕xg2 14 ♕h4 ♕g4, Kosikov-Kaminsky, Leningrad 1974, 15 ♗xd7 ♕xh4 16 ♗xh4

♘xd7 17 ♗xe7 ♖e8 18 ♘d5, threatening ♘d6, and White is much better – Razuvaev and Matsukevich) 13...♕xg2 (13...a6 14 ♗xd7 ♘xd7 15 ♕e3 was very good for White in Me.Sharif-Mantovani, Aosta 1988) 14 ♕h4 h6 15 ♗xh6 ♕g4 16 ♕h2 ♘c5 17 ♗xg7 ♔xg7 18 ♘e3 ♕h5 19 ♕g3 ♗e6 20 ♗e2 ♕h3 21 ♕e5 and White should win, Timman-Lautier, Wijk aan Zee 1997.

c2) 9...a6! (Black seems to hold on after this move, but note that White can avoid this option with 8 0-0-0) 10 ♘xd7 ♗xd7 11 ♗xf6 ♗xf6 12 ♕xd7+ ♕xd7 13 ♗xd7+ ♔xd7 14 0-0-0+ and now, rather than 14...♔e8? 15 ♘d5 ♗e5 16 ♖he1 ♗d6 17 ♖xe7+!, as in Dvoretsky-Grigorian, Leningrad 1974, Illescas thinks that Black can equalize with 14...♔c6 15 ♘d5 ♖he8 16 ♖he1 ♖ad8 17 ♘xf6 exf6 18 ♖xe8 ♖xe8 19 ♔d2 ♖d8+ 20 ♔e2 ♖e8+ 21 ♔f3 h5.

7 ♕d3 (D)

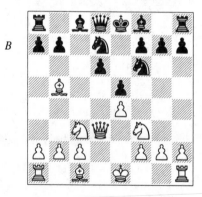

7...h6 (D)

This move is essentially linked with Black's previous move, for if White is allowed to play ♗g5, he will either obtain complete control over the d5-square or win the d6-pawn. One example is Kasparov-Svidler, ICC Blitz 1998: 7...♗e7? 8 ♗g5 0-0 9 ♗xd7 ♘xd7 (9...♗xd7 10 ♗xf6 ♗xf6 11 ♕xd6, Torre-Christiansen, San Francisco 1991, is similarly favourable for White) 10 ♗xe7 ♕xe7 11 0-0-0 ♘f6 12 ♕xd6 ♕xd6 13 ♖xd6 ±.

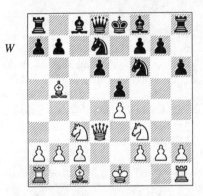

W

8 ♗e3

This natural move currently enjoys the best reputation, presumably due to its flexibility. White has a number of different plans he can pursue. The most popular is to keep the light-squared bishop, usually by retreating it to c4 – this idea is often prefaced by a4. Another idea is the knight manoeuvre ♘d2-c4. Both these strategies can still be implemented after 8 ♗e3, but a third one, namely castling queenside, is also very interesting, despite its rarity. Thus we consider a few alternatives:

a) 8 a4 ♗e7 (8...a6 might be more accurate, e.g. 9 ♗c4 ♘c5 10 ♕e2 ♗e7

11 h3 ♗d7 12 0-0 0-0 13 ♖d1 ♘xa4 14 ♘xa4 b5 15 ♗b3 bxa4 16 ♗xa4 ♗b5! = Madl-Nunn, Hastings 1994/5) 9 0-0 0-0 10 ♖d1 a6 11 ♗c4 ♕c7 12 ♕e2 ♘b6 (12...♘c5 13 ♘d5 ♘xd5 14 ♗xd5 ♗e6 15 a5 gives White a pleasant advantage) 13 ♗b3 ♗e6 14 ♘h4! ♖ad8 15 a5 ♘c4 16 ♘f5 ♖fe8 17 ♘e3! with an edge for White, Shamkovich-Valvo, New York Open 1987.

b) 8 ♘d2 ♗e7 (here it is not advisable to throw in 8...a6 since after 9 ♗xd7+ ♗xd7 10 ♘c4 ♗e6 11 ♗e3 ♖c8 12 ♘b6 ♖c6 13 ♘bd5 White is much better, M.Tseitlin-Rajković, Yugoslavia 1976) 9 ♘c4 0-0 10 ♗xd7 ♗xd7 11 ♘e3! ♗e6 12 0-0 ♖c8 13 ♗d2 ♕b6 14 b3 ♕d4 = Heidrich-Lau, Bundesliga 1981/2.

8...♗e7 *(D)*

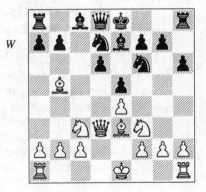

W

9 0-0

Again there are a number of other options:

a) 9 a4 0-0 10 0-0 ♕c7 (10...♘b8 11 a5 ♘c6 12 ♘d5 ♘xd5 13 exd5 ♘b8 14 ♘d2 ♘d7 15 ♘c4 ♕c7 16 b4 ± Rozentalis-Smirin, Klaipeda 1988)

11 ♗c4 ♘c5 12 ♗xc5 (this is better than 12 ♕e2, which allows Black to equalize by 12...♘cxe4 13 ♘xe4 ♘xe4 14 ♗xh6 ♗f5 15 ♗e3 ♘f6, I.Wells-Fedorowicz, Brighton 1979) 12...♕xc5 13 ♘d5 ♘xd5 14 ♗xd5, Dvoretsky-Geller, USSR Ch (Erevan) 1975, and now Black's best is 14...♖b8 with an approximately equal position.

b) 9 ♘d2 0-0 10 f3 ♕c7 11 0-0-0 a6 12 ♗c4 (Tal also analysed 12 ♗xd7 ♗xd7 13 ♘c4, giving the continuation 13...♗b5 14 ♘xb5 axb5 15 ♘b6 ♖xa2 16 ♕xb5 ♕c6 as unclear) 12...b5 13 ♗b3?! (better is 13 ♘d5 ♘xd5 14 ♗xd5 ♖b8 15 ♔b1 = Tal) 13...♘c5 14 ♗xc5 dxc5 15 ♘d5 ♘xd5 16 ♗xd5 c4 17 ♕e2 ♖b8 ∓ Dvoretsky-Tal, USSR Ch (Erevan) 1975.

c) 9 h3!? 0-0 (9...a6 10 ♗xd7+ ♗xd7 11 g4 ♖c8 12 0-0-0 ♕a5 13 g5 hxg5 14 ♗xg5 ♖xc3! 15 bxc3 ♕a3+ 16 ♔d2 ♗b5 17 ♕e3 0-0! was unclear in Quillan-S.Pedersen, British League (4NCL) 1997/8) 10 g4 a6 11 ♗xd7 ♗xd7 12 g5 hxg5 13 ♗xg5 ♘h5 14 ♗xe7 ♕xe7 (Ivkov-Chiburdanidze, Monaco Women vs Veterans 1994) and now White should try 15 0-0-0 ♕f6! 16 ♕xd6 ♗e6 17 ♕d3 (17 ♘xe5? ♖ad8 18 ♕c5 b6 19 ♕c7 ♖c8 20 ♕d6 ♖fd8 ∓) 17...♘f4 18 ♕f1 ♖ac8 with an unclear position – Ivkov.

9...0-0 10 ♗c4!? *(D)*

Since White is now planning to keep his bishop (or at least not to exchange it for Black's knight), he retreats the bishop immediately.

10...♘b6

10...♕c7 11 ♘d2 ♘b6 12 ♗b3 ♗e6 13 ♘b5 ♕c6 14 c4 is slightly better

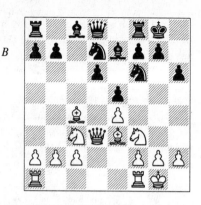

for White, while Black also fails to equalize by liquidating White's dark-squared bishop: 10...♘g4 11 ♖fd1 ♘b6 12 ♗b3 ♘xe3 13 ♕xe3 ♕c7 14 ♘d5 ♘xd5 15 ♖xd5 ♔h8 16 ♖d3 ± Bhend-Korchnoi, Montreux 1977.

11 ♗b3 ♗e6 *(D)*

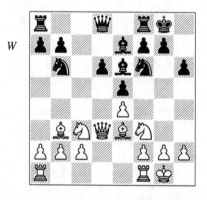

12 ♘h4

Intending ♘g6. Another interesting plan was seen in Yudasin-Avrukh, Beersheba 1996: beginning with 12 ♖fe1!?, White plans the manoeuvre ♘d2-f1, ♗xb6 and ♘e3, thereby controlling the d5-square. The game went

12...♜c8 13 ♞d2 ♞g4 14 ♝xb6 ♛xb6 15 ♖e2 and White was ready for ♞f1, h3 and ♞e3. This explains why the rook should be on e1.

12...♜c8 13 ♞g6 ♖e8 14 ♞xe7+

14 ♖fd1 ♞c4 15 ♝xc4 ♜xc4 16 ♞xe7+ ♖xe7 17 ♛xd6 ♛xd6 18 ♖xd6 ♞xe4 19 ♞xe4 ♖xe4 20 b3 a6 21 c4 with a slight advantage for White, Chandler-Mestel, Brighton Z 1984.

14...♖xe7 15 ♖fd1 ♖d7

15...♞c4 transposes to the note to White's 14th move.

16 ♞d5

White is better, Shaked-Ashley, Bermuda 1997. See the introduction to this chapter.

B)

5...a6 6 ♝xd7+ ♞xd7 (D)

6...♝xd7 7 dxc5 ♛a5 8 cxd6 ♞xe4 9 ♛d5! ± (Van der Wiel); 6...♛xd7 7 dxc5 dxc5 8 ♛xd7+ ♞xd7 9 ♝f4 e6 10 a4 ♝e7 11 ♞d2 also gives White the better chances, Van der Wiel-Kupreichik, Leeuwarden 1993.

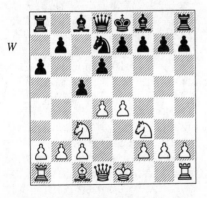

W

7 0-0

7 ♝g5!? leads to a more complicated position if Black takes up the challenge and plays 7...h6 8 ♝h4 g5 9 ♝g3 ♝g7:

a) 10 dxc5!? ♞xc5 11 e5 (11 ♛d2 ♛b6!) 11...g4 12 ♞h4 ♛a5 13 0-0 dxe5 14 ♖e1 f6 15 ♞g6 ♖h7 16 ♞d5 (16 ♞xe7!?) 16...e6 17 ♞de7 with an obscure position, Ansell-Sadler, British League (4NCL) 1997/8.

b) 10 0-0 g4 11 ♞h4 cxd4 (after 11...♝xd4 12 ♞f5 ♝xc3 13 bxc3 ♞f6 14 ♝e5! ♝xf5 15 ♝xf6 exf6 16 exf5 h5 17 ♖e1+ ♚f8 18 ♛d5 White has good compensation for the pawn, Pavasović-Soffer, Budapest 1994) 12 ♞f5 dxc3 13 ♞xg7+ ♚f8 and now:

b1) 14 ♞f5 cxb2 15 ♖b1 ♞f6, Dvoretsky-Ljubojević, Wijk aan Zee 1976, and now White should play 16 ♖xb2 ♝xf5 17 exf5 with a complicated position, albeit probably good for Black.

b2) 14 ♞h5 is Razuvaev and Matsukevich's suggestion. This might be better, and after 14...cxb2 15 ♖b1 ♛a5 16 ♛xg4 ♛g5 (16...♛c3!?) 17 ♛f3 ♞c5 18 h3 Black still has to be careful.

7...e6

If Black wants to make sure that his knight stays within reach of the e5-square, he should play 7...cxd4 8 ♛xd4 e6, which leads to very similar play to the main lines, but cuts out dxc5 possibilities.

8 ♝g5

White can also take on c5 immediately, but this gives Black an additional (albeit not very good) possibility: 8 dxc5 ♞xc5 9 ♝g5 ♛b6 (9...♛c7 transposes to the note 'a' to White's

9th move) 10 ♖b1 ♗d7 (Keres-Ljubo-
jević, Petropolis IZ 1973) 11 ♖e1
gives White with the better game as he
is threatening ♘d5.

8...♕c7 *(D)*

8...f6!? 9 ♗e3 ♗e7 10 d5 e5 11 ♘h4
g6 12 f4 exf4 13 ♗xf4 0-0 14 ♕g4
♘e5 15 ♕g3 ♖f7 with unclear play,
Rogers-Sunye, Lucerne OL 1982.

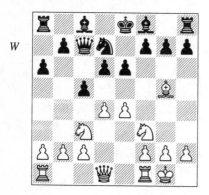

W

9 ♖e1

White has a rather big decision to
make, for he can also exchange on c5,
directing the black knight to the queenside rather than having it controlling
the centre. This issue is discussed in
more detail in the introduction to this
chapter.

a) 9 dxc5 ♘xc5 and here:

a1) 10 ♖e1 and now:

a11) 10...b5 11 ♘d5!? (I would
prefer to throw in 11 a4 b4 before
moving the knight to d5) 11...♕b7
(11...exd5?! is too dangerous: 12
exd5+ ♔d7 13 ♘d4! ♕b6 14 ♕f3 f6
15 ♗xf6 ♔c7 16 b4! ±) 12 ♕d4!? e5
(12...exd5 13 exd5+ ♔d7 still looks
extremely suspicious; amongst several

promising continuations White might
choose 14 ♖ac1!?, e.g. 14...♔c7 15 b4
♘a4 16 c4 ♔b8 17 ♖e8 with a probably winning attack) 13 ♕b4 ♗e6 14
♖ad1 h6 15 ♗h4 ♖c8 16 b3 g5 17 ♗g3
♗g7 with unclear play, Peng Xiaomin-
Pigusov, Beijing 1997.

a12) 10...f6 11 ♗h4 (another possibility is 11 ♗d2) 11...b5!? (11...♗e7
is more solid and fully playable) 12
♘d4 b4 13 ♘d5 (this can hardly come
as a surprise) 13...exd5 14 ♕h5+ ♕f7
15 exd5+ ♗e7 16 ♕e2 0-0!? (a good
practical decision, rather than stubbornly trying to hold on to the piece)
17 ♕xe7 ♕xd5 18 ♖ad1 ♗b7 19 ♘f3
♕xa2 with a very unclear position,
Ricardi-Gallagher, Benidorm 1991.

a2) 10 ♕d4!? f6 11 ♗e3 ♗e7
(11...b6!?) 12 a4 b6 13 ♕c4 (an interesting idea; White threatens b4 and
simultaneously eyes the slightly weak
e6-pawn) 13...♗d8 (the best move;
13...a5?! is positionally miserable after 14 ♘d4 and 15 ♘db5) 14 ♘d4
♘b7 15 ♕a2 ♕f7 16 f4 0-0 17 f5 (17
♘f3!?) 17...♖e8 18 ♖ad1 exf5 19
♕xf7+ ♔xf7 20 ♘xf5 ♗xf5 21 ♖xf5
and White has an edge, Liang Jinrong-
Zhu Chen, Beijing 1997.

b) 9 a4 h6 10 ♗h4 cxd4 11 ♘xd4
♘e5 12 ♔h1 (12 f4 g5!? 13 fxg5 ♘g6!?
is fine for Black) 12...g5 13 ♗g3 h5 14
f3 h4 15 ♗f2 h3 16 g3 b6 with a promising position for Black, Kamsky-
D.Gurevich, USA Ch 1993.

c) 9 d5!? (it is not clear how Black
should best react to this) 9...e5 (an
idea is 9...b5 10 dxe6 fxe6 11 ♖e1
♗b7 followed by ...♘e5, but this looks
risky) 10 a4 g6?! (Glek recommends

10...h6 11 ♗e3 ♗e7 12 ♘d2 ±) 11
♘d2 ♗g7 12 ♘c4 ♘b6 13 ♘xb6
♕xb6 14 a5 ♕c7 15 ♕d2 0-0 16 ♘a4
± Glek-Belichev, Cappelle la Grande
1998.

Returning to the position after 9
♖e1 *(D)*:

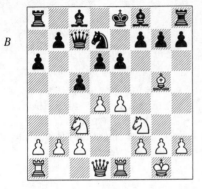

B

9...cxd4

Black is a long way behind in development, and this move even seems to
help White activate his major pieces.
However, Black wants the central tension clarified and to obtain a good
square for his knight on e5. However, I
am not sure I can recommend this idea
for Black. The reason is that when the
knight has gone to e5, there will be serious problems covering the sensitive
b6-square. Other moves:

a) Van Wely tried the highly pro-
vocative 9...b5 in a recent game, and
was probably doing OK after 10 a3
♗b7 11 ♕d2 h6 12 ♗h4 cxd4 13
♘xd4 g5!? 14 ♗g3 ♘e5 15 a4 ♘c4 16
♕e2 b4 17 ♘a2 ♗g7 with a complicated position, Curdo-Van Wely, New
York Open 1997. However, 10 a4! is

more critical, when play might continue 10...b4 11 ♘d5 ♕b8.

b) 9...f6 10 ♗h4 ♗e7 11 e5! dxe5
(11...fxe5 12 ♗xe7 ♔xe7 13 dxe5 d5
14 ♕d2 ± Von Gleich) 12 dxe5 0-0
(12...♘xe5 13 ♘xe5 fxe5 14 ♗xe7
♕xe7 15 ♕h5+ g6 16 ♕xe5 0-0 17
♖ad1 is horrible) 13 exf6 ♘xf6 14
♕e2 with a clear advantage for White,
Maiwald-Kengis, Bonn 1995.

c) 9...h6 is worth considering. 10
♗h4 cxd4 11 ♕xd4 ♘e5 should be
compared with the main line, but 10
♘d5! ♕b8 (Kr.Georgiev points out
that 10...♕a5? loses to the clever 11
♕d2!) 11 ♗h4 g5 12 ♗g3 exd5 13
exd5+ ♔d8 14 ♕e2 ♘f6 15 dxc5 ♕c7
16 ♘e5!? looks most fun for White.

10 ♕xd4

10 ♘xd4 ♘e5 11 f4 h6 12 ♗h4 g5!
is not a problem. Capturing with the
queen, however, gives Black more difficulties finishing his development.

10...♘e5 *(D)*

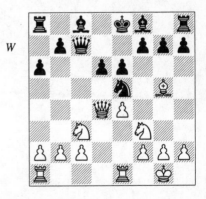

W

11 ♘a4!

I predict a dark future for Black after this move.

Previously, 11 ♖ad1 had been the most common move in this position, but then 11...♗d7 enables Black to solve his problems:

a) 12 ♗f4 f6 13 ♘d2 ♗e7 14 ♗g3 b5 is equal, Gufeld-Ljubojević, Belgrade 1974.

b) 12 ♘xe5 dxe5 13 ♕d2 b5 (Kasparov suggests 13...♖c8!?) 14 a3, Ljubojević-Kasparov, Amsterdam 1991, and now Kasparov thinks that Black is OK after 14...f6 15 ♗e3 ♗e7 16 ♗b6 ♕xb6 17 ♕xd7+ ♔f7.

11...h6 *(D)*

11...b5 12 ♘b6 ♘xf3+ 13 gxf3 ♖b8 14 ♘xc8 ♖xc8 15 a4 is very good for White, but 11...f6 12 ♗d2 ♗e7 might be Black's best.

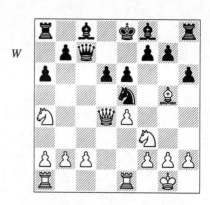

W

12 ♘b6 ♖b8 13 ♗d2!

White is clearly better, P.H.Nielsen-S.Pedersen, Copenhagen 1998. For further explanation see the introduction to this chapter.

Index of Variations

1: Rossolimo Variation with 3...g6
1 e4 c5 2 ♘f3 ♘c6 3 ♗b5 g6 *20*

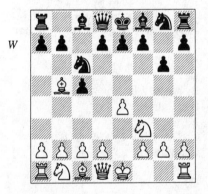

2: Rossolimo Variation with 3...e6
1 e4 c5 2 ♘f3 ♘c6 3 ♗b5 e6 *56*

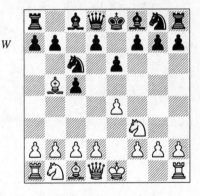

3: Rossolimo Variation: Other Third Moves
1 e4 c5 2 ♘f3 ♘c6 3 ♗b5 *69*
A: 3...♘a5 *70*
B: 3...♘d4 *71*
C: 3...♘f6 *72*
D: 3...♕c7 *72*
E: 3...♕b6 *73*

4: Moscow Variation with 3...♗d7
1 e4 c5 2 ♘f3 d6 3 ♗b5+ ♗d7 *80*

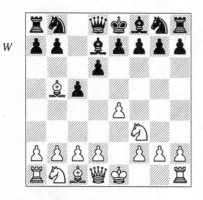

4 ♗xd7+ *80*
A: 4...♘xd7 *81* 5 0-0 ♘gf6 *81*
A1: 6 ♖e1 *81*
A2: 6 ♕e2 *82* 6...e6 *82*
A21: 7 c3 *83*
A22: 7 b3 *84*
B: 4...♕xd7 *86* 5 c4 ♘c6 *86*
B1: 6 ♘c3 *87*
B11: 6...♘e5 *87*
B12: 6...g6 *89*
B2: 6 d4 *91* 6...cxd4 7 ♘xd4 ♘f6 8 ♘c3 *92*
B21: 8...♕g4 *92*
B22: 8...e6 *93*
B23: 8...g6 *95*

5: Moscow Variation with 3...♘c6
1 e4 c5 2 ♘f3 d6 3 ♗b5+ ♘c6 *99*

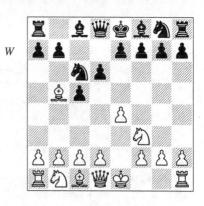

4 0-0 ♗d7 5 c3 ♘f6 6 ♖e1 a6 *100*
A: 7 ♗xc6!? *100* 7...♗xc6 8 d4 ♗xe4 9 ♗g5 *101*
A1: 9...d5 *102*
A2: 9...♗d5 *104*
B: 7 ♗a4 *106*
B1: 7...b5 *106*
B2: 7...c4 *108*
C: 7 ♗f1 *109* 7...♗g4 *109*
C1: 8 d4 *110*
C2: 8 h3 *112*
C3: 8 d3 *112*
C31: 8...g6 *113*
C32: 8...e6 *114*

6: Moscow Variation with 3...♘d7
1 e4 c5 2 ♘f3 d6 3 ♗b5+ ♘d7 *118* 4 d4 ♘f6 5 ♘c3 *118*
A: 5...cxd4 *119* 6 ♕xd4 *119* 6...e5 7 ♕d3 *120* 7...h6 8 ♗e3 *121* 8...♗e7 9 0-0 0-0 *122*
B: 5...a6 *123* 6 ♗xd7+ ♘xd7 7 0-0 e6 8 ♗g5 ♕c7 *124* 9 ♖e1 *125* 9...cxd4 *125* 10 ♕xd4 ♘e5 11 ♘a4! *125*